Prohibition Gangsters

Also by Marc Mappen

Witches and Historians: Interpretation of Salem (editor)
Jerseyana: The Underside of New Jersey History
Murders and Spies, Lovers and Lies: Settling the
Great Controversies of American History
Encyclopedia of New Jersey (coedited with Maxine N. Lurie)
There's More to New Jersey Than the Sopranos

Prohibition Gangsters

The Rise and Fall of a Bad Generation

Marc Mappen

Rutgers University Press

New Brunswick, New Jersey, and London

Library of Congress Cataloging-in-Publication Data

Mappen, Marc.

    Prohibition gangsters : the rise and fall of a bad generation / Marc Mappen.

      p. cm.

    Includes bibliographical references and index.

    ISBN 978–0–8135–6115–8 (hardcover : alk. paper) — ISBN 978–0–8135–6116–5 (e-book)

    1. Prohibition—United States—History. 2. Organized crime—United States—History. 3. Mafia—United States—History. I. Title.

HV5089.M327 2013
364.106′6097309042—dc23   2012033375

A British Cataloging-in-Publication record for this book is available from the British Library.

Visit our website: http://rutgerspress.rutgers.edu

Manufactured in the United States of America

*This book is dedicated to a man I never met:
my great uncle, Harry Mappen, who was born
in 1895 to an immigrant family on New York's
Lower East Side. He was a pickpocket, drug
dealer, jewelry fence, and stool pigeon with a long
arrest record. In 1925 he committed suicide in prison
by swallowing cyanide poison. My shared DNA
with Great Uncle Harry is a genetic connection
I have with the Prohibition generation.*

Contents

Prohibition Gangsters

The Bluebird Tattoo

The patient admitted to Saint Mary of Nazareth Hospital Center, Chicago, on May 14, 1992, was an eighty-six-year-old retired businessman, gray-haired, feeble, and dying from congestive heart failure and acute respiratory failure. There was little the doctors could do to save him, and his family sorrowfully agreed that he should be removed from life support. He quietly passed away on the evening of May 27. After he died his corpse was taken to the hospital mortuary and then picked up by the Montclare-Lucania Funeral Home, where the body was prepared and placed in a casket. A Catholic priest led a brief prayer service, after which the body was driven in a hearse to the Queen of Heaven Cemetery for burial.[1]

It's probable that among the nurses, physicians, orderlies, and undertakers who ministered to him at the time of his death one or more might have spotted an unlikely, faded relic on the weathered and wrinkled skin of the man's right hand. It was a tattoo of a bluebird, with wings outstretched. When the man was alive, moving his thumb and trigger finger gave the bird the appearance of flapping its wings in flight. Perhaps the caregivers who saw that tattoo wondered how this old man came by this young man's adornment and reflected on the passage from lively, frivolous youth to the somber end of life.

The old man's baptismal name was Antonino Leonardo Accardo, but he picked up other names as he made his way through life: Joe Batty, Joe

Batters, Big Tuna, and just plain Tony. His business was crime. He started his criminal career while still a teenager, running errands for the Chicago gang known as the "Outfit," which came to be headed by Al Capone. Accardo early on demonstrated the ability to use violence and got the nickname "Batters" for his aggressive beating of people who ran afoul of the gang. He moved up the ladder to become one of Capone's trusted bodyguards. His rise continued after Capone went to prison, and by the mid 1970s Accardo was the leader of the Outfit.

Accardo acquired his bluebird tattoo in Atlantic City in May 1929, shortly after his twenty-third birthday. He was providing protection for Capone at a conference of mob leaders. Maybe the spring weather and the pleasant breeze from the Atlantic Ocean inspired him to get a tattoo incised on his hand. Capone, thinking it a bad idea for the young man to give himself that identifying mark, is supposed to have said, "Kid, that will cost you as much money and trouble as it would to wear a badge with the word 'thief' on it."[2] As Accardo grew older and became a respected mob capo, he came to dislike the tattoo as too undignified, and he covered it with his left hand when appearing in public.[3] That bluebird tattoo might serve as a symbol of a different time in organized crime: the prosperous era of Prohibition, when young, ambitious criminals were on the make. Accardo was one of the last survivors of that era, and his tattoo offered him a constant reminder of that long ago time.

THE PROHIBITION GENERATION

Cultural observers often speak of generations that shared common experiences. Consider, for example, the Lost Generation that came of age in World War I, their Greatest Generation offspring who went on to win the Second World War, and their self-centered children who comprise the Baby Boom generation. More recently, pop culture analysts have identified Gen X, Gen Y, Gen Z, and the Millennial Generation. Traditionally, a generation is reckoned as a twenty-five-year span; anybody born in those years is considered a member of that generation. One of the finest analyses of the place of generations in American history was applied by historians Stanley Elkins and Eric McKitrick in a celebrated 1961 article, "The Founding Fathers: Young Men of the Revolution," which sees the authors of the U.S. Constitution as members of a younger generation who viewed the world differently from their elders.[4]

This book applies a generational perspective to the gangsters of the Prohibition era, men born in the quarter-century span roughly from 1880 to 1905, men who came to power with the Eighteenth Amendment when most were in their twenties. Virtually all were dead by the end of the twentieth century. This collective biography shows how these men were affected by forces in the larger society, such as morality, immigration, economic conditions, and government crackdowns, and what befell them as the decades unwound. It also seeks to strip away fact from myth in the traditional history of American gangsterdom.

Seeking Status

Most of the Prohibition gangsters were Italians or Jews. This was a period when immigration from the rural villages of Italy and the agricultural shtetls of Poland and Russia was at its height. The gangsters who came from this generation were mostly brought to America as children or were born in America to newly arrived immigrants.

Sociologists have examined how immigrant groups like the Prohibition generation found it difficult to achieve status and wealth in American cities because the more established ethnic groups had preempted them. The newcomers at the turn of the twentieth century found themselves stuck at the bottom of the career ladder—toiling in jobs such as ditch diggers, railroad track-layers, shoemakers, barbers, and garment workers. (Tony Accardo's father was an immigrant from Palermo who became a shoemaker in Chicago.) Sociologist Daniel Bell observed that the immigrants' children "became wise in the ways of urban slums" and found that crime could provide a route to wealth and power.[5] This was particularly true for those youths who were school dropouts with a taste for violence and who got their education on the streets and in penal institutions. It is possible that many of them might have grown out of youthful crime and graduated to everyday working-class jobs or perhaps even business and professional positions. But for many in the Prohibition generation, that's not what happened.

Crime writer Thomas Reppetto observed that bootlegging was "a quick and equal opportunity pathway to the American dream."[6] Prohibition was a unique economic opening for this generation—an opening unlike anything that previous generations of criminals had known, an opportunity whereby a man who might today be described as an underachiever or social misfit could achieve status.

That status-seeking can be seen in gangsters' apparel. Major Prohibition criminals favored hand-tailored suits with cuffed pants, silk ties, and fedora hats, which they wore with a swagger. Some at the top were flashy dressers like Al Capone with his diamond-studded belt buckle and $50,000 ring; some were more conservative, like Lucky Luciano with his oxford gray suit and herringbone cashmere topcoat.[7] Guns, which brought a sense of power, were a part of the criminal culture, too. "I always carried a gun," said one mobster, recalling the Prohibition era; "It was just like wearing an overcoat."[8] Writer Gay Talese claims the gangster bought into the image that the world had of him, "for it made him larger than he was, more powerful, more romantic, more respected and feared."[9] Nobody could confuse the Prohibition mobsters with the manual laborers their immigrant fathers had been.

For a few top mobsters, their status was also displayed by the elaborate funerals that followed. Or to put it another way, they showed they had arrived by the way they departed. The elaborate, costly gangster funeral of the Prohibition era was invented in Chicago and spread to New York and other cities, large and small. The most striking example was the November 14, 1924, Chicago funeral of Dion O'Banion, shot dead in a gang hit four days earlier. His funeral featured a $10,000 casket with silver angels as well as $50,000 worth of floral displays made of roses, orchids, and lilies.

Thousands of people watched the mile-long cortege to the cemetery of cars carrying mourners and trucks carrying flowers. There were also three bands playing somber music. Family members sobbed, and among the sorrowful throng were the men who had arranged for O'Banion's murder.[10]

ACCOMPLISHMENTS

What made these symbols of status possible were the Eighteenth Amendment, which went into effect on January 17, 1920, and the Volstead Act, which enforced Prohibition by outlawing "the manufacture, sale, or transportation of intoxicating liquors within, the importation thereof into, or the exportation thereof from the United States and all territory subject to the jurisdiction thereof for beverage purposes." As one crime writer memorably put it, "Nothing like it had happened before. An entire industry—one of the most important in the country—had been gifted by the government to gangsters."[11]

Before Prohibition, organized crime in America was a small-stakes affair that primarily involved hurting or threatening to hurt people in one way or another through protection schemes, shakedowns, loan sharking, extortion, robbery, serving as thugs for hire, or prostitution. (The last was once regarded as victimless crime, but now we know better.) Prohibition changed all that. Members of the Prohibition generation discovered that the amendment created a vast and lucrative new line of business, which would find favor with millions of Americans who would do anything they could to drink illegal alcohol. This discovery could be said to compare to other important findings made in the 1920s, like astronomers' observation that there were other galaxies in the universe besides our own Milky Way and archeologists' unearthing of the three-thousand-year-old tomb of King Tut in Egypt. In fact, this generation of criminals realized that a majority of the American public would do whatever it took and pay whatever it cost to defy Prohibition.

The Prohibition generation accomplished an expansion of the level of crime in the nation. The gangs that participated in bootlegging were different in many ways from the Sicilian Mafia or the isolated back alley gangs of late nineteenth-century American cities. Although the activities of the Prohibition generation were mercenary, illegal, and violent and although they often sought to kill each other, the Prohibition gangsters should be recognized, but not admired, for their organizational accomplishments. They never managed to create an all-powerful, nationwide syndicate that was imagined by their opponents, but they were able to build partnerships, assign territories, and negotiate treaties, however shortlived. They were able to transform the loosely organized gangs of the pre-Prohibition era into sophisticated, complex organizations that employed not just thugs and pimps, but truckers, lawyers, accountants, brew masters, chemists, warehousemen, bail bondsmen, nightclub waiters and chefs, casino card dealers, and racetrack operators. In the 1920s, in fact, the term "gang" was replaced by "syndicate" or "combination" to mean a criminal operation with many working parts. The Prohibition generation also inspired an enduring icon in American popular culture—the gangster, a character type that appears in countless books, movies, comics, and television shows and who, for all his evil, demonstrates the ingenuity and initiative valued by the American public.

Only a few of the Prohibition mobsters made it safely to old age, like Tony Accardo, who carried the bird tattoo he had acquired at the Atlantic City conference to the grave at Queen of Heaven Cemetery. It was the same burial ground where sixty-eight years earlier Dion O'Banion had been interred so ostentatiously. The difference was distinct: only five cars drove in Accardo's cortege and two sprays of roses stood beside his coffin.

This book recounts the lives of that Prohibition generation of mobsters from the time they were young men until the ends of their lives. In essence, it explores a unique group of Americans at a unique moment their nation's history.

PART I

The Rise

"You can get a lot further with a smile and a gun than you can with just a smile."

—Remark attributed to Al Capone

CHAPTER 1

The Big Fellow in the Windy City

"Honey, you have a nice ass, and I mean that as a compliment." The year was 1917, the place was the Harvard Inn, a bar and restaurant in the Coney Island section of Brooklyn, and the speaker of these unwelcome comments was a young waiter, Alphonse Capone, who had been eyeing the girl that evening. Her name was Lena Gallucio, and she was sitting on her much-admired posterior at a table with her brother Frank Gallucio. When Capone made his insulting remark Frank leaped to his feet, and the two men began a fierce struggle, in the course of which Frank pulled a knife and cut deep slashes in Capone's face and neck. Frank and his sister fled the establishment, presumably without leaving a tip.[1]

If Gallucio's knife had severed the waiter's jugular vein, the world would never have heard of Al Capone. As it was, Capone survived the fight, but bore deep, embarrassing scars on his face for the rest of his life. At the urging of local underworld figures, Capone later made his peace with Gallucio and hired the man as a part-time bodyguard when the Chicago mob boss visited New York. This early episode in the life of the best-known crime lord of the Prohibition era demonstrates his impulsive nature and brawler instincts. It also demonstrates his gift for smoothing things over with words. Although he was just a waiter at the time he was already known in the New York underworld. A sixth-grade dropout, he had run errands for a noted mobster, John Torrio of Brooklyn, who in turn recommended

Capone to the owner of the inn, Frankie Uale. (Frankie must have had a thing about the Ivy League because he changed his last name to Yale and chose Harvard as the name of his establishment.)

After the Gallucio incident, Capone moved on with his life. He married an Irish girl, Mae Coughlin, and they had a baby boy. World War I was raging in Europe, and having a family enabled Capone to avoid the draft. For a time he worked in Baltimore, where he did legitimate bookkeeping at a construction company. But at some point in 1920–1921 he left behind that occupation to move to Chicago, the fast-growing metropolis of the Midwest, where John Torrio had a job for him in the world of crime. He purchased a home at 7244 South Prairie Avenue, where he was joined by his wife, son, mother, and siblings who moved to the Windy City from Brooklyn.

A *Chicago Tribune* reporter, writing a decade later, described the newly arrived Capone as a loud dresser, "stout muscled, hard-knuckled; a vulgar person; a tough baby from Five Points, New York City."[2] Capone's patron, John Torrio, was very different. Seventeen years older than Capone, Torrio was described by another Chicago newspaperman as a "short, dumpy, sallow" figure, with a potbelly, chubby cheeks, and the demeanor of a "mild, benevolent little man."[3] He was soft-spoken and conservative, understated in the clothes he wore and the life he lived. Despite his immersion in the world of prostitutes, he remained faithful to his wife. Capone, however, had no such compunctions. Similarly, Torrio was not personally violent like so many other gang leaders and claimed later in life that he never fired a gun, a claim that certainly never fit Capone.[4] But Torrio knew how to hire men who could commit the violence he sought.

Torrio had left New York in 1909 to go to Chicago, where he handled business for Big Jim Colosimo, a flashy Chicago figure from an older generation whose specialty was running brothels. Colosimo had become rich in the prostitution business and was reluctant to branch out to bootlegging. Torrio, however, saw Prohibition as a way to make vast amounts of money. Colosimo was assassinated on May 11, 1920, and Torrio took over by expanding into bootlegging and bringing Capone to Chicago to assist him in the expansion of Big Jim's empire. There is speculation that Torrio arranged for the Colosimo murder, and no culprit was ever found.

Under Torrio, Capone began by managing the whorehouses that Colosimo had established. Chicago was notorious for its prostitution industry. Statistics on the sex trade are hard to come by, but a 1910 Vice Commission report estimated that fifteen thousand prostitutes in Chicago performed twenty-seven million sex acts each year.[5] Capone was based at the Four Deuces brothel and gambling den, which took its name from the address, 2222 South Wabash Avenue. The building had no elevator so customers had to trudge up the stairs. There was a bar on the first floor, a horse-betting operation on the second floor, and casino gambling on the third. On the fourth floor was the prostitution, suffused with the aroma of incense and perfume.

Jack McPhaul, a Chicago reporter who began his career in the 1920s, described that floor with a familiarity that suggests he had on occasion trod up those four flights: "The brothel was a colorless, no-nonsense sex mill designed for results. In a small drab parlor the buyer made his selection from a half-dozen or so women in thin slips. Nudity was rejected as an impairment to traffic; eye-feasting customers would stall overly long before decision. Choice made, the patron retired to a cubicle containing a cot and a chair for his garments. He was followed by the apple of his eye carrying a towel and a washbasin. Two dollars changed hands."[6] A clarinet player in a jazz band that performed in another of Capone's bordellos recalled how prostitutes approached customers: "Those girls were always competing with each other: one would come up to you, switchering her hips like a young duck, and whisper in your ear, 'Want to go to bed, dear, I'll show you a good time honey, I'm French,' and a minute later another one would ease along and say coyly, 'Baby, don't you want a straight girl for a change?'"[7] "French" in this context meant oral sex, which was popularized in America by the doughboys who served in France during the First World War.[8]

THE LANDSCAPE OF CHICAGO CRIME

With Big Jim out of the way and with the assistance of Capone, Torrio expanded the business into liquor through the acquisition of breweries idled by Prohibition. The beer they produced, along with hard liquor they smuggled, was used in their own brothels and gambling parlors and sold to speakeasies. All of this required skilled manpower, and among their top aides were Jack (or Jake) Guzik to handle the money and Frank Nitti to provide enforcement. Bribes were provided to a widening circle of police, judges, and politicians. But the Torrio-Capone organization faced competition from other gangs seeking to profit from Prohibition. Indeed, no city in the nation had such entrenched and fiercely defended gang territories. So out in the open were these gangs that Chicago newspapers were able to publish maps of the city with the territory of each gang delineated like warring Greek city-states of antiquity.[9]

The Torrio-Capone empire comprised most of south Chicago. In the north they faced a mob led by Dion O'Banion and his associates Hymie Weiss (who despite his Jewish-sounding name was a devout Polish Catholic whose real name was Earl Wojciechowsky), Vincent "The Schemer" Drucci, and later on George "Bugs" Moran (also Polish). The Genna brothers, along with John Scalise and Albert Anselmi, dominated the Little Italy section of Chicago. This gang specialized in "alky cookers," small home stills that Italian families used to produce whiskey that the mob collected. For this the families that operated the stills were paid $15 a day, a large sum of money in the 1920s but still low enough for the Gennas to make an estimated 200 percent profit from the sale of this low-grade, rotgut alcohol.[10] Smaller pockets of predominately Irish gangs consisted of the Regan Colts, for whom Ralph Sheldon handled bootlegging, and the Valley Gang of Terry Druggan and Frank Lake. Another enclave, located in the Chicago southwest, was the gang of Irishman Frank McErlane and Pole Joseph Saltis, more or less an extension of the Torrio-Capone empire. And to confuse the picture, two separate Irish gangs were run by two unrelated

O'Donnell families—the South Side O'Donnells consisting of brothers Ed, Steve, and Walter, and the West Side O'Donnells led by brothers William, Myles, and Bernard.

The interaction of these gangs—the incessant feuds, betrayals, defections, and alliances—created the violent world of Chicago crime in the 1920s. John Torrio, who clung to the idea that compromise could bring about peace between warring gangs, sought to work out cooperative arrangements. Some lasted for a time, notably Torrio's agreement with the Genna brothers to respect their authority in Little Italy in exchange for which the Gennas agreed not to hijack Torrio's beer trucks as they drove through that neighborhood's streets. Other truces were shorter lived, such as Torrio's proposal to make peace with Dion O'Banion by giving him a share of the income from prostitution in return for a percentage of the Irishman's operation in Cicero—a proposal that O'Banion rejected because, as a Catholic, he was opposed to making money from fornication.[11]

A challenge to the Torrio-Capone gang came with the 1923 election of a reform administration in Chicago, led by a new mayor, William Emmet Dever, a Democrat, who replaced the gang-friendly Republican William "Big Bill" Thompson. Whereas the Thompson administration had looked the other way on brothels, gambling, and bootlegging, Dever directed the police to make raids and arrest lawbreakers. Given these threats from law enforcement and rival gangs, Torrio and Capone saw the wisdom of branching out beyond the city limits of Chicago. Right over the border was the bustling suburb of Cicero. There they boldly took over town government and openly operated a gambling casino, betting parlor, brothel, and nightclub, while still holding on to their extensive operations in Chicago. Capone was put in charge.[12] Other suburbs, like Forest Glen and Chicago Heights, were drawn into the Torrio-Capone operation, adding enormous profits to the Outfit. But expansion was not without cost. April 1, 1924, was election day in Cicero, and Capone unleashed his mobsters to make sure his allies, the Republican candidates, won the vote. Thugs working for Capone kidnapped and beat up Democratic poll workers. Police from

Chicago were hastily deputized and sent to Cicero by a county judge (not coincidentally a Democrat) to fight back. A gun battle occurred on the city's streets, during which Capone's brother Frank was shot and killed. In the end Al Capone's allies won their election, and his control of Cicero was complete. Headlines such as "Gunmen Terrorize Primary in Illinois" reflected the shock felt across the nation by the blatant manner in which mobsters had subverted American democracy.[13]

The Capone operation in Cicero in the 1920s and 1930s has been used by Mark A. Haller of Temple University as an example of how illegal enterprises worked in that era.[14] According to Haller, it is a mistake to see Cicero as a hierarchical, top-down operation with Capone at the apex. Instead, he describes it as a "complex set of partnerships." There were four senior partners: Al Capone, his brother Ralph, Jack Guzik, and Frank Nitti. They were equals, each of whom looked after his assorted enterprises and shared the income jointly. The Hawthorne Smoke Shop was the center of the gang's gambling operation, in which they partnered with Frankie Pope to run bookmaking and Pete Penovich to run gambling games. The partners had other gambling establishments in Cicero, each in partnership with local managers. When they wanted to expand into slot machines they partnered with Sam Guzik, the younger brother of Jack. Partners like Penovich and Pope could form their own partnerships in other areas. This decentralized structure not only helped protect against law enforcement but also fit with the temperament of gangsters who, says Haller, did not have the management skills necessary to run complex organizations. Instead, they were hustlers and dealers who had a taste for risk taking and a willingness to use violence when necessary. Haller sees the violence as a handicap, but this seems unlikely. Violence, actual or threatened, kept down business rivals, a competitive advantage not open to legitimate business.

Around the time of the occupation of Cicero, Torrio entered middle age and began to think about his future. He took some long trips—a six-month stay in Italy with his wife and mother and another with his wife to the southern United States, including the gangster resort Hot Springs,

Arkansas. While in Italy Torrio deposited $1 million or so in Swiss and Italian banks, funds that he could draw on if he moved back to the old country.[15] After he returned to the Windy City, a series of events occurred that ultimately led to his permanent departure from Chicago.

A full-scale war had broken the uneasy truce between the North Side O'Banion gang and the South Side Torrio-Capone operation. A key event in this renewed gang war took place on May 19, 1924, when Torrio was arrested in a raid conducted by federal agents and Chicago police on a brewery he was planning to purchase from Dion O'Banion. It is believed that O'Banion set up the raid, got away with the purchase money, and then boasted about how he had pulled one over on the Italians Torrio and Capone. But O'Banion's glee was literally short lived. At midday on November 10, 1924, he was working in the flower shop he owned, a sort of hobby, on North State Street. A black employee, William Crutchfield, was sweeping the floor behind a partition. A customer had phoned in an order for a wreath for the funeral of one Mike Merlo. When three men entered the shop, O'Banion thought they had come for their order and walked forward to greet them, saying, "Hello, boys, you want Merlo's flowers?"[16] When he extended his arm to shake hands, one man grabbed it and pulled him off balance. Crutchfield heard six shots and found O'Banion, involuntarily twitching and oozing blood, sprawled on the floor.

Thinking about this incident leads one to conclude that it would be better to be killed with a shot to the head fired from behind without warning. In O'Banion's case he had to endure a few horrible seconds when he was grabbed by the arm and saw his killers pull out their guns.

Who did it? The best evidence is that Torrio and Capone had brought in their old colleague from New York, Frankie Yale, to head the hit squad. But if Torrio and Capone thought killing O'Banion would end the wars, they were mistaken. The next battle occurred on January 12, 1925, when the survivors of the O'Banion mob—George "Bugs" Moran, Vincent Drucci, and Hymie Weiss—tried to kill Al Capone by shooting up his car. That attack failed, but twelve days later they tried again. This time their target was Torrio, whom they ambushed while he was returning from a shopping trip with his wife, Ann. The gunmen intercepted Ann and John Torrio just as they had left their car and were heading into their apartment building. While Ann looked on in horror, her husband was shot repeatedly by the assassins, Moran and Weiss. Drucci served as the wheelman. Five shots went into Torrio's body, including one fired into his groin as a way to unman him. Moran was about to put a bullet into his victim's head, but he had run out of ammunition in his pistol and heard a truck approaching. He and Weiss made it back into the car and took off.[17] Miraculously, Torrio survived, though he suffered through a painful recovery and then served nine months in prison for the brewery arrest. He clearly saw the jail term as a time of refuge where, thanks to a cooperative warden, he was safe from further attack. At some point while he was in jail or shortly after his release, he turned the entire gang operation with its enormous profits over to Capone and departed once again for Italy before reestablishing himself in his hometown of New York.

Capone in Charge

Torrio's departure left Capone the master of an enormous criminal enterprise, known as the Outfit, at the age of twenty-six. He developed the gambling side of the business to include racetracks and dog tracks. He also got into the extortion racket, in which employees and bosses in butchering, construction, and dry cleaning were forced to pay for protection. There was even a gang-run union for movie theater ticket takers and ushers. This was a change from his first years in Chicago, when he lived in Torrio's shadow and was largely unknown to the public. Early on he had used the alias "Al Brown" and a spurious cover as an antique dealer—he took out a storefront near the Four Deuces in which he put in some furniture items. Even after his real name began to appear in the press, there was some confusion about his first name, which was sometimes reported as Toni or Alfred, or whether his last name was spelled Capone or Caponi. In 1924 "Scarface" first appeared in print, a nickname that he despised. A more flattering nickname that began to appear was "the Big Fellow."[18] As befitting the mob boss of Chicago, he purchased a custom-made Cadillac sedan with bulletproof glass and reinforced steel.

An episode from the Torrio years tells us something about how the Big Fellow operated. At 6:30 P.M. on May 8, 1924, at a Wabash Avenue saloon, he sidled up to Joseph Howard, a minor, nasty Chicago criminal. Capone pulled out a pistol and shot Howard four times in the face and twice in the shoulder, killing him instantly.[19] According to underworld tradition, Howard's crime was simple: he had previously slapped around Jake Guzik, the sickly, out-of-shape Jewish accountant whom Capone had befriended and upon whose managerial ability he depended. When Capone confronted Howard about this insult, the latter said, "Listen, you dago pimp, why don't you run along and take care of your broads." In other accounts Howard says, "Ahhh, go back to your girls, you dago pimp."[20] At that point Capone started shooting. There were witnesses in the saloon at the time: proprietor Hymie Jacobs and several customers, so the case against Capone seemed certain. But then occurred an outbreak of "Chicago Amnesia," a phenomenon that plagued law enforcement in the 1920s and beyond. Whether the witnesses were bribed with money or threatened with death, or both, they backed off by saying they could not identify the killer. This amnesia was exacerbated by the fact that police, judges, and other law enforcement personnel were routinely on the take. Bribes and threats also worked with juries.

Capone's biographers have identified key episodes in the Big Fellow's career as the top dog of the Chicago underworld after the departure of Torrio. One was a huge blunder. The Illinois state's attorney for Chicago from 1920 to 1928 was Robert Emmet Crowe, a notoriously ineffective lawman, whose attempts to clean up crime in Chicago were failures because he was either too timid or mobbed up; the reason is not clear. But a shining light in his office was one of his sixty-nine assistant state's attorneys, William Harold McSwiggin, known as the "hanging prosecutor" for his success in winning convictions of criminals that resulted in their executions.

McSwiggin was a young man from a good Catholic family. He was twenty-six years old and a graduate of De Paul University Law School. A photo of him shows a vigorously gesturing young man with slicked back hair and round eyeglasses. He had the making of a great career in law enforcement, but he had a flaw—an unseemly interest in associating with the underworld. In the present era this would be seen as a breach of ethical rules; in 1926 it turned out to be his doom.

McSwiggin lived with his parents and sisters in a home on the west side of Chicago. On the night of April 27, 1926, he told his parents he was going out with some friends. A car pulled up at the house to pick him up, and off he went, never to return alive (although his body did return). Traveling with him that night were two young men he had known since childhood, Tom "Red" Duffy and Jim Doherty. Tom and Jim were no angels; both were involved in bootlegging and were associated with the West Side O'Donnell brothers' mob. In fact, McSwiggin had unsuccessfully tried to convict Jim Doherty for murder, but there seem to have been no hard feelings. Also in the car that night was one of the O'Donnell brothers, Myles. Some accounts say that the other O'Donnell brother, William "Klondike," was with them too. The driver was a former cop and boxer, Ed Hanley. The car they traveled in was a Lincoln owned by the O'Donnells. The purpose of their jaunt seems to have been to do some bar-hopping in Cicero, the town dominated by Al Capone. At one point in this excursion, the car stopped at a saloon owned by Harry Madigan at 5615 West Roosevelt Road in Cicero. After some amount of drinking, they were emerging from the establishment when all hell broke loose as deadly machine gun fire cut down McSwiggin, Duffy, and Doherty. It was theorized that the other passengers were saved by ducking behind the Lincoln. Why had the shooting taken place, and who was responsible? The assorted theories boil down to two alternatives: either McSwiggin was the target because of his position as prosecutor, or the shooters were out to get the O'Donnell gang members and were not aware that the young prosecutor was among them.[21]

Gangland killings were common in Chicago, but this one with its prominent victim unleashed a furious reaction. The newspapers recounted how, when his coffin was brought home, his mother sobbed, "O, why did they kill him!" and her grim-faced husband vowed vengeance, "I'll never rest until I've killed my boy's slayers or seen them hanged."[22] State's Attorney Crowe crowed, "We are going to get to the bottom of this. I am going to root out this booze and gang killing business if we have to use all the peace officers in Cook County on the one task." Chief of Police Morgan Collins announced, "I have put every available man on the case. We shall stay at it until we have cleaned up the remnants of these gangs."[23] With uncharacteristic vigor, police, seeking evidence, ransacked speakeasies, whorehouses, casinos, and private homes. An inquest was held, and a succession of six grand juries deliberated for months.

From the outset suspicion fell on Al Capone. He had a grudge against the O'Donnell gang because it was trying to muscle in on his beer monopoly in Cicero. The saloonkeeper Harry Madigan stated that some time before he had switched from Capone beer to O'Donnell beer because it was cheaper and better. Eight days after the murder, State's Attorney Crowe, seeking to show that he was on top of the situation, issued a dramatic statement that was published on the front pages of Chicago's newspapers. Crowe asserted that Capone led the attack that resulted in McSwiggin's death. According to Crowe, a convoy of five automobiles filled with about thirty armed members of Capone's gang did the killing, and Capone himself used a machine gun "in order to set an example of fearlessness to his less eager companions."[24] Crowe's notice didn't say it, but the implication was that the O'Donnells, not McSwiggin, were the targets; McSwiggin evidently was at the wrong place at the wrong time in the wrong company. It may be that Capone, who had been at the nearby Hawthorne Inn in Cicero on the night of the shooting, got wind of the fact that the O'Donnell mob had been spotted at Madigan's saloon—the Lincoln automobile parked outside might have been the tip-off that led to the assault.

Capone wisely vanished after the murders, not to return for three months. When he surfaced again in Chicago he loudly expressed his innocence. "Of course I didn't kill him," Capone told reporters. He spoke of his friendship for McSwiggin, "a fine young fellow," and for the O'Donnells as well. And then he made the startling statement that he had given bribes to McSwiggin: "I paid him plenty and got what I was paying for."[25] Capone was acquitted of all charges and now seemed invincible against the forces of the law. But all was not well for him. The horrible murder of a prosecutor, however flawed the lawman was, angered the public. No longer could it be said that criminals just shot each other. An event that illustrates this changed attitude occurred shortly after the McSwiggin massacre, when locals from the suburban town of Forest View set fire to a large brothel, built and owned by Capone, in their community. A fire brigade arrived, but they made no effort to put out the blaze at the property. "Why don't you do something," pleaded one of the brothel employees, to which a firemen tersely responded, "Can't spare the water."[26]

The gang wars continued. Capone now focused on his long-time foes, the North Side successors to the slain O'Banion: Vincent Drucci, George Moran, and Hymie Weiss. On September 20, 1926, Capone was having lunch at the Hawthorne Inn in Cicero when a convoy of cars pulled up to the restaurant and the passengers fired machine guns into it, expending an estimated one thousand rounds of ammunition. Capone escaped harm when one of his bodyguards pushed him to the floor and jumped on top to keep him safe. After that episode, Capone tried to make peace among the warring gangs, following the maneuver he learned from his mentor John Torrio. But Weiss resisted any effort at compromise. Capone then returned to the old tried-and-true way of handling his enemies. On the afternoon of October 11, Weiss was gunned down in front of the Holy Name Cathedral on North State Street in Chicago by men firing machine guns and shotguns from a second-story window in a rooming house across the street. The hit had been carefully planned, with the assassins waiting for weeks by the window in the rooming house before the prey showed up. A lawyer accompanying Weiss was also killed in the fusillade, and three others in their group were wounded. Capone had an alibi for his whereabouts at the time of the killing, and no charges were brought against him. One crime writer surmises that the police and prosecutors were just as glad as the Big Fellow that the hot-tempered Weiss was permanently out of the picture.[27]

With Weiss disposed of, the push for a peace treaty advanced among the warring gangs. Although the impetus may have come from other gangsters, Capone was a main figure in making it happen. He was quite blunt in a press conference he held with reporters: "Hymie Weiss is dead because he was a bull-head. Forty times I've tried to arrange things so that we'd have peace in Chicago and life would be worth living. . . . There was, and there is, plenty of business for us all and competition needn't be a matter of murder, anyway. But Weiss couldn't be told anything. I suppose you couldn't have told him a week ago that that he'd be dead today. There are some reasonable fellows in his outfit, and if they want peace I'm for it now, as I have always been."[28]

And so on October 20, 1926, Chicago's top mobsters met at the Hotel Sherman. Among those present were Vincent Drucci, Bugs Moran, and Myles and William O'Donnell. It was a remarkably open event, held near City Hall and police headquarters. Like so many underworld affairs in 1920s Chicago, this meeting was not a secret. Newspapers covered both the meeting and the following party to celebrate the cessation of hostilities. Probably nothing was written down or signed, but the treaty was effective nonetheless. There had been sixty-seven gangland murders in the nine months and nineteen days of 1926 preceding the treaty, but none for the remainder of the year. Capone stated, "We shook hands and made peace and we promised each other that if anything ever came up between us that made us mad, we'd get together and talk it over peaceably and straighten it out."[29]

There was more good news for Capone toward the end of 1926—Big Bill Thompson announced that he was going to run for mayor of Chicago once again, which, if successful, would mean the end of the reformist Dever administration. Promising to open those speakeasies that Dever had closed, Thompson won a landslide victory in the April 7, 1927, election, with the support of Capone and other mobsters. And even more good news for Capone came just three days before the mayoral election, when his old enemy Vincent "Schemer" Drucci was shot to death in a scuffle with police. In this improved climate, Capone moved his headquarters from the Hawthorne Inn in Cicero to the Metropole Hotel in Chicago, where his outfit occupied more than fifty rooms.

But the peace treaty inevitably began to erode. The main force behind the erosion was Joseph "Joey" Aiello, whose burning ambition was to become the president of the Chicago branch of the Unione Sicilione. The Unione was a fraternal association dedicated to improving the lives of Sicilian immigrants to the United States. But to this noble mission was added a heavy involvement in criminal activities. Capone, seeking to use the Unione for his own purposes, was thwarted by the fact that his family originated in Naples. There were strong tensions between Neapolitans and Sicilians. Years later, one Neapolitan criminal in federal custody explained the extreme clannishness of Sicilians this way: "If you hang out with a Sicilian for twenty years and you have trouble with another Sicilian, the Sicilian that you hung out with all that time will turn on you."[30] Although Capone could not be a member of the Unione, he used his considerable influence in 1925 to ensure that his Sicilian friend Anthony Lombardo won the office. Aiello, who was allied with Bugs Moran's North Side gang, was furious that Capone had thwarted him and made it his mission in to take away Capone's life. In 1927 he reportedly offered to pay $50,000 to anybody who could off the Big Fellow, and Aiello tried to bribe a chef at a restaurant frequented by Capone to put poison in the gang leader's soup. Capone reinforced his bodyguards to defend himself and sent his own hit men to strike back at the killers hired by Aiello. The mounting deaths that this produced marked the end of the Hotel Sherman treaty. Aiello, fearing for his life, departed Chicago in November 1927.

About this time Capone began talking about retiring from the rackets, perhaps thinking he did not want to wait until he was bushwhacked like

Torrio had been. At a press conference at the Hotel Metropole on December 5, 1927, he announced to reporters that he was heading to Florida, "Let the worthy citizens of Chicago get their liquor the best way they can. I'm sick of the job. It's a thankless one and full of grief."[31] True to his word, he journeyed to Miami where he stayed for the winter at a rented bungalow. He liked Miami so much that he purchased a luxury home at 93 Palm Island built of white stucco, with fourteen rooms and a gatehouse, to which he added a swimming pool.

Here Capone entertained guests, zipped over the water in a powerboat, went fishing, and took seaplane rides. He went to sporting events at Hialeah racetrack and other venues, gambled, and hosted parties. All of this relaxation was possible because the Outfit in Chicago was able to run for long stretches without his being there, thanks to Frank Nitti, Jack Guzik, Al's brother Ralph Capone, and other gang members. Capone could stay in touch by telephone, or members of the outfit could come to Palm Island, or he could, when necessary, venture back to Chicago. For example, from his Florida vacation home on Palm Island Capone orchestrated the murder of Frankie Yale, his old mentor from his Brooklyn days. Yale's transgression against Capone was twofold: first, as the national head of the Unione Sicilione based in New York, Yale was reported to have been plotting with the banished Joseph Aiello to overthrow Joe Lombardo of the Chicago branch; second, Aiello was suspected of selling liquor to the Capone organization and then hijacking that same liquor so that he could resell it. On the afternoon of July 1, 1928, while he drove through his beloved Brooklyn, gunmen in a car with Illinois license plates caught up with Yale and murdered him with the customary shotguns and machine guns.

And also as customary, nobody was ever convicted of the crime. Capone demonstrated his innocence by proving that he had been in Florida at the time of the Brooklyn murder, but there was ample evidence that he had made arrangements with Chicago hit men and obtained the weapons in the Sunshine State. Murder was followed by murder. As revenge for the killing of Yale, three months later the Chicago head of the Unione, Antonio

Lombardo, was gunned down at midday at the intersection of Madison and State streets—the busiest intersection in the city. And three months after that, Pasqualino Lolardo, who succeeded Lombardo, was shot down in his home by people he thought were his friends. Being president of the Chicago branch of the Unione was probably the most dangerous job in the United States in the 1920s—seven of the eight incumbents during that decade died violent deaths.[32]

As for Capone, he kept moving back and forth from Miami to Chicago. He was spotted in the Windy City early in 1928 during the "Pineapple Primary," so called because of the unrestrained use of bombs to intimidate reformers who opposed Big Bill Thompson and his allies. Capone was also in Chicago on July 30, when he moved his operation from the Metropole into more extensive space at the nearby Lexington Hotel. In the winter of 1928–1929, he was ensconced in his Miami estate. On February 14, the weather in Florida was balmy, whereas in Chicago, 1,190 miles away, it was a dreary, cold, snowy day; however, more than the cold northern weather probably inclined Capone to be half a continent away on that date, which happened to be Saint Valentine's Day, 1929.

THE NORTH CLARK STREET MURDERS

The Saint Valentine's Day massacre remains the most notorious gangland rubout in history. A black car, with curtained windows and a bell in the manner of a detective squad car, pulled up at the SMC Cartage Company garage at 2122 North Clark Street. Two men in police uniforms and two men in civilian clothes left the car and entered the squat, one-story building. (In some accounts, there were three men in civvies.) Neighbors in buildings adjoining the garage heard loud, explosive noises coming from inside. About ten minutes after they had arrived the men returned to their car, with the two police holding guns on the other two, whose hands were in the air as if they had been arrested. The car then sped away.

A frantic dog was heard barking inside the garage. One neighbor, a Mr. C. L. McAllister, ventured inside the garage and quickly ran out, having observed a horrific scene. The victims had been in the garage when their killers arrived in their black car. They were lined up against the wall and methodically executed with seventy slugs from tommy guns followed by shotgun blasts. The victims' blood, brains, and guts splattered on the wall and the floor. Six were members of the Bugs Moran North Side gang, which used the garage for its beer-running trucks. The seventh, Reinhart H. Schwimmer, was a young optometrist who had added a bit of excitement to his life by hanging around with the Moran gang—an unfortunate choice for him.

Two creatures were actually still alive. One was the barking dog, whose leash had been attached to a truck. The dog's name was Highball, a good name for a bootlegger's pet. The other was Moran's gangster, Frank Gusenberg, who was still breathing even though he had fourteen bullets in his body. After the police arrived he was transported to a hospital where he later died. The episode created headlines around the world. Said the *Chicago Daily News*: "KILLING SCENE TOO GRUESOME FOR ONLOOKERS." Of course, the paper thoughtfully provided photos of that gruesome scene for its readers.[33]

In the minds of the populace, and among most crime writers as well, the Saint Valentine's Day Massacre is forever linked to Al Capone. He was never indicted or convicted of that crime, but neither was he convicted of other crimes or murders for which crime writers and the pubic believe him guilty—that is, the violent takeover of Cicero and the killings of Joe Howard, Dion O'Banion, William McSwiggin, Hymie Weiss, and Frankie Yale. Capone's guilt in the Saint Valentine's Day case is plausible, given his longtime, bloody struggle against the North Side mob. To reinforce the case against Capone, it has been argued that Joe Aiello, who had battled with Capone over the leadership of the Unione Siciliano, was affiliated with the North Siders (although Aiello was not in the garage on that fatal day). Others have suggested that Capone was motivated by a quarrel over the extortion racket in the Chicago dry cleaning industry or politics in an alderman election.[34] Whatever the motive may have been, the canonical view is that Capone was behind it and that he assigned the planning to his bodyguard Jack "Machine Gun" McGurn, who plotted the police car ruse, made up some scam to have the Moran gang assemble at the garage, and obtained the squad of hit men to do the job—all of this while Capone made sure to be in faraway Miami. George "Bugs" Moran's comment about the massacre summed it up: "only Capone kills like that."[35]

Despite the likelihood that Capone was to blame, there have been persistent claims that other persons were really responsible for the massacre. One theory suggests that the police committed the crime. The argument is that the killers looked like policemen because that is precisely what they were—corrupt cops out to get the Moran gang for some reason, such as revenge for the murder of one of their colleagues or a double-cross in an underworld scheme. In fact, just before he was taken to the hospital, Frank Gusenberg breathed, "Cops did it." A variant of the cop theory exists: a Chicago police sergeant's son had been murdered by the Moran gang, and, to avenge this wrong the policeman's cousin, a low-ranking Chicago gangster, William "Three-Fingered" White, organized the Saint Valentine's Day rubout.[36] Another group that has been suspected was the Purple Gang, a violent Jewish mob from Detroit that allegedly committed the massacre because the Moran gang had hijacked their liquor shipments. Still another theory focuses on Bugs Moran himself. Moran was not in the garage when the shooting took place because, it is said, he arrived at the 2122 North Clark Street location late for a meeting he had called and when he saw the bogus police car outside the building he walked on. Perhaps, however, he never had any intention of being there; perhaps he himself arranged the killing because he had discovered some disloyalty on the part of his men and had decided to have them executed.

So the arguments go. But one bit of tantalizing evidence does suggest a link between Capone and the massacre. As part of the investigation, police called on Calvin Goddard, one of the few experts in the emerging field of ballistics. Goddard employed microscopes to match bullets and shell casings with the guns from which the bullets were fired. By applying this matching technique to the North Clark Street garage, Goddard concluded that two Thompson machine guns had been employed in the murders. Later that year, two tommy guns were found by police in a St. Joseph, Michigan, hideout of the criminal Fred "Killer" Burke, who was being sought for the murder of a local traffic cop. Goddard tested the two tommy guns and found that both had been used in the Saint Valentine's murders; moreover, one of them had also been used in the 1928 murder of Frankie Yale in Brooklyn. This one weapon was connected to two separate crimes that Capone is suspected of commissioning. Burke was unfortunately never investigated by lawmen regarding either case. He did go to jail for the murder of the Michigan policeman and died of a heart attack in a Michigan prison in 1940 without revealing anything about the Saint Valentine's butchery.

One comic element emerged from the brutal tragedy of the Saint Valentine's Massacre. The police arrested Jack "Machine Gun" McGurn as part of the inquiry into crime. But he had an alibi—his girlfriend Louise Rolfe, a twenty-two-year-old blonde described in the press as a "slim, smart beauty," stated firmly that she and Jack had been in a hotel room all that day. McGurn was released; what he and Louise had been doing in the hotel was never specified, but her testimony was referred to ever after as the "Blonde Alibi," and she even got her own mob nickname, "Lulu Lou" from reporters.[37]

Less than three months after the Saint Valentine's Day Massacre came another multiple murder that has been attributed to Capone. On May 8, 1929, police in Indiana found the bodies of three men by the side of a road: Albert Anselmi, John Scalise, and Joseph Giunta. All three Sicilians had been repeatedly bludgeoned and shot. The dapper Giunta, known as Hop Toad for his dancing ability, was the president of the Chicago branch of the Unione Sicilione; the hulking Anselmi and Scalise were gunmen who worked for Capone. The first assumption was that Bugs Moran was taking revenge for the Saint Valentine's Day attack; "MORAN 'TROOPS' TAKE 3 FOR 7 IS POLICE THEORY" was the headline in the *Chicago Daily News* after the murder. But over the years, the crime has been pinned on Capone. The assumption is that Anselmi and Scalise were secretly plotting with Giunta to overthrow Capone but that the wily crime boss learned of this treachery and decided to punish the conspirators in dramatic fashion. He arranged for a dinner on May 7 at an Indiana roadhouse over the state line from Illinois. The three Sicilians were the guests of honor. After the attendees had been well fed, Capone and his henchmen turned on them in a murderous fury. Some accounts depict Capone himself beating the three with a baseball bat and muttering, "This is the way we deal with traitors."[38] But no indictments ever came forth, and one Caponeologist, Jonathan Eig, feels the roadhouse story is purely fiction.[39] Chicago reporter Fred Pasley, however, in the first biography of Capone, reported the account as genuine, and most Caponeologists agree.[40] Somebody killed Giunta, Anselmi, and Scalise, and Capone was certainly capable of the kills.

The decade of the 1920s was drawing to a close. Capone had begun it as the manager of a whorehouse in the Torrio crime empire, but by end he was unquestionably the most prominent mobster in the nation, the master of a vast empire of casinos, dog tracks, horse racing, prostitution, extortion, and bootleg alcohol that dominated Chicago and its neighboring suburbs. He had survived attempts to topple him by rival gangsters, lawmen, and reformers. He was a Chicago celebrity who gave informal conferences for reporters and who was seen by the public at operas and sporting events. But an invisible enemy army at work on Capone could not be eliminated by charm or tommy guns. This army consisted of billions of twisty bacteria known as spirochetes that for decades ate their hungry, wiggly way into his brain and nervous system. The condition was syphilis, a sexually transmitted disease he had contracted early in his career. Among the symptoms of advanced syphilis are violent behavior and megalomania. Says Capone's biographer Laurence Bergreen, "If Capone's syphilis had healed itself, as most cases did, it is unlikely he would have developed into the high-profile, feared gangster he became."[41] Those spirochetes were eventually able to extract a great price from Capone for his sexual transgression.

Syphilis aside, was Al Capone a criminal genius or just a lug who had gotten lucky? There are a surprisingly large number of crime writers who believe the latter. Thomas Reppetto in his book *American Mafia* referred to Capone as a thug who lacked business skills. Jay Robert Nash described him: "Capone was a murderous thug without remorse . . . a near-illiterate who acquired countless millions and knew not where to spend a dime of it. . . . Worse, for a decade the city of Chicago embraced this bragging, boasting, strutting killer." Stephen Fox said of Capone that he was a stupid, chuckleheaded buffoon, "a thrashing, flailing white elephant whom even his friends gave a wide berth." Arthur Madden, a treasury agent who investigated the Big Fellow, said flatly, "Capone was a fathead." New York mobster Joe Bonanno contemptuously pointed out that in Italian, Capone's name translated to "castrated male chicken." Capone's first biographer, Fred Pasley, said he was "Neapolitan by birth and Neanderthal by instinct."[42] Capone's critics believe that his rise was due to the brains of other, smarter men, like Jake Guzik and John Torrio.

Capone biographer Robert J. Schoenberg, however, contends that Capone was far more imaginative and intelligent than most criminals of that era. To prove his point, Schoenberg cites transcripts of Capone's testimony in legal proceedings to show the mobster's deft ability to control an interrogation.[43] Another way to gauge the level of Capone's mind is to read his frequent statements to reporters. He was able to come up with words that served his needs. During the McSwiggin investigation, when the slain prosecutor was being portrayed as a martyr, Capone stated that he had been paying regular bribes to the so-called hero. By cleverly portraying McSwiggin as not much better than a common criminal, he was able to reduce the fervor of the public campaign to solve the murder. In his other interviews, Capone consistently sought to shape his image—to portray himself as a family man who loved his wife and child, who wanted to achieve a lasting peace between warring mobs, and who was a civic-minded public benefactor. "Public service is my motto," he said on one occasion.[44] To show his patriotism he had pictures of George Washington and Abraham Lincoln on display in his office where visitors could see them. It is hard to imagine his contemporaries like Hymie Weiss and Bugs Moran being able to devote any thoughts to their brand in quite the same way. Some nimbleness of mind was also demonstrated by Capone's ability to come up with off-the-cuff jokes to fit the occasion. Early on in his Chicago career when he was running the Four Deuces brothel and pretending to be a dealer in second-hand furniture, he was asked what kind of stuff he sold, and he replied, "any old thing a man might want to lay on."[45] On another occasion he was arrested in Joliet, Illinois, for carrying a concealed weapon. When he stepped up to pay the fine, the judge said, "Maybe this will be a lesson to you." The cheerful Capone replied, "Yes, judge, it certainly will. I'll never tote a gun again—in Joliet."[46]

CHAPTER 2

Big Battles in the Big Apple

New York City in the 1920s is an iconic place and time in American memory. With six million people, it was the largest city in the nation. Chorus girls danced at the *Ziegfeld Follies*, nightclub hostess Texas Guinan greeted tipsy partiers with a cheery "Hello, suckers," Babe Ruth smacked out home runs at Yankee Stadium, Charles Lindbergh and Queen Marie of Romania got ticker tape parades down Wall Street, Langston Hughes wrote poetry in Harlem, barbers exchanged Wall Street tips with their customers, Duke Ellington and his band belted out jazz at the Cotton Club, ocean liners steamed into New York harbor with immigrants in steerage and the rich in first class, and street corner newsboys in cloth caps shouted "Extra! Extra!"

Crime too was part of the New York landscape in the 1920s, but it was not a subject for picturesque nostalgia. As two New York reporters later recalled the era, "Rum runners and hi-jackers were pistoled and machine gunned. They were taken for rides on the front seat of sedans and their brains blown out from behind by fellow mobsters they thought were their pals. . . . They were slashed into unconsciousness and placed in burlap sacks with hands, feet, and necks so roped that they would strangle themselves as they writhed. Charred bodies were found in burned automobiles. . . . Bootleggers and their molls were pinioned with wire and dropped alive into the East River."[1]

Crime in Chicago was checkered with the same kind of violence, but there the story was essentially Al Capone's conflict with his competition.

New York was the most diverse city in the world's most diverse nation, and its underworld was more complex, with several centers of influence. One way to describe the crime scene in the Big Apple is to look at a sample of the leading mobsters from separate ethnic groups, keeping in mind that this is a somewhat leaky concept because the Italians, Jews, and Irish were frequently thrown together for their mutual profit. An example of the diversity of New York crime was the Sicilian-born mobster Francisco Castiglia, who changed his name to the Irish Frank Costello, married a Jewish girl, and had a mistress of unknown ethnic background. He was a one-man melting pot.

And there were more like him. Italian American gangsters in New York and elsewhere frequently used names that originated in the British Isles; names that carried a tone of respectability, long pedigree in America, and, in the case of Irish names, athletic prowess. Vincenzo Gibaldi changed his name to Jack McGurn, Paulo Antonio Vaccarelli became a boxer under the nom de punch Paul Kelly, Girolmo Santucci became Bobby Doyle, James Plumari called himself Jimmy Doyle, Gandolfo Curto became Frank Marlow, Guarino Moretti for a time used the name Willie Moore, John Torrio sometimes took the name Frank Langley, and Lucky Luciano used Charles Ross. This casual changing of names was easier in that era before social security numbers. Gangsters lived in a world where everything, including their ethnic identity, was malleable.

Let us now trot out on the stage some leading gangsters from the New York City region in the 1920s. Although this chapter is divided into sections on Jews, Italians, and Irish, keep in mind that men of different ethnicity frequently crossed boundaries like billiard balls on a pool table.

Jews

Arnold Rothstein

The most prominent Jewish gangster in Prohibition New York was Arnold Rothstein. He was very different from other Jewish and Italian gang leaders of his generation, who either immigrated to America at a young age or were the American-born children of immigrants. Rothstein was Jewish, but he was the grandson of an immigrant so he had longer antecedents in America. He completed two years of high school, which made him the one of the best educated of the Prohibition gangsters. And unlike the crushing poverty and obscurity that most gangsters were born into, Rothstein's well-to-do family was prominent. New York governor Al Smith and U.S. Supreme Court Justice Louis Brandeis were among the admirers of Abraham Rothstein, Arnold's father, a wealthy businessman and Orthodox Jew. The Rothstein family lived on the prosperous West Side of New York, safely distant from the tenements of the Lower East Side Jewish ghetto.

Arnold was born in 1882, the second of the five children of Abraham and his wife Esther. His parents found Arnold to be moody and withdrawn, with a fierce sibling rivalry directed at his older brother Harry, a brilliant student and devout Jew who studied to become a rabbi. Arnold went in another direction, feeling little connection to his family's faith. Arnold put it this way to his father: "I'm an American. Let Harry be a Jew."[2] By his early twenties he had left home to become a gambler. A reporter who knew Rothstein described him as "a quiet, medium-sized man, inconspicuously dressed." He had dental problems, and when he grinned his small, even, sharklike false upper teeth became visible to observers. His complexion was described as feminine in its pallor.[3]

Rothstein's pallor probably stemmed from the fact that he slept most of the day and went out in the evening. He loved to stroll along Broadway, dine at Lindy's famed restaurant, and immerse himself in the world of gamblers, hoods, and newspapermen. Unlike most of them, however, he did not smoke tobacco or drink alcohol. He was married, but after his death his wife confessed to an interviewer that Arnold could not find his way to her bedroom.[4] One biographer finds an explanation in the field of psychiatry, claiming that gamblers "exhaust themselves emotionally in their gambling" and obtain "orgiastic pleasure" in that pursuit, with little time or enthusiasm for amatory activities.[5] Gambling turned the introvert Rothstein into a full-blown man about town possessed of wit and charm.

He loved to wager and had an extraordinary mathematical skill that aided his success. In sum, gambling was his life.

He owned gambling establishments, bet on horse races and boxing matches, and played poker, pool, craps, and other games of chance for enormous stakes. One game provided a quick adrenalin rush: he and an opponent would each pull out a fifty-dollar bill from their wallets, and they looked at the serial numbers to see who could put together the best poker hand, such as a full house or three of a kind; the winner took the other person's fifty dollars. At the other end of the gambling scale was a celebrated series of pool games that Rothstein played against a champion player from Philadelphia who was visiting New York in 1909. The marathon match ran nonstop for more than thirty-two hours, from 8:00 P.M. the evening of Thursday, November 18, to 4:00 A.M. on the following Sunday. Rothstein won a decisive victory, and thousands of dollars were bet by the two opponents and by the gamblers in the large crowd of onlookers. This historic competition helped to launch Rothstein's underworld status as a bold gambler.[6]

What really lifted his reputation was fixing the 1919 baseball World Series. Rothstein's role in this scandal is not clear, and he was never convicted of any involvement (in fact, he was never convicted of any crime), but he certainly participated at some (even long-distance) level in the bribery plot whereby White Sox players conspired to lose the 1919 World Series to the Cincinnati Reds, enriching those who bet on the underdog Cincinnati team.

The so-called Black Sox scandal broke at around the same time Prohibition became the law of the land. At the outset of Prohibition, the advocates of the Volstead Act predicted that once the saloons were closed, money that had been spent on booze would instead go to reputable amusements, such as Broadway theaters and amusement parks. The Adams Gum Company promoted their Chiclets brand as an alternative to cocktails.[7] But Rothstein concluded that the demand for alcohol would not go away and that major profits (certainly more than came from selling Chiclets) could be made by flouting the law of the land. One biographer says that Rothstein realized that he could provide "money, manpower, and protection"—all at a steep price—to those who made alcohol available. He was able to offer loans for criminal activities that a law-abiding bank could never undertake.

One of Rothstein's first Prohibition clients was Max Greenberg, a bootlegger from the Midwest who needed $175,000 to expand his business of smuggling booze from Canada. In 1920, Irving Wexler, a low-level New York mobster who knew the gambler, brought Greenberg to see Rothstein. Greenberg asked Rothstein to provide him the money. Rothstein thought it over and came back to him with a larger proposition; he wanted Greenberg to change the source of the liquor to Europe, rather than Canada. This contraband cargo would be brought across the Atlantic Ocean to a thirsty America. As his part of the expanded deal, Rothstein would supply the $175,000 that Greenberg wanted and would include his own additional funds into the operation, but several conditions were added. The $175,000 was to be considered a loan that Greenberg had to repay. Greenberg also had to guarantee payment by putting up as collateral the trucks and real estate he owned in Detroit, and he had to take out a life insurance policy for the highest amount he could obtain, with Rothstein as the beneficiary. That way Rothstein would be compensated if Greenberg voluntarily or involuntarily took the easy way out—that is, died. This insurance model became a characteristic of Rothstein's business practices, and he subsequently set up a life insurance company that enabled him to squeeze even more out of deals like these.[8]

With Greenberg now a junior partner in his own scheme, Rothstein made the big arrangements. He hired an agent in Europe to buy the alcohol and arrange to get a Norwegian ship to transport it. He had speedboats built to carry the cargo from the ship to the shore and arranged for trucks to take the booze to a warehouse. The whole project was successful, and the cargo ship made some eleven ocean crossings. On the last of those journeys, Rothstein was secretly the buyer of the smuggled alcohol, which enabled him to get an even larger share of the profits. The venture, profitable on all sides, launched

Wexler (who had invested in the project) and Greenberg on a partnership as major New York bootleggers. Crime writer Patrick Downey has questioned the details of the Rothstein-Greenberg-Wexler story because Greenberg was heavily involved in the St. Louis, Missouri, underworld in the early 1920s.[9] This uncertainty demonstrates the difficulty of getting to the truth about an illegal enterprise that all parties sought to hide from the authorities. One incontrovertible fact is that Wexler left behind his humble origins as a pickpocket and emerged as one of the most wealthy and successful of New York bootleggers in the 1920s.

Rothstein found it too much trouble to directly manage a liquor smuggling operation, given the tremendous risks and the major effort it required. He found it easier to be a silent investor in underworld enterprises and to smuggle in products that took up less cargo space, notably diamonds and narcotics. He retained a squad of lawyers and spun off companies that provided insurance, bail bonds, and other services, both legitimate and illegitimate. His companies, located in an office building on Forty-seventh Street, operated under names like Rothmere Investment Company, Redstone Material and Supply Company, and Pan-Continental Film Distribution Company. Little wonder that his nickname, coined by newspaper columnist Damon Runyon, was "The Brain," a moniker that made Rothstein proud. Along the way, Rothstein employed men from many different ethnic backgrounds who played important parts in Prohibition crime, including Frank Costello, Jack "Legs" Diamond, Irving Wexler, Meyer Lansky, Louis Lepke, Lucky Luciano, Dutch Schultz, and Bugsy Siegel. Working for Arnold was for New York's criminals what West Point was for army leaders. Legs Diamond seems to have been a somewhat insubordinate cadet. He served The Brain as bodyguard and defended bootleg shipments against hijacking. With Rothstein's approval, Diamond did some hijacking himself, aimed at his fellow Irishman Big Bill Dwyer. Rothstein and Diamond had a falling out, and in July 1927 Rothstein tipped off the police that Diamond was smuggling narcotics.[10] All of this demonstrates the complex interethnic relationships in the New York underworld.

Rothstein was such a central figure in the New York underworld that he was consulted like a guru. At one point the rebellious garment union locals, dominated by communists, were splitting the industry apart. The communists contacted Rothstein for help in their strike activities. He arranged to loan them $1,775,000, which was to be used to bribe police and judges so they would be neutral in the labor wars, and he made the phone calls and contacts to make sure it was spent effectively. It's intriguing to think about that encounter between (a) a radical group that dreamed of the time when the international proletariat would seize the means of production and (b) a dapper gambler who dreamed of drawing to an inside straight in poker.[11]

In fact, Rothstein's love of poker did him in. He was shot in a hotel room at the Park Central Hotel on the evening of November 5, 1928. The wound was in his abdomen, and he died the next day. It is likely that he was killed over a $320,000 loss he suffered when playing poker at the hotel, a loss he refused to pay because he thought the game was rigged. We will never know for sure. Although he was conscious and able to talk in the hospital for a brief time before he died, he put a finger to his lips when a detective tried to question him.[12] The code of silence had prevailed once again.

Louis "Lepke" Buchalter

Rothstein became prominent in the underworld mainly for his ability to bankroll criminal enterprises. Another Jewish gangster, Louis "Lepke" Buchalter, made his name in labor racketeering. He was born in 1897 to a large, poor Jewish immigrant family on the Lower East Side. His family nickname was "Lepkele," an affectionate Yiddish way of saying "little Louis." As happens with family nicknames, it morphed into something shorter—"Lepke." Sometimes during his adult life the nickname was used as his last name so he was called Louis Lepke, other times Louis Lepke Buchalter, or Lepke Buchalter—much to the confusion of later indexers of crime books. But whether used as his nickname or his surname, he liked the term Lepke because it humanized him to the Jewish garment workers he sought to exploit.

Lepke did quite well in elementary school, which in those years ended with the eighth grade and was the last year of compulsory education. Lepke dropped out of school at that point, like most other poor kids. Afterward he followed the usual gangster pattern of associating with young toughs. It is possible to speculate that his father's death when Lepke was ten and the breakup of his family had something to do with his dive to the depths. Or maybe it was because, like Rothstein, he came to resent his brother, who achieved a respected academic career. Or, throwing aside all this social and psychological analysis, maybe Lepke was just a natural-born thug. The voluminous FBI files on Lepke include an account of his first arrest, which took place in 1916 when he was nineteen years old. His crime was committed in Connecticut, where he stole five hundred dollars in property from the car of a salesman. For this crime he was sent to the Connecticut Reformatory at Cheshire. The medical director of the reformatory was clearly impressed by Lepke and wrote an upbeat report for the files about the young man: "Inmate is a clean cut intelligent Hebrew, who led a normal life in spite of little supervision. . . . [He] went to New York, got in with a bad crowd doing petty jobs. His delinquency was probably result of mental conflict coupled with companions. *Outlook is excellent* [emphasis in the original]."[13]

This intelligent Hebrew was subsequently arrested multiple times and served sentences in New York prisons for crimes that included burglary, armed robbery, and grand larceny. He was a hardened criminal when he was paroled at age twenty-five on March 6, 1922, by which time the landscape of crime had changed dramatically.[14]

Lepke reunited with a childhood friend, Jacob Shapiro. Where Lepke was a slim 5 foot 7 ½ inches, 160 pounds, with what his rap sheet described as "eyes alert—shifting," the stocky Shapiro was two inches shorter but 42 pounds heavier, with a curling lower lip, broken nose, and hulking demeanor. He slurred his words, pronouncing a grumpy "Get out of here," as "Gurrah," which became his nickname. At the time Shapiro was involved in labor slugging, and Lepke joined him in that endeavor.

Labor violence was something that by the 1920s had a long and nightmarish history in New York. Starting in the late 1800s, gangs armed with lead pipes and other weapons were paid by factory and sweatshop owners to wade into crowds of striking workers and beat them savagely. Labor unions paid other gangs—sometimes the same gang used by the owners—to attack scab strikebreakers and threaten the bosses. The gang members were known as "labor sluggers" (or "shlammers" in Yiddish). The gang Lepke and Shapiro joined was led by Jacob "Little Augie" Orgen. Little Augie was locked in competition for leadership of the labor slugging field against Nathan "Kid Dropper" Kaplan. All were from the Jewish underworld, and they sought to dominate the needle trades—men's clothes, women's clothes, hats, and furs—that constituted a major part of New York's economy. In these businesses most bosses and workers were Jewish.

On behalf of their boss, Little Augie, the team of Lepke and Shapiro came up with a plan to dispose of Kid Dropper. The two mobs, led by Kid Dropper and Little Augie, had been shooting at each other with some regularity, and, in a remarkable violation of the "don't squeal" underworld rule, Shapiro told the police that Dropper had wounded him with a shot fired from an automobile. Dropper was summoned to the Essex Market Court in Manhattan on August 28, 1923, to answer Shapiro's accusation. But when the two men faced each other that day, Shapiro stated that he had been wrong in identifying Dropper as one of the shooters. The judge dismissed the case, and Dropper was turned over to the police, who escorted him outside to be taken to the West Side Court by taxi to answer another charge, this one of carrying a concealed weapon without a permit. In the presence of two police captains, fifteen detectives, ten uniformed policemen, and civilian onlookers, Dropper was hustled into the cab, accompanied by detective Jesse Joseph and Captain Cornelius Willemse, with cab driver Ernest Goldfinger at the wheel. Before the taxi started moving, one Louis Cohen elbowed his way through the crowd and fired shots through the rear window, killing Dropper, wounding Goldfinger, and putting a bullet through Willemse's hat. When Dropper's wife struggled with Cohen, he threw her to the ground.

Cohen, described as undersized and emaciated, was arrested and ultimately sentenced to twenty years. Most crime writers who have examined this episode believe that Lepke and Shapiro put Cohen, a Little Augie mob hanger-on, up to the murder by getting him high on cocaine and telling him that he would be rewarded for doing the job. With the death of Kid Dropper, Little Augie was now the most powerful figure in the labor racket business, with Lepke and Shapiro as his high-ranking lieutenants.

Ever more strikes and leadership struggles in the garment district increased the demand for Little Augie's labor sluggers, so much so that Augie turned to the Irish gang of brothers Jack and Eddie Diamond to take on some of the work and also to provide bodyguard service to Augie. The entrance of the Diamond brothers into the business displeased Lepke, Gurrah, and another Augie gang member, Curly Holtz. The three men were also displeased by the fact Little Augie did not seem able to see the larger possibilities of the labor racket. According to the traditional method gangsters were workers for hire. A previous labor slugger chief from the earlier years of the twentieth century, Benjamin "Dopey Benny" Fein, had even established fixed prices: $150 for breaking up a small sweatshop or $600 for a larger one; $60 for shooting somebody in the leg or clipping off part of an ear; $200 for injuring a boss by breaking his arm or thumb or throwing him down an elevator shaft or flight of stairs.[15] Lepke, Shapiro, and Holtz reasoned it would be so much better to actually infiltrate the unions and get their hands directly on union bank accounts, but Augie clung to the old ways and resisted this innovation.

The dispute between Lepke on one side and Augie on the other surfaced over a labor issue in Brooklyn. Council 29 of the International Brotherhood of Painters, Decorators, and Paperhangers had gone on strike against an organization that represented the bosses of painting companies in the borough. The bosses gave $50,000 to Augie to end the strike by threatening to kill the union's leaders, a threat that ace New York reporters Craig

Thompson and Allen Raymond described as "as good as a call from the undertaker if disregarded."[16] The news of this got back to Lepke, Shapiro, and Holtz, who thought it a bad idea, believing it would be better to cultivate the union members than to alienate them. Augie ignored their protest and instead decided to split the $50,000 between him and the Diamond brothers, who would proceed to intimidate the union. The outcome of this issue came at approximately 8:30 on the evening of October 15, 1927. Augie and Jack "Legs" Diamond were in a car on the Lower East Side when another car pulled up and three men jumped out and started shooting. Augie was killed and Diamond wounded. Most likely Lepke and Shapiro committed the murder, possibly with Holtz. When the police interrogated the wounded Legs in the hospital he replied, "Don't ask me nothing, and don't bring anybody here for me to identify. Even if I knew they did it, I wouldn't put the finger on them."[17] Lepke and Gurrah were questioned by police, but they claimed that on the night of the killing they had been at the movies. As usual in these cases, neither an indictment nor a conviction followed; the killers simply walked away.

Was this really a matter of philosophical differences between Little Augie and Lepke over the proper way to operate the labor racket or just an old-fashioned power struggle? In this case the proof of the pudding was obvious: once he was in charge of Augie's gang, Lepke infiltrated labor unions just as he apparently advocated. In other words, the gangs who had been called in by the garment unions for assistance never left.

Dutch Schultz

One Jewish mobster who emerged late in the Roaring Twenties was Dutch Schultz. He was born in 1902 to German Jewish parents in the Yorkville section of Manhattan and later moved to the Bronx. His real name was Arthur Flegenheimer, but he was called Dutch Schultz after a legendary nineteenth-century rowdy Bronx kid. Years later, Shultz told a newspaper reporter that as a youth in elementary school he had been an avid reader. Among his favorite books, he said, were the works of Horatio Alger, an inspirational nineteenth-century American writer whose novels portrayed boys born in poverty who succeeded through hard work and honesty.[18] Schultz got the hard work part right, but he had trouble with the honesty component. After dropping out of school in the seventh grade, he worked to support his family as a roofer, newspaper boy, and printing press assistant, but he found that even more money could be made by holding up crap games and burglarizing other peoples' property as a member of the tough Bergen Gang. For his crimes the teenage Schultz spent fifteen months in New York correctional facilities. Years later when he was a notorious New York mobster, he still identified himself as a roofer.[19]

For most of the Prohibition era he was an obscure crook. But in 1928 he formed a business partnership with Joseph Noe (inevitably called Joey Noey by his peers), and together they opened a speakeasy in the Bronx called the Hub Social Club, with Schultz as the bartender. They invested in other Bronx bars and decided to branch out into bootlegging by trucking in beer from a Union City, New Jersey, brewery, which they used in not just their own drinking establishments but also others they could threaten into purchase. When Schultz and Noe encountered rival Bronx bootleggers John and Joe Rock, they responded with violence by kidnapping and beating (possibly even blinding) one of the brothers. Schultz and Noe prospered, making an estimated annual income of two million dollars. They built up a gang with men like Bo Weinberg, Fatty Walsh, and Vincent Coll and expanded their Bronx operation into other sections the city. One mobster who fought back against the expansion of the Schultz-Noe operation was Jack "Legs" Diamond. On the night of October 15, 1929, Noe was fatally wounded in a shootout outside the Chateau Madrid Hotel on West Fifty-fourth Street near Sixth Avenue in Manhattan. Noe's attacker was one Louis Weinberg, who himself was killed in the exchange of gunfire. Weinberg was said to have been a member of Legs Diamond's gang. The biographers of Dutch Schultz and Legs Diamond agree that the Chateau Madrid murders could have been the outcome of the rivalry between the two mobsters.[20]

The Chateau Madrid killings were of course never solved by the police, but two months after the shooting evidence that something was up was provided when police swooped down on one of the Schultz-Noe speakeasies and found five hundred shotgun shells, fifteen hundred rounds of pistol ammunition, six pistols, two bulletproof vests, and a loaded magazine for a tommy gun.[21] The partnerless Schultz knew he was now swimming in dangerous waters and was preparing for competition to come.

In movies like *The Cotton Club, Billy Bathgate,* and *Hoodlum,* Dutch Schultz has been depicted as a psychopath who flew into deadly rages. But part of his behavior may have been calculated. Crime writer Rich Cohen observed that Schultz "knew his power lay in the threat of violence."[22] He dressed in cheap suits and shirts, and he also had the tough guy habit of talking out of the side of his mouth. This was thought to be a characteristic of men who had spent time in prison where talk was not allowed and was made famous by the movie actor Edward G. Robinson in his portrayal of gangsters. This tic now seems extinct. Cohen also opined that Schultz had the eyes of a killer, a notion that stems from the ridiculous belief that the eye is a mirror of the soul, when in fact it is just a mirror of blood vessels, vitreous humor, retinas, and other material objects.[23]

ITALIANS

Joseph Masseria and Salvatore Maranzano

Markets have been a fixture of New York since the Dutch colony was established on Manhattan Island in the early seventeenth century, when an area was set aside where Indians and settlers could trade for fur pelts, fish, and corn. The New York Stock Exchange was established in 1817, and by the 1920s more than fifty outdoor markets operated in the city. It was therefore natural that, when Prohibition became the law of the land, an open market for the wholesale liquor business was soon established at Mulberry and Broome streets on the Lower East Side.[24] Here deals were made for liquor deliveries, and here genuine and counterfeit "permits" were bought and sold. (These permits authorized the holder to withdraw liquor from warehouses for medicinal purposes, an exemption allowed by the Volstead Act.) One problem with the market was its location—a mere block away from a local police station. Cops could look the other way just so much, and the blatant curbside market ended in 1922. Out of the ferment over control of the market emerged one Giuseppe Massseria.

Born in Sicily in 1879, Masseria was older than most of the Prohibition mobsters. He came to America in 1903 as a twenty-four-year-old adult and joined the Morello gang that ruled over the Lower East Side before Prohibition. He was arrested for kidnapping, extortion, theft, larceny, and breaking and entering, for which he went to prison. When the Morello gang was weakened by the imprisonment and death of its leaders, Masseria clawed and shot his way up to become by 1920 a dominant figure in the Lower East Side and was dubbed "Joe the Boss."

But uneasy is the boss that wears the crown, and Masseria had to fight the last enemy standing, one Umberto Valenti, a veteran of the Morello gang. The struggle came in three cinematic style rounds. First, on May 8, 1922, Masseria launched an ambush of Valenti on the streets of the Lower East Side. Five bystanders were wounded, a henchman of Valenti received a fatal wound, and Valenti got away. The police did manage to arrest Masseria, but he was not convicted.

Scandal erupted around the fact that Masseria had a permit for the pistol he used in the shootout; a permit issued by Selah B. Strong, a justice of the New York Supreme Court assigned to Suffolk County, bypassed the stricter gun permit standards of New York City. A Brooklyn magistrate charged that Justice Strong had given out dozens of such permits to criminals and was thus an enemy of law and order. When reached in his chambers, Judge Strong stated that he had no comment. Not coincidentally, the records of the permit disappeared from the court's files, another indication of the pervasive level of corruption in the Prohibition era.[25]

Round two came on August 8, 1922, when four men in a blue Hudson touring car pulled up near the brownstone at 80 Second Avenue where Masseria lived. It is probable that one of the men in the car was Valenti himself. He was rumored to have killed twenty men in his underworld career so he wouldn't have any qualms about adding another to the list. Two men got out of the car and walked to a restaurant across the street where they snacked on coffee and cake while watching the brownstone. Around 2:00 P.M. they saw a throng of people emerge onto the sidewalks from the Beethoven Music Hall. They were cloak makers from the International Ladies' Garment Workers' Union who had been attending a union meeting at the Beethoven auditorium. Also in the crowd was a street vendor selling lemonade to the thirsty union members from his donkey cart. At about the same time, Masseria came out of his house and started walking down the street. In front of the startled cloak makers, the two men in the restaurant started running after their target.

Once he realized he was being pursued, the unarmed Masseria dashed into the Heiney Brothers women's wear store at 82 Second Avenue, followed by one of the hoods with a Colt automatic in hand. The horrified shopkeeper, one of the Heiney brothers, saw the gunman fire twice at Masseria from close range. But by leaping and ducking the Boss dodged both bullets. Three shots were fired, two of which smashed the shop window. Massseria then fled to his home. Realizing that their quarry had eluded them, the two gunmen hastily returned to the car to make their getaway. But some men in the cloak makers group ran into the street to prevent the car from leaving. The panicked mobsters fired some twenty-five bullets into the crowd, wounding six men and the lemonade vendor's donkey. Police from the nearby Fifth Street station who got a glimpse of the tussle on Second Avenue commandeered an automobile and chased the fleeing Hudson through the streets of lower Manhattan. The hit men managed to elude the pursuers. Lawmen later found Joe the Boss sitting in his bedroom while soaking his aching feet in a basin of warm water after running for his life. There were two bullet holes in his hat form the attempted assassination.[26]

The third and final round in the Masseria/Valenti war came four days later. The location was seven blocks north the site of the previous shooting, and the time was 11:45 A.M. Bystanders on the street later said they had seen several young, well-dressed, short dark men walking down Twelfth Street, when somebody bolted away in fear, chased by the others who were shooting at him with drawn guns. The running man reached a taxi and tried to pull his own gun and fire back, but the bullets hit him first, and he fell dead. It was Umberto Valenti. Also wounded were a street sweeper and an eight-year-old girl who, as she fell to the sidewalk, said, "I'm hurt, Mamma." When the shooting ceased, the perpetrators scattered in different directions. The theory of crime writers is that Masseria had invited Valenti to meet him on the street to discuss peace between the two warring factions. Each agreed to bring bodyguards. Valenti fell—literally, as it turned out—for this bogus peace proposal. Masseria had no intention of arranging any sort of truce, but instead he had instructed his men to kill the rival gang leader.[27] When questioned by police, Masseria said that he had not been there and, in fact, had not left his home since the earlier shooting. The police noted that he was wearing a brand-new hat, casting doubt on the idea that he had been sequestered at home. Hat or no hat, he was not convicted of the crime, and at least for the moment was a major Mafia chieftain in New York City. The story of his miraculous ability to dodge bullets gave him a sort of supernatural credibility in the underworld.[28]

A different hat now enters the story; this one owned by Benito Mussolini, the Fascist dictator of Italy. In 1924, Il Duce came to a small town in Sicily to give a speech. This was unfriendly territory: Sicilians had long resented the rule of Rome and demonstrated it on this occasion by stealing Mussolini's hat from his chair when he got up to speak. It has been said that Mussolini, who had long resented the power of criminal networks in southern Italy, was so insulted by the hat incident that he now decided to focus his wrath on the Mafia. On his orders, between twelve hundred and two thousand suspected Mafia members were imprisoned—some without a trial, others in iron cages in the courtroom. A number of Mafioso decided to leave their country for the United States.[29]

One of them was Salvatore Maranzano, who was born in 1886 in the Sicilian town Castellammare del Golfo and immigrated to New York in the mid 1920s. He was far different from the American-raised school dropouts and reform school alumni who typified Prohibition gangsters. Maranzano had studied to be a Catholic priest and was able to speak Latin, Greek, and English, although the last was heavily accented. He immersed himself in the history of ancient Rome and Julius Caesar and was deeply steeped in the romantic tradition of the Sicilian Mafia as a patriotic resistance movement. He liked elaborate initiation rituals for his underlings, which involved things like sticking a pin in the trigger finger of new initiates to draw out a drop of blood.[30] He may have immigrated to the United States illegally because the U.S. Immigration Act of 1924 sharply reduced the flow of immigrants from Italy and Eastern Europe.

Maranzano had a charisma that attracted followers. One of his chief lieutenants was Joseph Bonanno, two decades younger, who by his own admission was smuggled into America from Sicily at the time of Mussolini's crackdown. Bonanno had known Marranzano in Italy and was thrilled to see him in New York. Bonanno said later, "He was a fine example of a Sicilian male: robust, about five feet nine inches tall, full-bodied, but with no excess flaccid flesh on him, deep chested, with sturdy muscular arms and legs. . . . He could make his face smile sweetly, or he could look severe enough to make you tremble." He added, "I felt honored and privileged just to be near him. I suppose it was like falling in love, only it was between men." Bonanno had a different feeling about Masseria, whom he regarded as a squat, fat, messy eater, drooling spaghetti from his mouth. Maranzano established himself in New York as a real estate broker, but he is also suspected of making money by smuggling his countrymen into the United States, and, like almost every other mobster, he entered the bootlegging business.[31]

Lucky Luciano

It was inevitable that the two ambitious Mafia bosses, Joe Masseria and Salvatore Maranzano, would clash over the leadership of the New York Mafia. As the antagonism grew, they each sought to recruit followers. One hot commodity in the New York underworld they vied for was one Salvatore Lucania, or, as he is known today, Lucky Luciano. He was born in Sicily in 1897 and immigrated with his parents to the Lower East Side in 1907. He followed the customary path of leaving school, committing street crime, going through reform school and prison, becoming a member of one of the youthful gangs that predated Prohibition—in this case the Five Points gang, called the prep school for crime. The Five Pointers also enrolled Al Capone, John Torrio, and Frankie Yale. Luciano changed his first name to Charles. He found "Sal" too feminine because it could be rendered as "Sally." Lucania later became Luciano—perhaps because the former had a feminine ending. He was a young man of medium stature and dark good looks. He learned to dress conservatively and mix easily with people born to a higher rank in society. Joseph Bonanno, who had reason to dislike him, said of Luciano, "He possessed a shrewd intelligence and level-mindedness that made him a good leader and superb organizer." A court-ordered psychological profile of Luciano has the ring of truth; he was "dominated by recklessness and a craving for action . . . his manner easy, copious, and ingratiating."[32]

In one respect Luciano's attitude was different from other Sicilian mobsters. The section of the Lower East Side where he was raised was also the home to a large Jewish population, and as a young man he befriended some rising criminals of that faith, notably Meyer Lansky and Benjamin "Bugsy" Siegel. Later in life he associated with other criminally inclined Jews. Because he was a Sicilian, Luciano had entree to the Mafia, but his association with Jews was frowned on by both Masseria and Maranzano. An oft-repeated story is how at a meeting of Luciano's mob in the late

1920s, one of his gang members, Vito Genovese, learned from Frank Costello that Dutch Schultz was being brought into the operation. The angry Genovese barked, "What the hell is this! What're you tryin' to do, load us up with a bunch of Hebes?" To which Costello sarcastically replied, "Take it easy, Don Vitone, you're nothin' but a fuckin' foreigner yourself."[33] The source of this story is *The Last Testament of Lucky Luciano*, which has been regarded as unreliable (see the Note on Sources in this book), but it's pleasing to believe that the account of easy tolerance in Luciano's circle is accurate.

With his Jewish and Italian colleagues, some as subordinates and some as partners, Luciano built a mob in the 1920s that engaged in bootlegging, narcotics, and brothels. It is estimated that his gang numbered two hundred men.[34] Others could be described as associates, each with their own operations. Among the partners were Longie Zwillman and Willie Moretti of New Jersey, Dutch Schultz, Joe Adonis, and the Bug and Meyer gang of Bugsy Siegel and Meyer Lansky. Luciano is supposed to have said, "At the top we were partners." But he went on to describe himself as the first among equals: "they all looked to me."[35] It should be emphasized that the structure was very loose. Anybody searching for an organizational chart with lines of authority would be disappointed. Luciano was not a remote CEO but somebody who was a hands-on criminal. During the 1920s he was arrested six times for narcotics, assault, carrying a concealed weapon, and grand larceny, but he was not convicted on any of these charges.

In the end, Luciano agreed to join Masseria's outfit. When did this happen? Some crime writers believe that it was as early as 1920–1922 and that he was one of the young, well-dressed shooters in the murder of Valenti. But others put it back to late 1927, when he stepped in as second to Joe the Boss.[36] There is a big difference between Luciano, still a kid in 1920, and Luciano the thirtyish mob boss of 1927. It is possible that Luciano did some work for Masseria early on, just as he also worked for Rothstein, Lepke et al., but he did not come on as a top aide to the Boss until 1927.

Frank Costello

The man who came to be called in the newspapers the prime minister of the underworld arrived in New York with his mother in 1896, when he was five years old. (His father and siblings had come over the previous year.) They settled in the Italian immigrant slum of East Harlem, and predictably Frank joined the hoodlum life. He was arrested twice for assault and robbery. When he was twenty-four he was sentenced to a year in prison for carrying a gun. It's probably misleading to think that a single event can determine the course of a person's life, but Costello's biographer believes the year in jail did just that; serving time convinced Costello that he should never carry a weapon.[37] Whether he packed a gun is irrelevant; Costello did not quit the criminal life, but rather he sought a higher level within it, beyond the stick-up man he had been. He had extensive dealings with Rothstein, and with the advent of Prohibition he set up a business office on high-toned Lexington Avenue. The organization he built was run in a businesslike manner, and thereafter he sought to act in the manner of a deal-making corporate executive, which ultimately led to his prime minister reputation.

In the 1920s the world of bootlegging was rough and tumble. One of the people whom Costello hired after an interview at the Lexington Avenue office was Fred Pitts, a maritime diesel engineer. Pitts was assigned by Costello to be the engineer on the *California*, a boat docked on the isolated north fork of Long Island. Once he got to the boat, a Costello gang member warned Pitts that the previous engineer was no longer there because he talked too much and that Pitts should learn to keep his mouth shut. He found that his job involved taking the boat out to sea to rendezvous with ships from Europe carrying liquor. The crew would transfer the cargo to the *California*.

On April 17, 1925, the *California* headed out to the meet the *Denise*, a cargo ship from Belgium. Pitts was told that one of the items the *California* would be receiving from the *Denise* were two suitcases, for the safe return of which the crew would receive a double bonus. Besides the two suitcases, the *California* crew took off the *Denise* a curious assortment of items—rifles, ammunition, motion picture machines, and a German shepherd puppy. They were also supposed to pick up two hundred cases of liquor, but before that could happen a Coast Guard destroyer spotted them and started a pursuit. As the *California* raced away as fast as it could the crew threw overboard the weapons, ammo, movie equipment, and suitcases; the latter weighed about sixty pounds each. The *California* was finally captured and brought back to the New London, Connecticut, Coast Guard station. The crew was let go, presumably because they no longer had anything incriminating on board, except possibly the puppy.

Other assignments were given to Pitts, among them a meeting on Block Island with six Coast Guard officers. Over much drinking and revelry, a payoff was arranged to allow the *California* to pick up a shipment of whiskey from another incoming cargo ship. On another occasion, Pitts was sent to Halifax, Nova Scotia, to negotiate the purchase of ten thousand gallons of alcohol. Pitts became worried about his survival in the Costello operation; one gang member suspected he was talking to the police, which he may well have been doing. He abruptly quit and went into hiding at his brother in-law's house on Long Island. Pitts hid in a closet when the gang came to kill him and afterward left the New York area. A quarter of a century later a federal investigator found Pitts residing in a wayside trailer camp in Ohio, still living in fear that the Costello mob would one day find him and kill him.

And what was in the two mysterious suitcases? Without a doubt, narcotics.[38]

Socks Lanza and Ciro Terranova

Extortion was a staple of criminal gangs in New York long before Prohibition. The basic equation was simple: if you don't give me money, then something bad will happen to you. This was as old as the sinister Italian "Black Hand" of the late nineteenth century and as common as a schoolyard bully threatening to beat up other kids if they don't fork over their lunch money. But in Prohibition the practice was expanded and improved. The term "racket" was loosely attached to this line of criminal activity, although the term could be used for any way of making money. In their 1940 book, *Gang Rule in New York*, the two veteran reporters Craig Thompson and Allen Raymond provided a "Guide to the Rackets," that included garment manufacturing, bread, milk, restaurants, taxi cabs, fish, chicken slaughtering, vegetables, and movies. In the classic racket scenario, the gang developed a trade association into which businessmen would be forced to pay. The rackets were often ethnic specific. Italians ran the construction racket because so many unskilled workers predominated in the building industry. Jewish racketeers Buchalter and Shapiro had a chokehold on the garment industry where most of the workers were Jewish.[39]

Notable among the Italian racketeers was Joseph "Socks" Lanza, whose career demonstrates how gangsters could suck income from legitimate businesses. Lanza was the founder and business manager of a union for the workers who handled the unloading of the six thousand fishing boats that each year docked at the Fulton Fish Market in lower Manhattan. Lanza charged each fishing boat a ten-dollar fee over and above the wages of the union workers; a captain who failed to pay up would discover that his cargo of fish had accidentally been dropped into the harbor. Peddlers who sold fish from pushcarts had to get a license from the city of New York; they also had to pay a fee to Lanza. Retail businessmen in the fish industry who came to the Market to purchase quantities of seafood were advised to pay a fee to a protective service that watched to make sure no harm came to their cars and trucks, such as slashed tires. The major wholesale dealers who sold to retailers were shaken down for around forty thousand dollars a year. Lanza's operation also got the inedible remains of fish for free, which he sold as feed to livestock growers at a profit. As in most protection rackets, a portion of what Lanza made went to bribe government and law enforcement authorities, which is why efforts to indict Lanza for his assorted protection rackets never got off the ground until the 1930s. But even after serving two prison terms, he continued to control the fish market, right up until his death in 1968.[40]

Another Italian racketeer was Ciro Terranova, a puffy-faced Mafioso who controlled the New York market for artichokes, a vegetable much desired by Italian households because it was a main ingredient in minestrone soup.[41] The enthusiasm for this vegetable may have also had something to do with an ancient Italian belief that artichokes had an aphrodisiac effect. Terranova came from a family of Sicilian immigrants with a Mafia pedigree that long predated Prohibition. There were three Terranova brothers—Ciro, Nick, and Vincenzo—all stepbrothers of Giuseppe Morello, a fearsome New York gang leader during the early years of the twentieth century. Morello was known as "Clutch Hand" because of his withered right arm, which had only the pinkie finger, giving the appearance of a claw.

The Terranova brothers were followers of Morello and suffered from the association. Rival gangsters shot Nick to death in 1916 and Vincenzo in 1922. The surviving Terranova brother, Ciro, moved into the artichoke racket, working from the large wholesale vegetable market in East Harlem, a part of the city that then had a large Italian population. Terranova skimmed tribute money for every truckload of vegetables brought into the market, and any retail merchant who tried to buy artichokes from another dealer would be punished. The stool pigeon Joseph Valachi later explained Ciro's racket this way: "The way I understand it he would buy all the artichokes that came into New York. . . . Being artichokes they hold; they can keep. Then Ciro would make his own price, and as you know, Italians got to have artichokes to eat."[42]

Terranova prospered in the business. He accumulated enough money to purchase a $52,000 home in the Westchester County town of Pelham. He and his wife had ten children, which, who knows, may have had something to do with all those artichokes. But Terranova had ambitions beyond his racket, and he dabbled in larger criminal goings-on in New York. He had a long arrest record that dated back to 1916. In a 1918 murder trial, he was acquitted of a double murder on a technicality, even though the entire courtroom, it is said, thought him guilty.[43] To help establish his bona fides as a leader of the underworld he provided a fifteen-foot-high floral tribute at the funeral of a slain gangster, and to protect himself he bought an automobile with armor plating and bulletproof glass. After all, if Al Capone could have an armored car, why not Ciro?

Terranova made headlines in 1929, when he was a suspect in the front-page slaying of Frank Marlow on June 24 of that year. Marlow, described in the papers as a "Broadway racketeer," was well known in the world of boxing, nightclubs, and horse racing. It was alleged that Terranova had been involved in the killing, but no charge was brought against him. In this incident he shared the publicity spotlight with an attractive twenty-year-old woman dancer named Minnie Seiden. Having at one time performed at the Rendezvous nightclub, she was dubbed "Mickey of the Rendezvous." It was established that on the night of the murder she had spent some time in a hotel room with Marlow until the hotel detective threw her out. At her appearance at a hearing to reduce her bail, she was described as wearing a beige silk dress with beige stockings, and brunette curls peeping out from her beige felt hat. The judge turned down her appeal and then expressed his Victorian disapproval to Minnie's mother who was in the courtroom: "It is you, madam, that we feel sorry for. Your daughter may be all that you believe her to be, but she has brought this on herself. Her associates have not been of the proper sort."[44]

Later that same year Terranova was implicated in another scandal. On December 7 he attended a political dinner held in honor of Magistrate Albert H. Vitale and sponsored by the Tepecano Democratic Club at the Roman Gardens, a banquet hall in the Bronx. The revelry and glowing remarks continued into the early hours of the morning, and Vitale was at the lectern gratefully acknowledging the appreciation of his supporters, when into the room came seven armed men who blocked the exits and trained their guns on the audience. Vitale and the attendees were robbed of their cash and jewelry, estimated at $4,500. The intruders also took away the guns brought to the dinner by court officers and a New York police detective and departed with their loot to a getaway car that was waiting outside.[45]

Nobody was hurt, but the stick-up touched off a furor. Shocking details were reported about the fact that several men with criminal arrest records had been in attendance at the magistrate's gala and that the police detective, Arthur Johnson, had his gun politely returned by the Tepecanoe club soon after the robbery. The whole affair was a huge embarrassment for the police and the city's political elite by exposing their connection with the criminal class. As the investigation dragged on without result, the police put forward a bizarre explanation, claiming that the Artichoke King had organized the robbery in order to grab from another hoodlum at the event a signed contract implicating Terranova in the murders of Frankie Yale and Frank Marlow. The contract was said to have authorized the killers of Yale and Marlow to receive $20,000, of which $5,000 had already been paid.[46] It is ludicrous to believe that an actual signed piece of paper had been drawn up for a gangland double assassination or that anybody in his right mind would choose a crowded banquet filled with witnesses as the place to retrieve such a document.

Terranova was without question mobbed up to his shifty eyeballs in criminal activities, but he was probably right when he stated that "the political fuss has reached the stage where I am being made the goat. Somebody had to be the goat, that's all."[47] He blamed the whole mess on Democratic politicians, including New York City mayor Jimmy Walker and former state governor Al Smith. Mayor Walker quickly struck back with a statement to reporters: "Terranova is right in his idea of an animal, but he got his animals mixed. He's not a goat, he's a jackass."[48] There has never been a solution to the mystery of who pulled the Roman Gardens stick-up, but Walker's assessment of Terranova as a weak fool has endured. It is said of the Artichoke King that he should never have become embroiled in the political rivalry, that the whole episode had dredged up his criminal career, and that he fumbled in his desire to become a Mafia boss.[49] A legend of the Prohibition era contends that on one occasion in 1931, Terranova was assigned to be the driver of the getaway car in a murder of a prominent mobster. He stayed in the limousine while four hit men entered a restaurant where their target was located, shot him, and then raced back to the car. Terranova was so shaking in fright that he could not get the car in gear, and one of the others had to push him aside and take over the wheel.[50] Terranova finally got out of the rackets in 1931, when he turned over the artichoke monopoly to an underling. But it was not a happy retirement. He was plagued with dwindling health and income and derided by the police as a "cheap pushcart peddler."[51] He died of a stroke in 1938, the last of the three brothers to die, and the only one who wasn't murdered.

Irish

Of the three main ethnic groups involved in crime during the Prohibition era, the Irish got there first. The potato famine of the 1840s brought massive numbers of Irish immigrants to the city. In the year 1850, for example, 117,000 immigrants from Ireland came to New York. On the eve of the Civil War, one out of four New Yorkers had been born in Ireland.[52] The newcomers' Catholic religion and poverty offended the Protestant majority in the city, but the Irish proved adept at politics and in the Civil War era firmly established themselves within the city's Democratic party. In 1925, the dapper Irishman, foe of Prohibition, and Tammany Hall politician Jimmy Walker was elected mayor. Though not as blatant as Mayor Thompson in Chicago, Walker eased the climate for bootleggers. In fact, that climate was already pretty balmy. In 1924 the New York City–born governor of the state, Al Smith, pushed a law through the legislature preventing the state from enforcing federal Prohibition statutes. It was a gift to gangsters.

Bill Dwyer and Owney Madden

William Dwyer, born in 1883, was a dockworker when Prohibition became the law of the land. Like Rothstein, he was one of the early visionaries who realized the profits that could be made in a large liquor smuggling enterprise. He drew on the help of businessman George J. Shevlin, who had expertise in the saloon trade. Together they assembled the infrastructure of trucks, boats, garages, and warehouses necessary to make it happen. When ships with contraband liquor began to sell their Rum Row cargoes off the coast of New Jersey, Dwyer's speedboat fleet brought the liquor to shore. A vital part of his operation was to provide generous bribes to the police. This led to an inquiry into corruption, but Dwyer resolutely refused to name names, a fact that endeared him to the members of the police force who were on the take. When the Coast Guard began to swoop down on the offshore rum-runner ships, Dwyer included them in his bribery too. At one point he bribed virtually the entire crew of a Coast Guard boat, giving each man seven hundred dollars to not only look the other way but also to actually pick up a shipment of 315 cases of booze from a rum-runner, *Ellis B*, and unload it on the shore. Whenever a policeman or Coast Guardsmen on his payroll was arrested, Dwyer paid for their legal defense; if they did have to serve time behind bars, Dwyer provided financial support for their families. Money also went to the judges and politicians of Tammany Hall.

All of this bribery added to his overhead costs, but Dwyer was still able to make a handsome profit on his booze by diluting the imported European or Canadian liquor with water, coloring, and cheap alcohol. This watering down was commonplace in the bootleggers' world, but Dwyer took it a step further by his attention to detail. He contracted to have counterfeit bottles made up, along with counterfeit labels, and even counterfeit revenue tax stamps. With the money he made Dwyer was able to buy a new home on Belle Harbor, Long Island, to invest in restaurants, a hockey team, racetracks, hotels, and prime Manhattan real estate, and to sport a diamond stick pin.[53]

Dwyer brought another Irishman, Owney Madden, into the operation. Like Dwyer, Madden was a guy who knew the docks and saloons. Born in 1892 to poor Irish parents in the port city of Liverpool, at the age of eleven he was sent to America to live with his aunt. He grew up as a tough guy with a "dese, dem, and dose" New York accent, spoken out of the side of his mouth like Dutch Schultz. In 1914 he shot and killed a fellow hoodlum in a fight over a girl and was sent to Sing Sing. He was released in January

1923, which made him available to throw in his lot with Dwyer as somebody who could prevent the hijacking of the combine's shipments against
rivals like Legs Diamond. Madden was the iron fist in the velvet glove of
the genial Big Bill.

In 1924, Dwyer and Madden opened the Phoenix (or sometimes Phenix)
Cereal Beverage Company, a block-long brewery at Twenty-sixth Street and
Tenth Avenue in Manhattan, where they produced a brand of beer dubbed
Madden's No. 1. The large structure was metaphor for the middle finger,
stretched out on Manhattan Island in defiance of the Eighteenth Amend-
ment. The man who protected Dwyer and Madden from arrest was a major
Tammany Hall Irish politician, James J. Hines. For twenty-five years Hines
served as alderman from the Eleventh Assembly District. He was tight with
New York's major criminals and relied on them to help win reelection.

In December 1925, the magic faded. In a sweep by federal Department
of Justice agents, dozens of men were arrested for violating the Prohibition laws, and at the top of the list of arrestees was Dwyer, described in the
papers as "the head of an international rum ring controlling many millions
in money, ships, and liquor"[54] Much came tumbling out from prosecution
witnesses at the trial—the bribery, the trips to Rum Row, the involvement of
Coast Guard members, the speedboat fleet. Madden, however, was not one
of the other suspects named in the indictment, and the Phoenix brewery
never came up. Moreover, Tammany judges and lawyers handled Dwyer's
appeals, and in the end he served only eleven months of his two-year sentence.[55] Perhaps Hines was able to do some damage control.

Frank Costello was also arrested in the 1925 sweep. His smuggling operation was not part of Dwyer's, but they did cooperate from time to time
in an informal partnership. Costello and thirteen codefendants went on
trial after the Dwyer case, which turned out even better for them; the jury
acquitted eight of the defendants and could come to no agreement about
Costello and the other six so Costello walked away. Years later he proudly
confided to his attorney that he had bribed the judge and the jury in the
case.[56]

Legs Diamond

The astute reader will notice that the name of Jack "Legs" Diamond has been mentioned several times in the above narrative of Prohibition era crime in New York City. He did seem to be everywhere, and during his career was arguably the nation's best-known mobster in the 1920s after Al Capone. He was born to Irish immigrant parents Philadelphia. After his mother died, Jack and his younger brother Eddie wound up in Brooklyn, where they ran in youth gangs and committed the usual crimes of burglary, robbery, and larceny. Jack seems to have been the more incorrigible; in 1914, when he was fifteen or sixteen—his date of birth is uncertain—he served time in the New York reformatory. In 1918, when America was at war with Germany, he was in the army, although it is uncertain whether he was there because he was drafted or because he enlisted in order to avoid another prison term. Theoretically, military service for his country might have turned him away from crime and started him on an honest career path, but he chose a different path. He deserted from Fort Dix in New Jersey, in the process stealing a pistol and attacking a sergeant with an iron bar. For this he was sentenced to hard labor at the federal penitentiary in Fort Leavenworth, Kansas. He was released in 1921 and returned to the streets of New York with his antisocial tendencies intact.[57]

Based on his rap sheet, his preferred crimes were burglary and theft, and stealing furs was a specialty. He was also adept at antagonizing New York's leading mobsters, as we have seen in the case of Arnold Rothstein, Louis Lepke, Gurrah Shapiro, Big Bill Dwyer, Owney Madden, and Dutch Schultz. Crime writer T. J. English observed that Diamond was an "underworld outsider," who did not seem to mind antagonizing other mobsters.[58] For Legs, somewhat like Luciano, the ethnicity of his few friends and many foes did not seem to bother his tolerance one way or the other; he didn't care whether they were Jewish, Italian, or Irish. There have been many suggestions on the origin of his "Legs" nickname. One opinion is that as a double-crosser, he was adept at running from his friends; another is that he was an energetic dancer. More likely but less ironic is the thought that his whippet-thin frame—5'9" and 140 pounds—emphasized his legs.

Diamond's reckless escapades frequently made headlines, which he did again in July 1929, when he demonstrated a particularly bad example of customer service at the Hotsy Totsy Club, a Broadway drinking establishment in which he had a share with mobster Charles Entratta. On the evening of July 14 a group of friends entered the establishment, among them two low-level hoods from the New York docks, Simon Walker and William "Red" Cassidy. Walker and Cassidy were drunk as skunks and itching for a fight. They shoved the staff around and pounded on the bar. Diamond and Entratta confronted the two. Legs is reported to have said to Walker, "I'm Legs Diamond and I run the place. If you don't calm down I'll blow your head off," to which Walker replied, "You no-good bastard, you can't push me around." Diamond and Entratta pulled out their pistols and started shooting at Walker and Cassidy, while the Hotsy Totsy band played louder to overcome the noise. When the smoke cleared, Walker and Cassidy were dead, and Red's brother Peter was wounded.[59]

By the time the police arrived, Diamond and Entratta had fled the scene. New York City Chief of Police Grover Whalen vowed to apprehend the two "notorious gunmen and racketeers" and thereby "send a message to gangdom that the police will give them no quarter."[60] This was the usual empty bluster from the authorities. Diamond and Entratta remained in hiding, and, during that time, four of the Hotsy Totsy Club staff members were rubbed out, including waiter Walter Wolgast and manager Hymie Cohen. This mightily discouraged other witnesses from testifying, and neither Diamond nor Entratta was convicted.[61]

Diamond was as experienced at being shot at as he was in shooting other people. On four separate occasions he was wounded in attacks by rival mobsters, sometimes so seriously that he was not expected to recover. But recover he did. "Nobody can kill Legs Diamond," he once boasted.[62] That statement ultimately proved wrong.

CHAPTER 3

Smaller Cities

New York and Chicago were the biggest cities and the biggest crime centers in America during the Prohibition era, but the wave of crime extended to smaller cities as well. The underworld conducted business and adapted the roles of different ethnic groups in three urban centers: Detroit, where one tough Jewish mob gained dominance; Kansas City, where an Irish political boss allied himself with an Italian consigliore; and Cleveland, where a governing Jewish syndicate brought a measure of order while a war was fought in the Italian neighborhoods.

DETROIT, MICHIGAN

Starting in the late nineteenth century Detroit witnessed an influx of Jewish immigrants from Eastern Europe. Between 1910 and 1920 alone, the Jewish population of the city increased by an astonishing 247 percent—faster than the overall population growth. A 1903 article in the *Detroit Free Press* praised the Jewish newcomers as "intelligent, sensible, hard-working people, sober and religious, of good moral character and determined to get ahead in the world. They are men with characteristics that make any nation strong."[1]

One of those hard-working immigrants was Henry Bernstein, a Russian Jew who arrived in Detroit in 1902 and established a shoe repair shop. Although Henry might well have been of good moral character, his four sons—Abe, Joseph, Ray, and Isadore—were decidedly not. The local Bishop School had two tracks—an academic one for the brightest, and a vocational, reform school track for those not so promising. Except for Abe, who did not attend the school, the Bernstein brothers took the lower track.[2] The trade they really learned was not taught in the classrooms, but rather outside, where they shot dice in the school yard and joined with other disaffected boys to roam the rundown, crowded streets of Detroit's grittiest sections, stealing from pushcarts, robbing drunks, and beating up other kids. As they grew older their crime became more sophisticated—extorting money, stealing cargo from railroad freight yards, and working with established criminals. The four Bernstein brothers and their friends came to be known as the Purple Gang. Several stories circulate about the origin of the name. According to one, a Jewish fruit peddler who had been robbed by the gang complained, "They're tainted, those boys. Their characters are discolored, they're purple. They'll come to a bad end." But this story is dubious—the Purple Gang name did not appear in the newspapers until late in the decade, long after the boys had moved into the big time.[3]

The four brothers came to maturity just at the right time to take advantage of a new line of business that eventually rivaled Detroit's mainstay automobile industry—bootlegging. Had it not been for Prohibition with its promise of vast criminal wealth, the streetwise Bishop School kids might have grown up to lead normal lives.

For several reasons, Detroit was uniquely positioned to violate the Volstead Act. The state of Michigan had gone dry two years before national Prohibition went into effect, and enterprising scofflaws had already established a smuggling network along U.S. Highway 25, dubbed the Avenue de Booze, that brought liquor to Detroit from Toledo, Ohio, where it was still legal.[4] Once Ohio and the rest of the states went dry, the thirsty residents of Detroit turned their attention to Canada, where the manufacture of liquor was legal. The southernmost city in Canada was Windsor, separated from Detroit by the narrow Detroit River, which in places was less than a mile wide. The American side of the river boundary also had remote areas where contraband could be unloaded without detection. Once Prohibition was enacted in the United States, shrewd Canadian businessmen built distilleries in Windsor; the whiskey they produced could be easily smuggled to Detroit, which in turn became the main liquor distribution center for the entire Midwest. Boats were the usual method for smuggling, but booze was also conveyed by railroad freight cars, ferries, and even airplanes. One especially ingenious technique was an underwater pipe that carried whiskey produced in a Windsor distillery directly to a bottling plant in Detroit. The Windsor-Detroit route provided the major share of the foreign whiskey smuggled into the United States from Canada.[5] Looking back on the Prohibition era, a veteran Detroit newspaperman joked about how the city had been awash in illegal liquor: "It was absolutely impossible to get a drink in Detroit unless you told the busy bartender what you wanted in a voice loud enough for him to hear above the uproar."[6]

Early in the Prohibition era, bootlegging in Detroit was an amateur affair, with families sneaking over whiskey for themselves and their friends. By the mid 1920s, however, the business had been taken over by mobsters, in particular, the Purple Gang. Their early specialty was hijacking cargo brought across the Detroit River by other rum-running mobs. For their exploits on the water, a segment of the gang was known as the Little Jewish Navy. The Purple's activities attracted the attention of Henry Shorr and Charles Leiter, the proprietors of the Oakland Sugar House, which sold to the public the supplies needed to make home brew alcohol, a legitimate activity under the Volstead Act. Corn sugar was in high demand because home brewers needed six pounds to produce one gallon of whiskey.[7] The Sugar House expanded into the illegal side of the business, brewing and distilling liquor and running "blind pigs," a midwestern term for a speakeasy. An alliance was created between the Sugar House Gang and the Purple Gang, with funds coming from the Sugar House and muscle from the Purples. One of the best-known products that emerged from the alliance was Old Log Cabin whiskey, which the Purples sold in vast quantities to Al Capone's Chicago Outfit.

Oldest brother Abe Bernstein was nominally the Purple Gang's boss. Described as "small and dapper with the soft hands of a woman and a quiet way of speaking," he was given to smoothing relationships with the city's Italian criminals in the East Side of Detroit.[8] His brother Joey, wirier and younger by six years, was quite the opposite. Crime writer Paul Kavieff describes him as a "shtarker," Yiddish for a thug or hoodlum, a tough guy.[9] Joey's violent approach came to characterize the group. The gang's violence was exemplified by the Milaflores Apartment Massacre of March 28, 1927, when three mobsters were machine gunned to death on the third floor of an apartment building at 4:45 in the morning. Two Purples were arrested for the crime, but the case against them was dismissed for lack of evidence. The rubout was most likely revenge for the 1926 shotgun murder of a Purple Gang booze distributor. The Milaflores incident is said to have a place in Prohibition history as the first murder using a Thompson submachine gun, although that distinction may arguably belong to Capone thug Frank McErlane in Chicago.

In January 1928, ten months after the Milaflores Apartment incident, the Purple Gang murdered a Detroit policeman named Vivian Welch, who earned the gang's enmity by shaking down bootleggers and saloonkeepers. (Despite Welch's first name, he was a male.) Abe Bernstein was one of those arrested for Welch's murder, but the case was dismissed for lack of evidence before it could go to trial. Later the same year, Samuel Polakoff, an independent businessman in the cleaning and dying industry, was brutally beaten to death with a hammer. Once again, suspicion fell on the Purples, who were heavily involved in labor racketeering. The gang operated a union that used dynamite, stink bombs, and theft to enforce the sucking of money from both workers and management in the dry cleaning industry. It is likely that Polakoff was murdered for not cooperating with the union. Polakoff's accused killers went on trial but—no surprise—were acquitted for lack of evidence. The Purples' reputation for violent retribution kept potential witnesses from testifying against them. "There is something radically wrong with law enforcement in Detroit," observed a local high-ranking federal law enforcement official who resigned in 1925; in fact, a Rockefeller Foundation report characterized Detroit as the most corrupt city in the United States.[10]

In sum, the Purple Gang was utterly ruthless, even beyond the norm for gangs of this era, and up through the early 1930s the group was able to get away with it all. Federal Bureau of Investigation files released under the Freedom of Information Act contain a 1932 report that sheds light on the Purple Gang and enables us to know more about them than any other group of criminals in the Prohibition era. Fred Frahm, chief of detectives of the Detroit police, prepared the FBI report, which contained information on the forty-nine members of the gang, including physical descriptions, photos, and accounts of their criminal activities. FBI Director J. Edgar Hoover himself commended Frahm for the scope of his report.[11] Of the forty-nine gang members, four were dead, ten in prison, seven wanted by law enforcement, and twenty-eight not currently behind bars; of those still alive in 1932, 30 percent were in their twenties, 60 percent in their thirties, and the remainder in their forties and older. One elderly gangster, Willie Laks, was in his fifties—advanced old age in the risky world of Detroit crime. The Purples had aged from their origins in the Bishop School playground. The following entries from the police report provide a flavor of their lives:

> Edward Shaw. Approximate age: 25. This man has been arrested in Eastview, N.Y. charge Narcotics; New York City, Homicide; Los Angeles, Calif. Charge Suspicion Burglary; and in Detroit on charge of Robbery Armed. He is wanted on the charge of Homicide in New York City.
>
> Philip Keywell. Approximate age: 31 This man has a long record of arrests by the Detroit Police on charges Grand Larceny, Robbery Armed, Assault With Intent to Kill, Fugitive, Kidnapping and Murder. He is now serving a Life Sentence in Jackson Prison, having been sentenced by Judge Cotter on Oct.10.1930 for the Murder of a Colored Boy who found some liquor that had been planted by Keywell and some of his gang.

Issie Kaminski. Approximate age: 41. This man is a Bootlegger, and has been picked up for possession of Burglary Tools and for Extortion. He is not in jail at this time.

Jack Stein. Approximate age 34. This man has been arrested by the Detroit Police on charges of Murder, Robbery Armed, and he did a 5 year stretch in Leavenworth on a charge of Violating the Harrison Narcotic Act out of Detroit. He has been arrested in Buffalo N.Y. and served time for 2nd degree Grand Larceny (Pickpocket) and got a sentence of 2 to 3 years in the New Jersey State Prison out of Jersey City N.J. on charge of Pickpocket. He is not in jail at this time, and he was picked up here in July 1932.

These biographies and the dozens of others in the report suggest that the Purple Gang was a loose assortment of men with eclectic specialties, including bootlegging, burglary, narcotics, pickpocketing, receiving stolen property, kidnapping, extortion, and murder, who frequently journeyed out of Detroit to California, New Jersey, Ohio, Kansas, New York, and elsewhere to ply their trades. They did not get a regular salary from being members of the Purple Gang, but they did get the benefit of being associated with a notorious organization that struck fear in witnesses and rivals. In this notoriety they were similar to other established gangs of the era that sought to intimidate their enemies.[12]

KANSAS CITY, MISSOURI

There have been many big city bosses in American history—men able to build political coalitions by providing jobs and other services to immigrants and the lower classes. These bosses offered a social safety net before the post–Word War II welfare state emerged.

The political clout of the bosses rested on their ability to turn out a large quantity of votes for whatever candidate they chose. Sometimes the boss took over the job of mayor; other times the boss worked behind the scenes with some modest title. In either case, the bosses amassed sums of money for themselves from kickbacks and bribes and fended off challenges from reformers. Among the top bosses were William Daley of Chicago, James Michael Curley of Boston, Enoch "Nucky" Johnson of Atlantic City, and Frank Hague of Jersey City. Most, but not all were of Irish descent, Catholics, and Democrats. But they should not just be considered anarchistic crooks; they knew that they and their underlings had to govern the city with some degree of responsibility to its residents.

In Kansas City, Missouri, the Pendergast political machine was unusual in its longevity, which outlasted a single individual. Two brothers, born six years apart, reigned for roughly half a century. The so-called "House of Pendergast" began with Jim Pendergast the founder; his successor was brother Tom. Jim got his start in Kansas City by opening a saloon in the gritty West Bottoms neighborhood. He went on to buy other watering holes and became a long-term alderman on the city council. His ability to turn out the vote made him a power in the city, and he engaged in epic battles with reformers like "Colonel" William Rockhill Nelson, owner of the *Kansas City Star* newspaper. Tom Pendergast entered the scene late in Jim's career by helping his brother keep the books and manage his saloons. Through his political connections, Jim was able to get brother Tom appointed superintendent of streets, a powerful municipal position that enabled the younger Pendergast to learn the ins and outs of Kansas City politics literally at the street level. Everybody who encountered Tom was struck by his remarkable appearance: an enormous head resting on a thick, powerful body.[13] Unlike his brother, Tom was willing to use his fists on his opponents, a brawler's skill that other political bosses customarily subcontracted. When poor health caused Jim to retire in 1910, Tom took over the Pendergast organization.

Tom far exceeded his elder brother in the level of control he held over Kansas City, and the entire state of Missouri as well. Early in his career as boss, Tom concentrated on building a network of ward leaders, precinct captains, and block leaders to control election turnouts. This paid off in the election of 1916. The vast Irish bedrock of the Democratic Party in Kansas City and Jackson County had long been divided into two charmingly named factions, the Goats and the Rabbits. The Goats were Tom's faction; the leader of the Rabbits was another Irishman, Joseph B. Shannon. In 1916 the Rabbits were in a strong position, with the incumbent mayor and the leadership of the police department on their side. In the primary preceding the election, the Rabbits' slate won the party nomination. Not about to give up, Tom Pendergast fought back with the political strategy known as "knifing"—that is, to work against candidates from one's own party in order to gain an advantage. He sent word out to his precinct apparatus that in the fall election Goat voters should spurn the Democratic ticket and instead cast their ballots for the opposition Republican candidate for mayor and for the city council slate of aldermen that Pendergast had selected. On election day the police tried to prevent the Goats from voting. But Pendergast prevailed: the Republican candidate for mayor won, as did five of Pendergast's alderman candidates. Shortly thereafter, Pendergast won control of the Jackson County Democratic Committee. As Tom's biographer, newspaperman William Reddig, observed of the 1916 triumph, "Boss Tom Pendergast had arrived."[14]

Tom also demonstrated his political acumen in 1924–1925 when Kansas City voters approved a new, nonpartisan charter for municipal government designed by reformers to overthrow the political bosses. Tom cannily supported the reform movement, and in 1926 installed one of his cronies, Henry McElroy, in the all-important post of city manager. By controlling McElroy, Tom controlled Kansas City and cleverly twisted the reform plan to his own advantage. He installed another loyalist to serve as his man at the county level: Harry S. Truman, a veteran of the First World War and failed co-owner of a haberdashery. In 1922, the Prendergast machine successfully ran Truman as a candidate for the position of judge of the County Court's eastern district. This was not a judicial position, but rather a post equivalent to a county commissioner. Much later Truman was elected U.S. senator (known as the "Senator from Pendergast") and still later became vice president and then president of the nation—a spectacular political trajectory.

While amassing power at the city and county level, Tom Pendergast himself kept a low public profile. His first office was in the rundown Jefferson Hotel. He later moved to a cramped office on the second floor of a two-story office building at 1908 Main Street, where he had a steady stream of visitors asking for the favors that only the boss could provide. He was known as a devout family man who went to mass every day. He made it a point to serve his constituents with jobs, food, clothes, and coal for their furnaces. Behind his life as a humble servant of the public (which we can assume he practiced sincerely), he indulged in some extravagancy. He quietly amassed enormous wealth as the owner of the Ready-Mix Concrete company, a firm that was regularly awarded lucrative contracts from the city. A builder who started using cement from a rival company would be flunked by the city's building inspector.[15] A Pendergast company handled garbage collection in Kansas City and was paid by the ton. The weight of the garbage was increased by pumping water into the garbage trucks before they were weighed on the public scales. The garbage was fed to pigs; "the only honest creatures that fed at the public trough," observed a critic.[16] Pendergast also made money from other companies that handled construction projects and manufactured everything from cigars to plumbing pipes. He spent a staggering $175,000 to buy a luxurious mansion in the upper-class Ward Parkway section of town and squandered great amounts of money in bets on horse races.

In addition to McElroy and Truman, Tom needed another lieutenant to handle the illegal aspect of the organization. The North End of Kansas City was a center for the Italian population. Old Jim Pendergast had installed an Irishman, Mike Ross, as the political go-to guy. But in a 1928 referendum over a bond issue, Ross was overthrown by one Johnny Lazia, who used kidnapping and violence to win a victory at the polls. Recognizing Lazia's talents, Tom put him in charge of keeping bootlegging, gambling, and prostitution in line and made sure tribute money was extracted

from them; Lazia's official position was head of the North Side Democratic Club. With the backing of Pendergast, Lazia was given the authority
to determine who would be hired for the police department—as blatant
an example of the fox overseeing the hen house as any in American history.[17] Like Tom Pendergast, Johnny Lazia started his own business, a soft
drink company that won contracts with the city.

Even before he came to the attention of Tom Prendergast, Lazia was well
known in Missouri. As a teenager he had worked as a respectable clerk in
a lawyer's office, but he earned extra money on the side as a gun-wielding
thief. Although he was convicted of armed robbery and sentenced to a term
of fifteen years, Lazia was paroled by the lieutenant governor of Missouri,
with the proviso that Lazia enlist in the army, then fighting on Europe's
Western Front. Lazia never got around to enlisting; instead, he returned to
his criminal career in Kansas City, assisted by his burly bodyguard Charles
Carollo. There was something likeable about Lazia that won him friends.
He was a trim 140 pounds, dapper in his attire, a gum-chewing, enthusiastic fellow who loved jokes and snappy conversation and who donated to
charity. Women found him irresistible.[18] Although he had a limited education, he filled the shelves in his office with the classics.

Criminals who entered the city had to pay obeisance to Lazia. Those
who stepped out of line would be arrested by the police force Lazia oversaw or die at the hands of the underworld force he controlled. Under
Lazia's oversight, petty crimes like pickpocketing and holdups were sup-
pressed so that the public could enjoy the more established illegal world
of whorehouses, saloons, and gambling casinos. One vignette from wide-
open Kansas City in the days of Prohibition has a waiter from a speakeasy
sitting outside alone in a police car while handling incoming radio calls
from police headquarters; his service was a favor for members of the force
who were inside drinking at the bar.[19]

Beginning in the 1920s, and expanding into the thirties and forties,
Kansas City established a rich musical culture, where Count Basie, Ben-
nie Morton, and other talented performers played pioneering ragtime and

jazz music. This outburst of creativity might have reminded the historically minded visitor of Renaissance Florence, with John Lazia and Tom Prendergast in the role of the Medici rulers. But as in the case of the Medicis, the rule of John and Tom would one day end.

CLEVELAND, OHIO

The man at the top of the Cleveland underworld during Prohibition, Moe Dalitz, got his start in Detroit, where his Jewish immigrant father went into the laundry business, ultimately owning the Varsity Cleaners in the college town of Ann Arbor. It's been said that Dalitz as a young man was a high-ranking member of the Purple Gang, but more likely he was on the periphery of that violent organization.[20] Known as "Puller" for his ability to get contraband whiskey across the border from Canada, he borrowed his father's laundry trucks to distribute the booze. Dalitz used over sixty aliases in the course of his early career, his favorite being Moe Davis.[21] At some point in the years 1925–1928, he relocated from Detroit to the Cleveland area. Why? Perhaps he was caught in some kind of vendetta with Italian gangs, or was perhaps he was appalled by the violence of the Purple Gang. Most likely he saw an opportunity to make more money with less violence than he would smuggling booze in Detroit. Once in Cleveland he established what came to be known as the Cleveland Syndicate, aka the Cleveland Four.

Cleveland was a good place for Dalitz to set up shop. It had a history of white-collar crime conducted in corridors of power, rather than in saloons and back streets. This high level of crime in Cleveland dates back to Mark Hannah, a late nineteenth-century businessman who put William McKinley into the White House, and to Harry Daugherty, an early twentieth-century lawyer who did the same for Warren G. Harding. In building his own crime regime, Dalitz established a headquarters in the Hollenden Hotel, a swanky, upscale city landmark—no tables in the back of speakeasies or rundown offices in decaying buildings for him! He drew together three partners, like him from Jewish immigrant families: Samuel "Sambo" Tucker, Morris Kleinman, and Lou Rothkopf. The partners worked quietly behind the scenes, dividing profits evenly and leading modest personal lives—although Dalitz enjoyed female companionship and was married four times in his career.[22]

Dalitz's biographer, Michael Newton, identifies thirteen key participants at a level below the four partners, a mix of Italians, Jews, and Irish that include the well-connected Jewish attorney Samuel Haas and an Irish saloonkeeper and bootlegger with the appealing name Thomas Jefferson McGinty. Like his Founding Father namesake, McGinty believed in the pursuit of happiness, but in his case happiness consisted of profits from bootlegging. The Italian contingent consisted of the mobsters known as the Mayfield Road gang, named after a section of Cleveland's Little Italy. One crossover figure in this operation was Charles "Chuck" Polizzi. His name at birth was Leo Berkowitz, but when his parents died the orphaned Jewish boy was adopted by the Polizzi family who renamed him. Perhaps his Jewish background explains why in 1936 he was selected to serve on the Syndicate board while one of the four partners, Morris Kleinman, was behind bars.[23] What did Dalitz's syndicate do? Legitimate investments, like laundries, steel, railroads and real estate, coexisted with illegal operations like gambling establishments. This being Prohibition, the biggest enterprise was liquor, and the Syndicate spent money on trucks, speedboats, and barges that could transport booze across Lake Erie, which was nicknamed the Jewish Lake.

The Syndicate made connections with organized mobs in Chicago and the East Coast, but was more insular at the lower levels. A case in point occurred when two pistol-packing, would-be extortionists from Philadelphia, Jack Brownstein and Ernest Yorkell, tried to push their way into the Cleveland crime scene. In younger years the tattooed, bull-necked Yorkell had been a sideshow strongman known as Young Hercules. Brownstein was a slick dresser who dabbled in the jewelry trade. In Cleveland they walked into stores and speakeasies and threatened the owners with violence if they did not pay up. They did not manage to scare anybody and were thrown out of establishments by outraged owners, among them Dalitz's ally Thomas Jefferson McGinty. Brownstein and Yorkell did manage to impress two waitresses they encountered by telling the young women, "Yeah, we're tough guys and we're looking to shake a bootlegger down" and boasting they would soon get their hands on $5,000 from one of their victims. But the two Philly would-be mobsters never showed up for their date with the waitresses. A milkman making his rounds early next morning found in a local park the dead bodies of Brownstein and Yorkell, tied up with clothesline and shot repeatedly. Suspicion fell on Charles Polizzi and others in the Mayfield Road mob, but they were released by police. The whole thing was treated as a laughable episode by the Cleveland underworld, police, and reporters.[24]

Far less amusing was a violent feud between Italian crime families that took place in the Italian ghetto of Woodland on the eastern part of town, far from the posh world of the Dalitz syndicate at the Hollenden Hotel. Perhaps Moe looked down on it all as the bloodthirsty actions of Italians, and perhaps he asked Charles Polizzi to explain it all to him. At the center of the feud was corn sugar, "zucchero di granturco," that fueled the home manufacture of whiskey. Italian families in the Woodland district purchased the product, along with stills, from the Lonardo brothers, headed by "Big Joe" Lonardo. Big Joe would then buy back the whiskey produced in the stills, which would be resold on the market, giving Big Joe a profit estimated at $5,000 per week. He was a respected leader in the Italian community, with an expensive home, nice clothes, and bodyguards. But some became envious of Big Joe Lonardo's success, chief among them the Porrello brothers, who came from the same town in Sicily as the Lonardos and for a time worked with them in the Cleveland bootlegging business. The Porrellos decided to strike out on their own in competition with the Lonardos, setting up a stressful situation for Big Joe, who decided in the spring of 1927 that this might be a good time to for him to get away from it all by taking a vacation in Italy. He left the management of his operations with his brother John and one of his top employees, Salvatore "Black Sam" Todaro. Big Joe's Italian vacation stretched on for half a year, quite likely extended because he met an attractive woman who became his mistress.

While Big Joe Lonardo was busy in Italy being unfaithful to his wife, Sam Todaro back in Cleveland was being unfaithful to Big Joe by allying himself with the Porrello family. The Porrellos, while expanding their corn sugar business, won customers away from the absent Big Joe. Learning what was going on, Big Joe headed back home, with his mistress in tow, and fired Black Sam. Big Joe's fury against Black Sam increased to a murderous rage when he saw his former employee flaunting his fancy Lincoln automobile without acknowledging that money from Big Joe had made the purchase possible. This motive may seem petty to the modern reader, but it was a factor that helped to fan the flames of a long-lasting blood feud in Cleveland.[25]

Big Joe did not break off his ties with the Porrellos, and from time to time he met them for a friendly game of cards at a Porrellos-owned barbershop. On October 13, 1927, Big Joe Lonardo and his brother John, unaccompanied by bodyguards, came over to the shop. There then ensued a hail of bullets fired into the back room directed at the two Lonardos. Big Joe was killed immediately. The wounded John was able to stagger out of the shop after the assassins but collapsed, ironically enough, in front of a local butcher shop.[26]

To pose the Latin question "Cui bono," who stood to gain from the murder of the two Lonardos? The answer is clear: the Porrello brothers and Black Sam Todaro. As a result of the murder, the Lonardo family's fortune declined as the Porrellos' rose, and the title "Big Joe" passed to Joseph Porrello, the leading Porrello brother. Police suspicion fell on brother Angelo Porrello, who claimed he was in the backroom of the barbershop when the killings took place. But the case against him evaporated when, fifty-four days after the double murder, the proprietor of the butcher shop, Anthony Caruso, was shot to death outside his home by an unknown gunman. It was rumored that Caruso saw the murderers fleeing the barbershop hit and had to be killed so he would not identify them.

The corn sugar business was declining as the result of the increased availability of quality liquor smuggled in from Canada, far superior to the rotgut produced by household stills. Despite the decline, the deadly feud between the Lonardos and the Porrellos unleashed by the barbershop killings continued unabated, among them the following assassinations:[27]

June 11, 1929: Black Sam Todaro shot and killed by Angelo Lonardo, son of the deceased Big Joe Lonardo.

October 19, 1929: Frank Lonardo, brother of the deceased Big Joe, shot and killed probably on the order of Frank Alessi, brother-in-law of Black Sam Todaro.

July 5, 1930: Joe Porrello and his bodyguard killed, probably by members of the Mayfield Road gang.

July 26, 1930: Vincenti "Jim" Porrello, Joe's brother, shot to death while in a grocery store.

February 25th, 1932: Raymond Porrello, his brother Rosario, and their bodyguard killed.

These deaths were typically followed by elaborate burial ceremonies with expensive coffins, elaborate floral displays, vast crowds of mourners, and sobbing wives and mothers. The corn sugar business may have been on the skids, but funeral parlors and florists were doing fine. A 1931 *New York Times* article revealed that undertakers had a cost-cutting measure they employed in mob burials. The families of the deceased gangsters were charged extra to have their loved one buried in a fancy silver coffin. But after the mourners departed the silver case would be removed leaving a standard cast iron coffin to be buried underground. The silver case was reused at other funerals, with the families that paid for it none the wiser.[28]

Early in this chain of revenge, murder, and funerals in Cleveland came a curious event. The police got wind of the presence of a large number of suspicious-looking Italian men who had registered at the Statler Hotel on December 5, 1928. How they learned of this group is unclear; perhaps an observant policeman saw the Italians entering the hotel, or perhaps the hotel staff noticed the crowd, or perhaps the rival Syndicate or Mayfield Road gang tipped off authorities. Whatever the case, police descended on the building and rounded up twenty-three men who surrendered without any resistance. The arrested men shared several distinguishing character-istics: they were well dressed, right down to their silk underwear, carried nice luggage, and possessed guns and large amounts of cash; moreover, on further inspection it turned out that they were all of Sicilian ancestry and came from around the country, including Philadelphia, Buffalo, New York, Newark, Tampa, and Brooklyn. According to a story, in the course of the raid the police, forcing a desk clerk to act as a human shield, pushed him into a hotel meeting room in case any mobsters started shooting. But nobody fired a shot so the desk clerk's ordeal (if it actually took place) was not necessary. Reporters described the arrestees as the "Grand Council of the Mafia," but that designation seems too grandiose. Many suggestions have been put forward about the purpose. Perhaps they were members of the Unione Sicilione, who were there to discuss what to do about the recent rubout of two Unione leaders, Frankie Yale of New York and Tony Lombardo of Chicago. Or perhaps they were there to sort out the turmoil in the Cleveland corn sugar industry, possibly by ratifying Joe Porrello as the new boss. We will never know because the police arrived before the meeting began. Most of the arrested men were let out of jail on bond and later released on the condition that they stay away from Cleveland for at least a year.[29]

The meeting had failed, but the underworld learned some lessons in time for the next crime conference, which was held in Atlantic City.

PART II

Atlantic City Interlude

"Let's give each other a break. We're a bunch of saps killing each other this way and giving the cops a laugh."
—Maxie Eisen, Chicago fish market racketeer, 1926

CHAPTER 4

Gangsters in the Surf

From Monday, May 13, to Thursday, May 16, in 1929, top gangsters in the Prohibition generation came to Atlantic City for a conference. Spring in the resort town was a perfect time for the gathering; the temperature was in the comfortable upper 50s, and the summer vacation season with its tens of thousands of visitors had not yet descended. There was still room on the Boardwalk, in hotels, and on the beaches. Many organizations traditionally chose this time of year to hold their annual conferences and galas in the resort. The same time as the gangster conference was town, the society pages of the *Atlantic City Daily Press* covered the arrivals of the New Jersey State Master Barbers, the New Jersey Bankers, the Grand Court of the New Jersey Foresters of America, the Catholic Daughters of America, the Junior Hadassah, and the Women's Auxiliary of the Atlantic County Medical Society.

The gangster conference was different; its arrival in the city received no coverage in the society pages or any other part of the newspaper during the meeting. The attendees did not wear nametags; there was neither printed agenda nor election of officers nor membership list nor minutes of the meeting. Given this secrecy, uncertainties about the event abound. In fact, there are two conflicting interpretations. One might be called the "big conference" view, which posits a sizeable attendance of top mobsters from around the nation who met to establish a national crime syndicate, but an emerging "small conference" interpretation believes the attendance was much less and the goals more narrow. This chapter begins with the more traditionally accepted big view and ends with the revisionist small view—a situation that resembles the parallel universes about which physicists hypothesize.

THE BIG CONFERENCE VIEW

According to that big view, the attendees included such established and frequently named leaders from the major crime capitals: Al Capone of Chicago; Lucky Luciano, Frank Costello, John Torrio, and Joe Adonis of New York; Charles "King" Solomon of Boston; and Moe Dalitz of Cleveland. More names from more cities have been suggested too, and the total number varies from a dozen to more than thirty. Two intriguing absences from the list are the feuding New York City Mafia bosses Giuseppe Masseria and Salvatore Maranzano. It is likely that these firm believers in the purity of the Mafia did not wish to mingle with Jews and other non-Sicilians. Also striking is that nobody from the western states and possibly nobody from the South attended. In the late 1920s, the majority of the nation's population and industry was concentrated in the Northeast and the Midwest. Similarly, until the post–World War II era no major league baseball teams resided west of St. Louis or south of Washington, D.C. This geographic imbalance extended to the world of organized crime.

Nucky Johnson's City

Why Atlantic City? Evidently the mobsters learned from the aborted Cleveland conference of five months before that they needed a location where the police would not bother them and where they could be at ease. Probably no place in America could provide those benefits as well as Atlantic City. Although the ocean resort publicized itself as a haven for the elite upper classes, the city actually catered to the middle and lower classes, who flocked there mostly by train from Philadelphia and crowded into hotels and rooming houses. There were seven miles of Boardwalk to explore and amusement piers to enjoy.

The master of the resort city was Enoch "Nucky" Johnson. Born into a politically active family in 1883, he was elected sheriff at age twenty-five, the youngest in the state. In 1913, he was appointed as the treasurer of Atlantic County, a position he held for the next forty years. Johnson knew that his prosperity and Atlantic City's were linked, and he made sure visitors got what they wanted—and what they wanted was the illicit and the exciting. A resident looking back on Atlantic City's notorious period described the resort's attitude: "If the people who came to town had wanted Bible readings, we'd have given 'em that. But nobody ever asked for Bible readings. They wanted booze, broads, and gambling, so that's what we gave 'em."[1] Thus, Johnson protected speakeasies, brothels, and gambling dens, and those establishments paid him for his protective services. He also got salary kickbacks from county and municipal employees, whom he personally hired, and there were kickbacks from government contracts as well. He lived life large, with a hotel suite at the best hotel in Atlantic City, an apartment in New York City overlooking Central Park, expensive cars, and a bevy of showgirls and other female companions.[2] Because Atlantic City was a landing spot for smuggled liquor, Johnson was well known to bootleggers and gangsters in the region. And he also knew that conventions were the lifeblood of the resort in the off-season so it is likely that he assented to hosting a gathering of Prohibition crime lords in Atlantic City.

Who proposed the conference? From the top ranks of gangsterdom several possible candidates emerge. Luciano claimed to have been the one who originated the idea. "I asked Meyer [Lansky] to put out a few feelers around the country, to see if the top guys were willin' to make a meet—you might say like a national convention of our own."[3] Other contenders for the organizational role are Al Capone, Frank Costello, Meyer Lansky, and Longie Zwillman. But the likeliest choice is the soft-spoken elder statesman John Torrio, a man with credibility in both Chicago and New York, who in his career had sought to bring about peace between warring mobs. Probably, like many ideas and inventions, this pioneering national gangster conference had several fathers.

The Agendas

What did the attendees hope to accomplish in Atlantic City? Undoubtedly they wanted what mainstream business people have always wanted—to create a stable environment for their endeavors. Crime was a particularly vicious cutthroat and tommy-gunning line of work, in which rivals for market share had one another killed and their trucks hijacked. Some mobsters thought that a commission or tribunal of some sort could settle disputes and restrain wildcatting. Another concern was the need to unite to lower the prices charged by suppliers, notably the liquor manufacturers of Canada, England, and the Bahamas. Longie Zwillman is supposed to have said that mobsters needed something like a National Association of Manufacturers. Lansky too wanted something larger than the close-knit Mafia crime families, each with its own narrow territory. Another concern was to explore new criminal opportunities given the prospect that Prohibition would eventually come to an end. Then they knew they would have to devote their energies to other parts of their business such as gambling, narcotics, prostitution, and labor racketeering.[4]

Beyond the obvious goals of cooperation, coordination, and stabilization, some crime writers have claimed other agendas afoot at the conference. Crime writer Leo Katcher argues that one such agenda, pushed by Frank Costello, was to divide the operations of the late Arnold Rothstein. Luciano and Buchalter were to get the narcotics smuggling; the bookmaking business would go to Frank Erickson, Las Vegas to Bugsy Siegel, and so on.[5] Another agenda, it has been said, sought to reduce the power and visibility of Al Capone. Scarface's reign over Chicago had become ever more violent; only two months before the Atlantic City conference, Capone had reputedly orchestrated the Saint Valentine's Day Massacre, an event that shocked the city, the nation, and even Capone's fellow mobsters. Capone's biographer Laurence Bergreen writes about the Atlantic City conference, "his jealous rivals wanted to strip him of his power and his profits, and the ill will generated by the St. Valentine's Day Massacre provided them with just the excuse they needed to do so."[6] Luciano is supposed to have phrased it more colorfully, "What the fuck are we gonna do 'bout Al? That fat bastard is gonna take us all down with his tommy gun hysterics."[7]

Not all crime writers are convinced that Capone was a pariah at the conference or that Capone was even responsible for the Saint Valentine's Day rubout. J. Robert Nash argues that the anti-Capone interpretation is simply absurd: Capone drove the agenda, and anybody who opposed him would have drawn the opposition of all the other attendees.[8] The crime writer T. J. English proposes another hidden purpose—to squeeze the Irish out of organized crime. The Jewish and Italian gangsters who attended the conference came out of the wave of eastern and southern European immigrants that began to arrive in large numbers at the tail end of the nineteenth century, while the Irish came generations earlier in the century and had established themselves comfortably in the police departments and city halls of major cities, where they were receiving hefty bribes from the gangs of newly arrived immigrants. By seeking to marginalize Irish gangsters, says English, the Italians and Jews were not motivated by ethnic prejudice; they were simply seeking their share of the leadership pie while willing to allow the Irish in subordinate positions. To support his argument, English cites the fact that only two sons of Erin attended the Atlantic City conference. One was Frank McErlane of Chicago, an ally of Capone while Big Al was driving the main Irish gangs to extinction. The other was Owney Madden of New York, who had moved far away from his Irish roots and was operating on his own.[9]

The Incident at the Breakers Hotel

The conference started off on the wrong foot. Atlantic City boss Nucky Johnson had made reservations for the attendees at one of the finest and most exclusive hotels in the resort community, the Breakers. To keep the convention under wraps, Johnson had made up assumed names for the gangsters. But when attendees showed up at the hotel in their limousines, something went seriously wrong. The Breakers only accepted WASP guests; Jews and Catholics were unwelcome. The hotel manager looked on in horror as the lobby filled up with people who were clearly not the WASPS whose names Johnson had provided for the reservation list. When the manager refused to let them sign in, the attendees telephoned Johnson, who advised them to go to the President Hotel. Nucky met the limousine motorcade on the road. Al Capone, furious at the whole incident, started a shouting match with both Johnson and Luciano. According to Luciano's version of what happened next, "So Nucky picks Al up under one arm and throws him into his car and yells out 'All you fuckers follow me!'" The limousines proceeded to the Ritz Hotel. Capone was still angry and tore down pictures from the walls and threw them at Johnson.[10]

The above is the gist of the Breakers story as accepted and repeated by generations of crime writers. But questions remain. How could it be that Nucky Johnson so badly misunderstood the prejudices in force at the Breakers? By the time the incident took place Johnson had been the undisputed boss of the city for a decade and a half, and he, more than anybody, knew about its businesses both legal and illegal and its people both great and small. And if the mobsters were told to go to the President Hotel, thirty blocks south of the Breakers, why did the destination change to the Ritz, twenty-one blocks south? The passage about Johnson carrying the corpulent, 255-pound, five foot seven boss of Chicago under one arm also sounds dubious.

The assertion that the Breakers Hotel catered only to WASPS also does not prove true. Research into Atlantic City hotels reveals that the Breakers was owned by a prominent Jewish family in the resort town, and the same week the gangsters were in town the hotel hosted a meeting of the American Jewish Congress. In the 1930s the Breakers became the first Jersey Shore hotel to become kosher.[11] Maybe Capone, Luciano, and company were turned away not because of their ethnicity, but because they were tough-looking thugs with female companions who did not seem to be their wives—not the clientele welcome at a family hotel. In sum, there is something fishy about the Breakers story. A major problem is that the story had its origin in *The Last Testament of Lucky Luciano,* a book that has been widely criticized as inaccurate. But for all these unanswered questions, it is hard to imagine why anybody would make up such a curious, inconsistent story. Let us therefore assume that saga of the mobsters being kicked out of the Breakers has at least an element of truth to it.

The Sex Life of Gangsters

With the Breakers embarrassment out of the way, the conference attendees settled down to the schedule of daytime meetings and evening partying.

Regarding the partying, crime writers accept without any doubt that it was riotous. "Plenty of liquor, food, and girls," says Luciano's biographer.[12] The ever-thoughtful Nucky Johnson was said to have provided fur capes for women who were with the gangsters, whether wives or girlfriends. For those men who arrived without women, Johnson was more than happy to provide prostitutes—one of his specialties as the boss of Atlantic City. It was almost obligatory for gangsters to overindulge—crime, after all is defined as deviant behavior that violates prevailing norms. Gangsters lived their lives in rebellion against lawful, moral society. Smashing ideals of chastity and monogamy was part of that rebellion. Some confirmation of the revelry at the conference comes from an article in an Atlantic City newspaper that reported of Capone, "The past few nights found him making whoopee, boom-boom, or what have you in several of the resort's best known night clubs."[13]

There is plenty of evidence about this aspect of gangster behavior. A pioneering 1927 sociological study of Chicago gangs talked about the prevalence of "unspeakable exhibitions" at gang parties: "Women dancers appear, first singly and later in groups entirely nude and proceed to participate in a licentious debauchery in which the men nearby join. The scene finally culminates in a raffle of one of the girl performers, the man holding the winning ticket being awarded the girl for the balance of the night."[14] One of Capone's biographers describes what the mob chief and his outfit typically did for recreation at their headquarters in a Cicero, Illinois, hotel: "It was here that he came with his pals and all their teenage mistresses to drink, to party, to make love until dawn and sleep to noon."[15] Capone himself is quoted as saying this about qualifications for being a member of his gang: "When a guy don't fall for a broad, he's through." Nucky Johnson's chauffer recalled what he saw in the rear view mirror during a ride with his boss (an incident that is probably post-conference). "There I am driving along talking to Mr. Johnson with a pretty little tart seated next to him. The next thing I know she's got her head in his lap and Mr. Johnson's grinning from ear to ear."[16]

One exception to the rule of enthusiastic lechery among mobsters was reputed to be Meyer Lansky. One of his biographers says that, unlike the other gangsters, Lansky was restrained in his sexual appetites because he thought sex a destructive urge that needed to be under control.[17] Lansky had gotten married a few days before the conference to Anna Citron, a demure and devout Jewish girl from Hoboken, and he took his bride to the Atlantic City conference as a sort of honeymoon; they stayed in the presidential suite at the Ritz Hotel, where Johnson supplied them with champagne.[18] One hopes the newlyweds spent a romantic moment or two on the Boardwalk watching the waves roll in and listening to the haunting cries of the shorebirds. But there are doubts about this as well—one crime writer claims that Anna did not accompany her husband to Atlantic City.[19]

Lucky Luciano also does not quite fit the mode of the lustful, orgiastic gangster. The *Last Testament of Lucky Luciano* has him saying that throughout his adult life he suffered from occasional erectile dysfunction, or, as he put it, "sometimes I'd go out with one of them girls and take her home without tryin' to lay her. . . . I lost plenty of good tail that way." It pained him that rumors circulated that "Big Shot Charlie Lucania couldn't get it up."[20] The story that Luciano had ED has some second-hand confirmation. In 1936, a New York City prostitute said that "Charles Luciano was diseased during the time of her visits to him at the Barbizon Plaza and that he used to give her money despite the fact that she did not have relations with him."[21] Luciano attributed his difficulty to contracting gonorrhea from sex with a prostitute when the gangster was in his early twenties, but he claimed he acquired the disease deliberately to avoid the draft in World War I by showing he was under a doctor's care for the malady. For all that, he enjoyed sexual conquests when everything was working. He recalled having sex with a beautiful society girl who cried out "Hijack me! Hijack me!" during their lovemaking.[22] ("Hijack" was a word coined in the Prohibition era.)

A minor vignette that has survived from the conference sheds light on mobsters' amusement during their spare time. As described in the prologue, Tony Accardo was the young Capone bodyguard who, during the conference, visited a tattoo parlor where he had the image of a bluebird tattooed on the back of his hand.

Police watch illegal beer being poured down a sewer, circa 1921. Enforcement of Prohibition was wildly unpopular with large segments of the American population and was repealed after thirteen years. (New York World-Telegram and the Sun Newspaper Photograph Collection, Prints & Photographs Division, Library of Congress)

The pugnacious New York gangster Dutch Schultz seems to be bursting out of this 1931 photo, which was cropped for a newspaper photomontage. A chorus girl memorably said of his looks that he resembled Bing Crosby with his face bashed in. (New York World-Telegram and the Sun Newspaper Photograph Collection, Prints & Photographs Division, Library of Congress)

The most notorious gangster in the world, Mr. Alphonse Capone of Chicago—by 1928, the time of this photograph, he had outmaneuvered his rivals to become the master of an empire of bootlegging, prostitution, and gambling. (New York World-Telegram and the Sun Newspaper Photograph Collection, Prints & Photographs Division, Library of Congress)

Born Salvatore Lucania in Sicily, in America he changed his name to Charles Luciano and was popularly known as "Lucky." This 1935 photo displays his droopy eyelid, the result of a 1929 beating. (New York World-Telegram and the Sun Newspaper Photograph Collection, Prints & Photographs Division, Library of Congress)

The city of Detroit is separated from Canada by a narrow river, a situation that made the city a major center for smuggling whisky over the U.S. border. This photo shows how the liquor was transferred from boats to cars. (Walter P. Reuther Library, Wayne State University)

UNLOADING BOAT

BOAT LIES HERE

HOLDING LINE TO BOAT

PUTTING LIQUOR INTO CAR

SECOND CAR WAITING FOR LOAD

RIODELLE STREET

SCOUT CAR

Gangster Louis "Lepke" Buchalter, shown in police custody in 1939. Five years later he was executed at Sing Sing Prison, the only crime lord to die in the electric chair. (New York World-Telegram and the Sun Collection, Prints & Photographs Division, Library of Congress)

A depiction of Buchalter that appeared in the comic book *Crime Does Not Pay*. The artwork exhibits the mix of mayhem and sex that characterized the popular publication. (Crime Does Not Pay ®)

Two of the most important Treasury Department sleuths appear in this 1940 photo of the opening of a pistol range in the Treasury Department building in Washington, D.C. On the far left is Elmer Irey, and on the far right is Frank Wilson; together they brought about the downfall of Al Capone. The men in the middle are exhibiting dangerously deficient gun handling behavior. (Harris & Ewing Collection, Prints & Photographs Division, Library of Congress)

This wistful looking woman was Nancy Presser, a prostitute whose testimony as a witness for the prosecution at a dramatic 1936 trial helped to convict Lucky Luciano of forcing women into the trade. Presser was also said to have been a sometime companion of bootlegger Waxey Gordon. (Courtesy New York City Municipal Archives)

Thomas E. Dewey, an unrelenting New York lawman, was able to win convictions against Lucky Luciano, Waxey Gordon, Lepke Buchalter, and other crime figures. Dewey used his reputation as a gangbuster to become governor of New York for three terms. (Prints & Photographs Division, Library of Congress)

Benjamin "Bugsy" Siegel was still a handsome young man when he stared into the camera in this 1935 photo. A New York triggerman, he later relocated to the West Coast. He was shot to death in Los Angeles in 1947, probably for his mismanagement of a Las Vegas casino project. (New York World-Telegram and the Sun Newspaper Photograph Collection, Prints & Photographs Division, Library of Congress)

Meyer Lansky was a boyhood friend of Lucky Luciano in the immigrant Lower East Side of New York. They remained friends throughout the years. Lansky was respected by gangsters for his financial acumen and trustworthiness. (New York World-Telegram and the Sun Newspaper Photograph Collection, Prints & Photographs Division, Library of Congress)

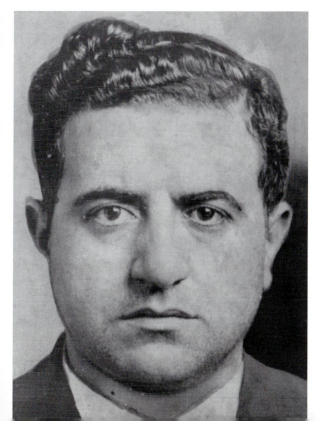

Known as the "Prime Minister" for his skill at underworld deal making, Frank Costello is shown here in 1951 testifying before a U.S. Senate investigating committee. (New York World-Telegram and the Sun Newspaper Photograph Collection, Prints & Photographs Division, Library of Congress)

Albert Anastasia was a racketeer on the Brooklyn waterfront and a figure in the Murder Incorporated gang, but he is best known not for what he did in life, but for the brazen manner of his death—in 1957 he was shot to death while sitting in a midtown Manhattan barbershop. (New York World-Telegram and the Sun Newspaper Photograph Collection, Prints & Photographs Division, Library of Congress)

Vito Genovese was a crime figure who rose in the ranks of the Mafia by eliminating rivals to his leadership. It is likely that he ordered the assassination of Albert Anastasia and also sought to kill Frank Costello. (New York World-Telegram and the Sun Newspaper Photograph Collection, Prints & Photographs Division, Library of Congress)

During his criminal career, Jack "Legs" Diamond survived four attacks on his life before being killed in 1931 in an Albany rooming house. This photo shows the coffin carrying his last remains. The man in the middle seems to have found it all quite amusing. (New York World-Telegram and the Sun Newspaper Photograph Collection, Prints & Photographs Division, Library of Congress)

One distinct photograph survives from the conference, but, like so much else about the event, it has been interpreted differently. The photo was published in the January 17, 1930, edition of the *New York Evening Journal* and shows six smiling, well-dressed men striding down the Atlantic City Boardwalk. The pattern of the Boardwalk's planks in the photo confirm the fact that this was Atlantic City. The caption identifies two of the men walking shoulder to shoulder as "Enoch ('Nucky') Johnson, a dapper duke with the smile of a sheik," and "'Scarface Al' Capone, the Chicago gang czar." The six are described as "sunny boys taking the air and anything else that they want at Atlantic City." The photo was part of an expose of Atlantic City corruption undertaken by William Randolph Hearst's newspaper. Hearst allegedly bore a grudge against Johnson because the Atlantic City boss had insulted Hearst's mistress, a showgirl at the Silver Slipper Saloon in New York. For his part, Johnson claimed that the photo was a hoax; the print had been tampered with by cutting and pasting a photo image of himself next to Capone. The proof, the fashion-conscious Johnson stated, was that he was shown wearing a white linen summer suit while the others in the photo were dressed for the spring. But a decade later, when Johnson was asked to pose for a photograph he was reported to have said, "Nothing doing. Some photographer caught me with Al Capone once. From now on I'm being careful."[23]

Getting Down to Business

Let us turn from such matters of gangster lust and idle amusement to focus on the business side of the conference, when the attendees met to forge agreements. Some accounts, including Capone's, say that the meetings were held in a conference room at the President Hotel; others say the meetings were shifted from hotel to hotel and room to room to avoid eavesdropping. According to *The Last Testament of Lucky Luciano*, in addition to meeting in hotels, the attendees would get in Boardwalk roller chairs to travel to a stretch of beach. Here they would take off their socks, roll up their pants, and stroll along the water's edge where they could discuss business without being overheard. But one crime writer regards this claim as "ridiculous" and "completely false."[24] The image of the nation's leading mobsters standing without shoes or socks as the waves lap their feet does conjure up an image of hefty, pistol-packing wading birds in suits, but it would certainly be an effective way for a small group of two or three to make sure nobody was close enough to hear the conversation. Moreover, there is clear evidence that the criminals made use of rolling chairs; the *Atlantic City Daily Press* newspaper described Capone this way: "Seated in a rolling chair at Kentucky Avenue and the Boardwalk yesterday afternoon, puffing on a big black cigar and surrounded by half a dozen henchmen, 'Al' took in the sights of the famous street and breathed deeply and freely of the ozone with apparently no care in the world."[25] In a racist mood, Luciano complained that the mobsters in the rolling chairs did not want to be overheard talking business within hearing range of the black men who pushed the chairs. Luciano called them "Niggers," which demonstrates that his tolerance of diversity did not extend to other races.[26]

A 1974 book by George Wolf with the assistance of George DiMona, *Frank Costello: Prime Minister of the Underworld*, contains an extended passage describing the opening meeting of the conference:[27]

> A large conference room had been provided by the President Hotel, and it was quite picturesque. A crystal chandelier dangled above the rich mahogany table and chairs, which gleamed from recent polishing.
>
> Now the great criminal chiefs from around the nation sat uneasily, wondering what was going to happen. Near one end of the table the Chicago delegation sat, menacingly. Frank "the Enforcer" Nitti, Jake "Greasy Thumb" Guzik, and a bodyguard named Frank Rio flanked the glowering Al Capone.
>
> The New York delegation sat at the other end, Frank [Costello], at the head, Torrio on his right. But Torrio, as the "elder statesmen," was the first one on his feet. Cigar smoke curled to the ceiling as the gang leaders looked at the little man. Torrio said, "The reason we called this meeting is we have to get organized. Everybody's working on his own, we got

independent guys muscling in, and that's got to stop. What we need is a combination [i.e., alliance] around the country where everybody in charge of his city is the boss, but we all work with each other."

With this preface he introduced Costello. Frank stood up and carefully kept his eyes away from Capone's. He said, "The reason we got to organize is that we got to put ourselves on a business basis. That's what we're in, a business. We got to stop the kind of thing that's going on in Chicago right now."

And so the account continues, with Capone getting increasingly hostile. Nitti leans over and whispers into his ear, "Stall them and let's blow," shortly after which Al and his henchmen storm out of the room, slamming the door behind them.

What are we to make of this account? The dialogue, including Nitti's whispered comments, is surely made up for dramatic effect, as are the details of curling smoke, the gleaming mahogany, and the direction of Costello's eyes. But perhaps there is a nugget of truth buried somewhere in this melodramatic passage. The principal author, George Wolf, was the friend and personal attorney of Frank Costello from 1943 to 1973 and may have learned from Costello that reining in the Chicago crime boss was one purpose of the conference. Although this scene has made-up dialogue presumably provided by Wolf's coauthor, DiMona, it may be as close to the truth of what happened behind closed doors as we can get.

If the attendees needed any more proof that Capone's notoriety was bringing unwanted attention to the crime world, then it came during the Atlantic City conference itself. The *New York Times* reported on May 16 that the resort city's director of public safety, W. S. Cuthbert, issued orders to the police "to pick up Al Capone if he is found in the city and arrest him as an undesirable." Evidently Cuthburt's edict was just window dressing, especially because the resort police force had long been under the control of Nucky Johnson. The local Atlantic City paper sent a reporter to ask a dozen or so policemen about Cuthbert's supposed order and found that none of them had heard of it. But window dressing or not, this newspaper account and others like it must have driven home the image of Capone as a problem for his fellow mob bosses.[28]

One important piece of business that transpired during the course of the conference was a sales pitch from a figure outside the mob, but one with the same willingness to skirt the law. The communications magnate Moses Annenberg was said to have been persuaded to come to the conference by his fellow resident of Chicago, Al Capone. At the time of the conference Annenberg was fifty-two years old, tall, thin, and craggy. Born to a Jewish grocer and his wife in East Prussia, the family immigrated to America when Moses was eight. He prospered in the New World and first came to prominence by winning circulation wars for the Hearst newspapers. His tactic was to use violent gangs to ensure that newsstands stocked Hearst papers to the exclusion of the competition. Annenberg eventually became a multimillionaire in the publication business. As part of his publishing empire he acquired the *Daily Racing Form*, a bible for those who bet on horses, and he decided to expand his hold on hardcore bettors by buying up a telegraphic horse-racing wire service known as the General News Bureau, which provided an accurate and fast source of information on the outcome of horse races around the country reported by spotters at the major tracks.

Moses Annenberg was in Atlantic City to expand the market penetration of his product by signing up gangs to control which horse parlors within their territories would be able to buy into the service. By having the major mobs franchise the wire network, the service would be denied to betting parlors that were not under mob control. At the Atlantic City conference, Waxey Gordon of Philadelphia reportedly agreed to pay $300,000 to set up the franchise in Philadelphia.[29] Others may have signed on at the conference or soon thereafter. The deals Annenberg worked out with the mobsters were evidently successful. In the depression year 1937 he made a profit of $1.1 million, and his horse racing service was the most lucrative component of his publishing empire.[30]

As with so much else about the Atlantic City conference, however, there is some ambiguity here. Although most crime writers affirm Annenberg's presence, often described as appearing under Capone's sponsorship, two separate biographers of Annenberg do not place him at the Atlantic City conference.

One of the two states that Annenberg never met or had anything to do with Capone; the second says the pitch for having the mob buy into a national race track network was done at the conference by Capone associate Frank Erickson.[31] It has also been said that at the conference Erickson was given wide control of gambling operations. That may be true, but it is hard to believe that the shrewd businessman Annenberg would not jump at the chance to attend a major gathering of his most important potential customers. Whatever the case, it seems likely that important negotiations over a wire service did take place in Atlantic City, whether they were led by Annenberg or Erickson.

The Legacy of Atlantic City

The conference ended on Thursday, May 16, when the attendees repacked their suitcases and headed back to their home cities. What had they accomplished in their brief time at the resort? Crime writers have concluded that the Atlantic City conference was a milestone in the establishment of an organized crime network in the United States, a belief that has been repeated in true crime books and articles ranging from the academic to the sensationalist. Humbert S. Nelli, a professor of history at the University of Kentucky, concluded that the conference was "an early effort to coordinate activities between syndicates composed of a number of ethnic groups and divide the market among them."[32] The establishment of an organization of East Coast mobsters known as "the Big Seven" is also seen as a consequence of the conference.[33] More strident was an entry on the conference in Jay Robert Nash's encyclopedia of organized crime: "The conference galvanized the gangs of America into a powerful single unit which was directed by a board of governors whose collective word was law, whose decisions were sacrosanct, and whose influence would affect every American in one form or other, for generations to come."[34]

A CONTRARY VIEW—THE SMALL CONFERENCE INTERPRETATION

Although the standard, big view of the Atlantic City conference has prevailed, all the contradictions, suppositions, and unanswered questions have allowed an alternative theory to emerge. Recently a radically different "small conference" view has been suggested by crime historian David Critchley in his book *The Origin of Organized Crime in America: The New York City Mafia, 1891–1931.*

Critchley points to primary sources on the Atlantic City conference that appeared soon after the event. Shortly after the conference Capone talked to a Philadelphia lawman: "I spent the week in Atlantic City trying to make peace among the various gang leaders of my city"; these men had agreed to "bury the hatchet and forget the enmities for the good of all concerned."[35] He further specified that in Atlantic City he had met with Bugs Moran "and three or four other Chicago gang leaders, whose names I don't care to mention."[36] An article in the May 18 *Chicago Tribune* was more specific, stating that besides Capone, the other attendees, who attended "in person or by proxy" were all Chicagoans: Bugs Moran, Joseph Aiello, Earl McErlane, Joe Saltis, and John Torrio. ("Earl" McErlane may be a typo for Frank McErlane.) In his 1930 biography of Capone, Chicago reporter Fred Pasley said that Scarface "had been sequestered at the President Hotel, Atlantic City, talking shop with other Chicago gangsters."[37]

Using these and other sources, Critchley casts doubt on the accepted version that gang leaders from New York, Philadelphia, Cleveland, Detroit, Boston, and other cities around the nation were there in addition to those from Chicago. This interpretation also contradicts the idea that the purpose of the conference was to establish a national syndicate and refutes the notion that the Big Seven emerged from the conference. Instead, Critchley sees the Big Seven as just a loose, short-lived consortium of bootleggers in the Northeast.

Supporting Critchley's small conference interpretation is Chicago-based United Press reporter Robert T. Loughran's *Literary Digest* article published shortly after the Atlantic City event; the piece conveys information about the pact agreed to by the mobsters. According to Loughran, the pact consisted of the following points, all of which solely concern Chicago:

1. That all killings be abolished and that all controversies be settled by an executive committee; all machine-guns and small arms to be relinquished under pain of extreme punishment should gangsters fail to adhere to the disarmament ruling.

2. That Johnny Torrio rule as the king and chief arbiter of the new syndicate.

3. That Capone disband his gang and aid the new combination to break up smaller gangs.

4. That Capone relinquish his hold on three dog tracks, vice, gambling, and beer throughout Cook County, including Chicago and Cicero.

5. Torrio, Aiello, Moran, and Capone to split all profits after deduction of expenses.

6. Torrio to handle all finances single-handed and to serve weekly notice on each of the "Big Four" of their earnings.

7. That a monthly audit be made with the "Big Four" sitting in and poring over the books to see that an equitable split has been made.

8. Joe Aiello to head the Chicago branch of the Unione Siciliano and its 6,000 members; Aiello to be responsible to Torrio.

9. Jack Guzick [sic] and Johnny Patton (boy mayor of Burnham) to give up their holdings in the Capone organization and turn it into a new syndicate.

10. Capone to agree on a national head for the reorganized Union Siciliano; Torrio to make the appointment.

11. Capone to turn over to the organization the "ship" in Cicero and other gaming houses still running, and to agree on locations for new gaming houses.

12. Everyone to forget all past grievances, such as the Saint Valentine's Day massacre, and hundreds of other gang violences of the past.

13. That all South Side and North Side gangs to be amalgamated under Torrio's jurisdiction.

14. That the peace be permanent and binding, subject to the extreme measures of the executive board.

Torrio, as head of the new syndicate will control single-handedly between $15,000,000 and $16,000,000 annually, reports estimate. He will collect annually from the following:

Hawthorne dog track . . . $1,000,000

Fairview Dog Track 1,000,000

Thornton Dog Track 1,000,000

Cicero gaming 3,600,000

Chicago gaming 3,000,000

Vice 2,000,000

Beer 3,000,000

Unione Sicialiano 500,000

Nowhere in this document does Loughran mention anything about conference attendees like Luciano, Schultz, or others, and he says nothing about any city other than Chicago. Loughran can be regarded as a reliable source on the underworld. He was a leading United Press crime reporter in the Windy City and was notable for arriving at the scene of the Saint Valentine's Day Massacre before the detectives.

If Critchley is correct in his "small conference" interpretation, how then did the "big conference" legend come into being? One of the first references (perhaps the first) came in a 1939 book about Lucky Luciano by New York investigative reporter Hickman Powell, who said that Frank Costello attended the Atlantic City event, and in fact arranged it, and that Luciano and other "gang chieftains" were there.[38] The idea of a Big Conference attended by the major East Coast gang leaders also appeared a 1958 book by crime writer Leo Katcher.[39] A burst of books in the 1970s offered expanding lists of the attendees and their cities. Fred Jay Cook's 1973 potboiler *Mafia!* listed a dozen attendees.[40] In the dubious 1974 book *The Last Testament of Lucky Luciano*, Martin Gosch expanded the guest list to more than two dozen and included delegates from Boston, Detroit, Cleveland, Kansas City, and a few other smaller cities. The Big Conference scenario has continued to grow; the anonymous 2012 entry in Wikipeida names some thirty-five attendees and speculates that there were still more delegates from Louisiana and Florida. No primary sources are provided for these assorted lists of attendees, with the exception of George Wolf's claim that Frank Costello had described the conference to him.[41]

In the end, the only certainty is that a gathering of mobsters occurred in Atlantic City in May 1929. But who they were and what they accomplished is in question. And unless some researcher finds long-lost May 1929 Atlantic City hotel registers from vanished hotels that were signed by gangsters using their real names, there is unlikely to be any clear-cut solution. However, the small conference interpretation is most in accord with primary sources, and by the standards of the historical profession is the more credible analysis.

THE TREATY OF ATLANTIC CITY

The treaty that Loughran reported and Capone described deserves some scrutiny. It certainly displays a keen knowledge of Chicago crime. The "Ship" was a Capone-run casino, and Johnny Patton, the youthful mayor of the Chicago suburb of Burnham, was associated with the Capone Outfit. But was Loughran referring to a real document that the gangsters signed? Al Capone said there was indeed such a document; in his Philadelphia conversation he related that the gang leaders had signed a pact "on the dotted line" that would stop gangsters murdering each other and that would have weapons, including machine guns, dumped into Lake Michigan.[42] But gangsters disliked putting agreements in writing that could later incriminate them. Capone biographer Laurence Bergreen thinks Loughran's report was designed to give an upbeat version of gangsters as public servants seeking peace and suggests that the reporter spun the event as the development of a treaty.[43]

The American public, including mobsters, was certainly attuned to the concept of treaties. The year 1929 was only a decade after the most famous treaty of all time, the one negotiated at Versailles in 1919, after the armistice that ended the First World War. And it is significant that Loughran reported that the gangsters' treaty consisted of fourteen points, just as President Woodrow Wilson's 1918 "Fourteen Points" formed the basis of the Versailles treaty. In the years after Versailles, much public attention was focused on negotiations between the major international powers to rein in the construction of warships. The *Literary Digest* article referred to Loughran's text as a "limitation of armaments" agreement, a

term undoubtedly derived from the Conference on the Limitation of Arma-
ment held in Washington, D.C., in 1922 and subsequent conferences to limit the
construction of warships by the major world powers.[44]

Al Capone certainly had international diplomacy on his mind when he
said that he and his fellow mobsters sat around a table in Atlantic City "discussing amity like a group of diplomats might gather in a peace conference."[45]
The highbrow *Literary Digest* compared the attempt of gangsters to achieve
internal order to similar efforts that had been instituted in other fields of
endeavor in the United States: "gunmen will have an executive council and
a 'czar,' whose duties will presumably be analogous to those of Judge Landis
and Will Hays in the domains of baseball and the movies."[46] (The magazine
was referring here to the appointment of the first commissioner of baseball,
former judge Kennesaw Mountain Landis, and of the appointment of the
first president of the motion picture association, William Harrison Hays Sr.,
former U.S. postmaster general. Both offices had been created in 1922.)

Perhaps the Chicago mobsters actually felt they had achieved a lasting
peace. Fat chance. Like the Treaty of Versailles, the Treaty of Atlantic City
went only so far. The killing of mob leaders did not end, and machine guns
were never confiscated for a mass dumping in Lake Michigan.

Finally, what did the people of Atlantic City say about having a gangster conference in their midst? While it was happening, the residents and tourists in the city
were unaware it was going on. Not until two days after the gathering ended did a
front-page article in the *Atlantic City Daily Press* reveal that the criminals had met.
On its editorial page two days later, the paper's editors angrily speculated about
why the event had been held in the resort: "Did these gangsters merely have reason
to believe that here they would be undisturbed and here they could foregather
without any undue police interference, a supposition which turned out to be the
correct one?" The paper lambasted the town's lax law enforcement: "Surely, our
police and detective departments did not cover themselves with glory when they
permitted a gangster convention to be held under their very noses." What most
seemed to gall the editors was that the name Atlantic City would forever be associated with gangsterism. The editorial lamented, "Why did Capone have to pick
out Atlantic City to bring his gangsters, friends, and enemies?"[47]

CHAPTER 5

The Conference as Comedy

No matter how it has been interpreted the May 1929 Atlantic City Conference was serious business. But it has spilled over into two comedic classics, one a short story by a noted American writer and the other a celebrated Hollywood movie.

"Dark Dolores"

The unique writing style of Damon Runyon has lead to the adjective "runyonesque," generally describing the kind of characters to which he was drawn—gamblers, dancing girls, hobos, outlaws, boxers, and other dubious people on the sketchy fringe of society. It has often been pointed out that Runyon's own life was runyonesque. Born in 1880, he was the offspring of a family whose American origins went back to the colonial era. His mother died when Runyon was a child, and parental oversight was provided by a remote, uncaring, hard-drinking father—a newspaperman whose career sank from publisher to typesetter and who drifted from Manhattan, Kansas, to Pueblo, Colorado. Young Damon was something of a wild child in Pueblo, kicked out of school after the sixth grade, living on the streets, and following in the footsteps of his dad by drinking, smoking, and whoring. While still in his teens he became a reporter for local newspapers. He enlisted in the army during the Spanish American War, though his only combat was with sobriety. After the service he kept on writing, lying prodigiously about his military service, and binge drinking. But his life changed as he matured and developed his writing skills. He got to work at better quality newspapers, got his stories and poems published in quality magazines, fell in love, and stopped drinking. He was hired by William Randolph Hearst's *New York American* as a reporter and columnist and eventually became the highest paid newsman in the nation. But he still had about him the gaunt look of a three-pack-a-day smoker and reformed alcoholic.

Runyon is best known today for his connection to the great New York thoroughfare of Broadway, where he spent his evenings immersed in low culture, eating at Lindy's Restaurant, smoking cigarettes, drinking coffee, and hobnobbing with celebrities and nobodies. He used the people he met on those late-night expeditions to create the characters in his newspaper columns, magazine stories, and books. The musical *Guys and Dolls*, based on his Broadway writing, is today his best-known legacy.

A significant part of his writing concerned gangsters, and Damon Runyon knew lots of them, including Frank Costello, Owney Madden, Lucky Luciano, Meyer Lansky, and Al Capone. Runyon actually had dinner at Capone's mansion in Florida a short time before the Atlantic City conference. He knew enough about the Atlantic City event to write a short story about it, "Dark Dolores," that was published in *Cosmopolitan* magazine in November 1929.[1] *Cosmopolitan* in those days was a literary magazine (unlike its present incarnation as a publication devoted to advising young women about how to attract young men by practicing sensual techniques).

"Dark Dolores" has all the aspects of Runyon's prose style. It is written entirely in the present tense, with a degree of affection for its dimwit characters and laugh-out-loud humor. The story begins with an unnamed narrator, who describes a chat he had with Waldo Winchester, Runyon's name for his friend and rival columnist Walter Winchell. Winchester bemoans the dearth of female murderers for him to write about, and he reflects on femme fatales from the past, including Cleopatra, Helen of Troy, the mermaid Lorelei, and the Greek goddess Circe. This brings the narrator to relate the story of Dolores, "a doll I met when I am in Atlantic City with Dave the Dude at the time of the big peace conference." Some crime writers use this line to claim that Runyon actually attended the conference, but this is improbable.

The narrator relates how he is strolling down Broadway one day, when a cab pulls up at the curb. Riding in the taxi is Dave the Dude, a character who appeared in many of Runyon's short stories. This time Dave is on his way to Penn Station to catch the train to Atlantic City. Dave pulls the narrator into the taxi and asks him to accompany him on this trip.

Dave the Dude has been called to the Ritz Hotel in Atlantic City to settle a gang war going on in St. Louis between three rival mobs, one headed by the Black Mike Mario, another by Benny the Blond Jew, and a third by Scoodles Shea. Black Mike is an Italian with a big scar on his cheek made by a Sicilian enemy. Scoodles Shea, the Irishman, is a "big red-headed muzzler with a lot of freckles and a big grin all over his kisser." Benny the Blond Jew is "a tall pale guy," and the narrator knows Benny has killed nine people.

The mobsters agree that they need somebody to mediate the gang war in their town. They consider getting President of the United States Herbert Hoover, Supreme Court Chief Justice William Howard Taft, or the hero aviator Colonel Charles Lindbergh as umpire, but, upon realizing that Hoover, Taft, and Lindbergh might be too busy, they decide to hold their conference in Atlantic City with Dave the Dude as mediator.

Before they leave St. Louis by train for Atlantic City, Mike, Scoodles, and Benny decide to run an errand. They sneak into a St. Louis speakeasy where they shoot to death Frankie Farrone, a lone wolf mobster whose crime is lack of respect for the three established gang leaders. In a typical Runyon bit of black humor, the narrator says that they would have fired more than four slugs into Frankie but had to leave quickly because their taxi was outside with the meter running, "and they know the St. Louis taxi jockeys are terrible for jumping the meter on guys who keep them waiting."

Thus all five men—the narrator, Dave, Mike, Scoodles, and Benny— wind up playing cards and drinking at the bar of the Ritz Hotel in Atlantic City. Black Mike suggests they go out looking for some "tomatoes"—that is, women, who are also known in Runyon's world as dolls, broads, pancakes, and cookies. Thus, putting aside the task of holding a conference, the group heads down to a cabaret near the Boardwalk, where they soon meet "half a dozen dolls of different shapes and sizes" with whom to drink, dance, and flirt. Dave and the narrator are a bit more restrained because Dave doesn't want to get in trouble with his wife back home, and the narrator finds the combination of bad alcohol, armed thugs, and loose women bad for his nervous system.

One of the tomatoes stands out. Her name is Dolores. Says the narrator, "She is about as good a looker as a guy will wish to clap an eye on. She is tall and limber, like a buggy whip, and she has hair as black as the ace of spades, and maybe blacker, and all smooth and shiny." Her large black eyes have a look "that somehow makes me think she may know more than she lets on, which I afterwards find out is very true, indeed."

Mike, Scoodles, and Benny, groggy from the bad booze, are utterly smitten by Dolores and ignore the other girls. When the bar closes at 5:00 A.M., the five men and Dolores head over to her shabby hotel on North Carolina Avenue. Mike, Scoodles, and Benny are elbowing each other out of the way to arrange a date. She suggests that whoever wants can meet her on the beach in front of the Ritz later that day. Dave reminds them that they have to start the conference in the afternoon.

But the conference never does convene because Mike, Scoodles, and Benny spend the days that follow with Dolores. Their afternoons are taken up with dipping in the ocean, the evenings with drinking at the cabaret as well as riding around the Boardwalk in rolling chairs and dining at the resort's hotels. None of them gets to see her alone, and their rivalry heats up to the level that only two things prevent the mobsters from shooting each other: (a) Dolores tells them she doesn't like that kind of thing, and (b) Dave the Dude confiscates their pistols. The narrator is struck by the unusual situation of three hoods "daffy over the same doll." Dave the Dude sticks around because (another Runyon witticism) he wants to keep the mobsters from giving a bad name to Atlantic City, the center of illegal gambling, drinking, and vice. It is also clear that Dave himself is torn between his lust for Dolores and his fear of his wife's fury if she learns about his interest.

Dolores proposes a dawn swimming party, and sure enough when the sun comes up Mike, Scoodles, and Benny, filled to the gills with booze, are on the beach in bathing suits. And so, strikingly, is Dolores: "She is in a red bathing suit, with red rubber cap over her black hair, and while most dolls in bathing suits hurt my eyes, she is still beautiful." She enters the water where she moves "like a big beautiful red fish." The St. Louis mobsters paddle around a bit and then lie next to her on the sand. The narrator and Dave the Dude, exhausted from their night on the town, are getting ready to leave, when Dolores does something quite unexpected:

> "She tears into the water, kicking it every which way until she gets to where it is deep, when she starts to swim, heading for the open sea. Black Mike and Scoodles Shea and Benny the Blond Jew are paddling after her like blazes. We can see it is some kind of chase, and we stand watching it. We can see Dolores' little red cap, bouncing along over the water like a rubber ball on a sidewalk, with Black Mike and Scoodles and Benny staggering along behind her."

Dolores swims circles around the three, coming tantalizingly close to each one and then teasingly pulling away, all the while gradually moving farther away from the shore. After watching this curious game of tag for a while, Dave and the narrator go back to the hotel to catch some sleep. Later that afternoon the two men are eating grapefruit, ham, and eggs in Dave's room when they realize they haven't seen the swimmers. At that moment comes a knock at the door. (Warning: plot spoiler follows.)

It is, of course, Dolores, beautiful as ever, but exhausted. She tells Dave that the three gangsters are dead. Mike and Scoodles are the first to die. They go out three miles from the shore. They try to turn around and swim back, but it is too late, and they sink to their deaths. She says, "I made sure of this, Mister Dave the Dude." Benny gets the furthest of any of the three, but he has a cramp and drowns. "I guess he loves me the most, at that, as he always claims." Dolores then explains that she is a champion swimmer and that she has used her athletic ability to bring about the three deaths. Why? Because she is none other than the widow of Frankie Farrone, the mobster who was killed in St. Louis. She promises her dead husband in his coffin that she will get revenge so she takes a flight to Atlantic City and is stationed at the cabaret when the mobsters arrive. How does she lure them into the sea? "I tell them I will marry the first one who reaches me in the water."

And thus the narrator and Dave leave Atlantic City to return to Broadway. Dave gets the final word: "You know, I will always consider I get a very lucky break that Dolores does not include me in her offer, or the chances are I will be swimming yet." The tale of Dark Dolores is, of course, fiction and does not pretend to be a historical narrative—nobody drowned at the real conference. But the story does suggest some reality of the event or at the very least what was thought at the time to be the reality.

For starters, several characters are based on real people. Runyonologists believe that Dave the Dude was inspired by the real-life underworld figure and Runyon friend Frank Costello, the prime minister of organized crime known for his managerial and negotiating skills.[2] The "Dave the Dude" moniker came from Costello's fondness for expensive tailored suits. He refused to wear cheap suits even when advised to do so by his lawyer, George Wolf, who thought it would make him look like a regular guy to trial jurors. Costello's presence in the story lends support to the "Big Conference" interpretation of the Atlantic City gathering. It has also been thought that Dark Dolores is based on Costello's girlfriend at the time Runyon wrote the story.[3] Black Mike Mario is clearly based on

Al Capone, both of whom are Italian mobsters with visible scars on their faces from youthful fights. Scoodles Shea, the Irishman, may have been an amalgam of Irish mobsters, such as Runyon's friend Owney Madden and Dion O'Banion. Benny the Blond Jew, the best looking of the three, might be Runyon's amalgam of up-and-coming Jewish gangsters known for their good looks, Benjamin "Bugsy" Siegel and Abner "Longie" Zwillman. By placing an Italian, an Irishman, and a Jew at the center of the story, Runyon is clearly reflecting the diversity of the conference attendees. White Anglo Saxon Protestants were not much in evidence among those mobsters who went to Atlantic City, and neither were they cast as main characters in Runyon's story.

Second, the idea that the Atlantic City event focused on cooling off the rivalry between warring gangs in one city corresponds to the "Small Conference" interpretation. The narrator describes how Mike, Scoodles, and Benny "all have different mobs in St. Louis, and who are ripping and tearing at each other for a couple of years over such propositions as to who shall have what in the way of business privileges of one kind and another, including alky, and liquor, and gambling." The narrator continues, "From what I hear there is plenty of shooting going on between these mobs, and guys getting topped right and left. Also there is much heaving of bombs, and all this and that, until finally the only people making any dough in the town are the undertakers, and it seems there is no chance of anybody cutting in on the undertakers, though Scoodles Shea tries." Runyon is obviously using St. Louis to represent Chicago as he uses Black Mike Marrio to represent Capone. One can also see in the story the pervasiveness of the Treaty of Versailles metaphor for what the conference attendees were trying to achieve. In the story, the narrator credits Scoodles for seeking a way to solve the gang wars in St. Louis. Scoodles fought in France during World War I and tells Mike and Benny how, "when all the big nations get broke, and sick and tired of fighting, they hold a peace conference and straighten things out."

Just as the conference attendees clashed with Capone, Black Mike comes across badly in Runyon's story. Says the narrator, "I can see at once that this

Black Mike is a guy who has little bringing up." The narrator also says that Mike looks the most unattractive and even inhuman in his bathing suit. And Dolores reveals that Mike is the one whom she most dislikes: "I do not wish to seem hard-hearted, but it is a relief when I see Black Mike sink. Can you imagine being married to such a bum?"

The time spent by the Dark Dolores character at the off-Boardwalk cabaret and the gangsters' predilection for sex reflects the partying that is said to have gone on at the real Atlantic City conference. Again, the real Al Capone did not drown in Atlantic City, but it is fair to say that the conference put him in hot water, as chapter 6 describes.

Some Like It Hot

The Atlantic City gangster conference manifested itself in another work of fiction—the classic 1959 film comedy *Some Like It Hot*, directed by Billy Wilder and starring Jack Lemmon, Tony Curtis, and Marilyn Monroe.[4] Wilder was a refuge from Nazi Germany who became a Hollywood screenwriter and later combined screenwriting with directing. His acclaimed films in the 1950s included *Sabrina* (1954), *The Seven Year Itch* (1955), and *Witness for the Prosecution* (1957). Wilder and his writing partner I.A.L. Diamond were looking around for a new project and were struck by two obscure European movies that had to do with men who dressed as women in order to play in female orchestras. Those early films no longer exist so it is unknown how much was borrowed, but Wilder and Diamond needed to come up with a framework–some more or less plausible plot justification of why men would wear drag for an extended period of time. They were also concerned that making the time period contemporary would not provide enough of a topsy-turvy environment. Wilder came up with the idea of basing the picture on the Prohibition world of the Roaring Twenties.

The movie is set in 1929, and the story begins in Chicago with a car chase, a shootout, and a speakeasy hidden in a funeral parlor. Two down-at-the-heels musicians, the saxophone-playing Joe (played by Curtis) and the bassist Jerry (Lemmon), stumble upon the Saint Valentine's Day Massacre as it is in progress. The scene is faithful in many ways to the actual event, with seven mobsters lined up against a wall in a Clark Street garage and killed with shotguns and machine guns. To escape being murdered by the Capone-like crime boss, "Spats" Colombo (George Raft), the two frightened musicians race away from the murder scene. Knowing that Chicago is now unsafe for them, they come up with a desperate plan: they dress as females so they can join a traveling all-woman dance band, "Sweet Sue and Her Society Syncopaters," which is booked to play in Florida. Joe takes the name Josephine, and Jerry becomes Daphne. As their train heads south, the boys in makeup and wigs, wobbling along in their dresses and heels, encounter the impossibly sexy and wide-eyed innocent band member Sugar Kane Kowalczyk (Monroe). There follows much opportunity for comedy as Sugar and the Society Syncopaters snuggle up to the two new band members in the train sleeping car, while the disguised boys struggle to control their raging testosterone impulses.

The band arrives at the Seminole Ritz, an oceanfront resort hotel in Miami, where new plot twists develop. The elderly millionaire Osborne Fielding III develops a crush on Daphne. Meanwhile, Joe develops a new male persona as a millionaire in order to romance Sugar. Now comes the gangster conference part: Joe/Josephine and Jerry/Daphne are shocked to find that a gathering of gangsters from around the nation has assembled at the resort hotel under the bogus name of the 10th Annual Convention of the Friends of Italian Opera. Of course, Spats Colombo and his gang are there and recognize the boys as the witnesses to the Saint Valentine's Day massacre who must be snuffed out. In the best tradition of slapstick, the mobsters frantically pursue the boys around the hotel. At one point Joe/Josephine and Jerry/Daphne hide under a table in the hall where the gangster conference is in progress. A gigantic birthday cake is wheeled into the room; it is supposed to be for Spats from a rival mobster, Little Bonaparte, who secretly wants to avenge the Saint Valentine's Day Massacre. As the gathering starts to sing the happy birthday song, a machine gun wielding mobster jumps out of the cake and mows down Spats and his mob.

After much more chasing around, Sugar, Joe/Josephine, and Jerry/Daphne finally flee the hotel and wind up in a motorboat driven by Fielding Osborne III. In the rear seats of the motorboat speeding over the ocean, Jerry reveals to Sugar that he is a man, and they embrace each other. In the front seats, Osborne professes his love for Daphne, who tries to resist. "I'M A MAN," Jerry finally shouts as he rips off his wig. To which the unfazed Osgood smiles and shrugs, "Well—nobody's perfect." Jerry looks into the camera as he considers the proposition.

Some Like It Hot was filmed at the MGM studies and at the Del Coranado Hotel in California and released in March 1959 by Mirisch Company and United Artists. It was a hit, and in 2000, the American Film Institute named it the funniest American movie of all time.

————

Both Damon Runyon's short story and Billy Wilder's movie are reminiscent of the remark by Karl Marx that history repeats itself, first as tragedy and then as farce.

CHAPTER 6

Capone's Long Trip Home

The Philly Pinch

The good citizens of Philadelphia who sat down to read their morning newspapers over breakfast on Friday, May 17, 1929, were met with an astonishing and entirely unexpected front-page headline. Said the *Inquirer* newspaper:

CHICAGO'S OWN "SCARFACE" HELD IN $35,000 HERE

RACKET DRAGNET YIELDS NOTORIOUS AL CAPONE, BEER BARON AND

UNDERWORLD LEADER

MUST FACE TRIAL FOR FIRST TIME IN LONG AND FRUITFUL CAREER

SAID TO HAVE NETTED HIM $2,000,000

The story told in the *Inquirer* and other Philly papers described how Capone and his bodyguard Frankie Rio appeared in the city the previous evening when they stepped off a train from the Jersey Shore. Two alert detectives from the Philadelphia City Hall Detective Bureau, James "Shoey" Malone and John "Jack" Creedon, recognized Capone and watched the two men enter the Stanley Theater at Nineteenth and Market streets. (The feature movie was a detective thriller *Voice of the City.*) The lawmen waited patiently outside. When the two mobsters emerged from the theater, Shoey, described as "demure, blue-eyed little chap," accosted Capone and confiscated a .38 snub nose revolver the gangster carried in his pocket. At the same time Creedon, who resembled "a back-country deacon with eye glasses," separated Frankie Rio from his pistol.

The *Inquirer* article, praising the two detectives, noted that they had previously received Philadelphia Citizen's Awards for bravery. The article went on to describe how Capone and Rio were charged with carrying concealed weapons, photographed, fingerprinted, and locked up in cells at City Hall. A lawyer for Capone appeared on the scene to argue for the release of the mobster and his bodyguard, but Magistrate Edward Carney refused the request and held an impromptu hearing. Carney observed, "There is no doubt in my mind that you have been responsible for a great many murders in America. You have intimidated police. You are known to every District Attorney in the Country. I am going to hold you in $35,000 bail each for court. Take 'em back."[1]

The next day, May 18, the citizenry learned more. A few hours after Carney set bail, Judge John E. Walsh presided over a quick trial. Capone and Rio admitted they were guilty of the concealed weapons violation, after which Walsh sentenced the pair to a year in prison. The sheriff's officers then put them in a van and took them to Moyamensing Prison in South Philly. It all happened with remarkable swiftness. Capone and his henchmen were arrested at 8:15 P.M. on May 16, brought before the magistrate at 11:55 that evening, indicted next morning, May 17, at 10:25, sentenced at 12:21 that afternoon, and in prison by 12:50 P.M.[2] The whole process, from arrest to prison, took a mere sixteen hours.

Philadelphians were filled with pride. The *Inquirer* carried an editorial entitled "Philadelphia Puts Capone Behind the Bars," which boasted that the City of Brotherly Love had succeeded in stopping Capone, where Chicago, Miami, and other parts of the country had failed. Chicago officials, by contrast, were a bit mortified. The deputy police commissioner of Chicago, John Stege, lamely said he had not been able to arrest Capone because the Illinois Supreme Court required the police to get a warrant before they could search a suspect for a gun.[3]

In the midst of all of this self-congratulation in Philadelphia and excuse-making in Chicago, some troubling news emerged. Voices were raised from Chicago to suggest something fishy about the whole business. Frank J. Loesch, president of the Chicago Crime Commission, said of Capone, "I believe it was his idea for some time to get himself in jail to escape the vengeance of rival gangsters." Tom Pettey, a reporter for the *Chicago Tribune* who was in Philadelphia to cover events, related the following rumors that he had picked up and tied Capone's desire to go to jail with the decisions made at Atlantic City:

> The Atlantic City conference broke up in a row when "Scarface" refused to "retire" or to come through with a large share of his fortune. Rival gang leaders told him that if he showed up in New York he would "get his head blown off" and that the minute he appeared in Chicago he would be "on the spot" [i.e., set up for assassination]. From Atlantic City, Capone went to his hotel and telephoned a Philadelphia friend. "Have 'Shoey' Malone tipped off that I'll be in Philadelphia tonight wearing a pistol" was the message. "Tell him I'll stand in for a pinch."[4]

Other rumors quickly surfaced: one was that Capone gave $20,000 to Malone and Creedon; when Capone was arrested he had voiced a friendly "Hello, Shoey." The *Philadelphia Inquirer* refused to believe that Capone had arranged the arrest or that there had been anything polite and friendly about the encounter outside the theater. Shoey himself angrily dismissed the implication that the arrest had been a sham: "It's enough to make anybody want to quit being a copper. Here we take a chance and pinch two of the most dangerous characters in the racket. They have guns on them and know how to use them. Then everybody hollers 'frame up.'" Shoey denied the allegation that Capone and Rio had willingly handed over their guns. Quite the contrary, said Shoey, he and Jack Creedon had found it necessary to use force to wrest the pistols away from the mobsters. "The story that they politely handed us their guns is all hokem." Agreeing with that statement, Capone told a reporter, "I didn't give myself up to the cops. If the automobile had not broken down coming from Atlantic City to Philadelphia they never would have seen me."[5] But then came news that Shoey and Creedon actually knew Al Capone. They admitted they had met him at his Miami home a few months before and that he had given them tickets to a major boxing match.

What else did the central figure in the story, Al Capone himself, have to say? Quite a bit, actually—he spoke about not only the arrest but also his life in general. At two o'clock on the morning after the arrest, Capone was interviewed by Major Lemuel B. Schofield, the director of public safety for the city of Philadelphia. In his remarks to Schofield, spoken with his usual rambling blather, the Chicago mob leader discussed the hardship of his career: "It's a tough life to lead. You fear death every moment, and worse than death you fear the rats of the game, who would run around and tell the police if you didn't constantly satisfy them with money and favors. I never was able to leave my home without my body-guard [Frankie Rio]." When Rio started to get belligerent during the interview, Capone cautioned him, "Listen, boy, you're my friend and have been a faithful pal, but I'll do the talking." Capone rhapsodized about his dreams of peace: "I have a wife, and a boy who is eleven—a lad I idolize, and a beautiful home at Palm Island, Florida. If I could go there and forget it all, I would be the happiest man in the world. I want peace and I am willing to live and let live."[6]

Capone revealed that there had been a conference among gangsters earlier in the week at Atlantic City—a revelation that made headlines, such as "Prisoner Tells Amazing Tale of Three-Day Peace Conference of Rival Gang Chiefs at Shore."[7] He also talked about the circumstances of his arrest. Whereas early reports said that he had taken the train from the Jersey Shore to Philadelphia, in Capone's version he was being driven by car from Atlantic City to Philadelphia via the White Horse Pike when the car broke down fifteen miles outside Camden, and he missed his train reservation to Chicago. Somehow the car was fixed and the reservation switched to later that evening—all of which explains why he wound up at the wrong place at the wrong time.

So was it a legitimate arrest or prearranged set-up? Capone did face serious criticism from his fellow mobsters at the Atlantic City convention so he may have sought a refuge in prison for a time. At the brief trial the day after his arrest, however, his lawyers sought to keep him out of jail by offering compromises to Judge Walsh, who rejected them.[8]

Serving a prison sentence was a new experience for Capone. He had been arrested before, but he had never been sentenced to prison. For years, he had been a public figure in Chicago—a man who loved to be in the spotlight at news conferences, baseball games, boxing matches, and horse races, dodging public attention when the heat was on by journeying to places like Miami and Wisconsin or back to his family in the house on Prairie Avenue. He lost that freedom once he was sentenced. The public, through the press, now had a different relationship with the mobster. Everyone knew where he was, and as a result newspaper coverage of Capone increased during the time he was caged in the Pennsylvania prison system.

BEHIND BARS

The first night after their arrest, Capone and Rio were locked up in holding cells in Philadelphia's massive City Hall. They were then taken to Moyamensing Prison, where they spent the next night, May 17. The Board of Prison Inspectors approved their transfer to Holmesburg County Jail, and at 2:15 P.M. on May 18, a prison van left Moyamensing with just two prisoners, Capone and Rio. The authorities had heard rumors that rival criminals were seeking to rub Capone out so a machine-gun attack on the prison van was considered a real threat. Three armed guards were in the front section of the van, with two more keeping an eye on the prisoners in the rear section. The van was followed by another vehicle with five city detectives, guns at the ready.

Holmesburg Prison, located in north Philly, was a horrible place. In 1928, an investigation into the prison revealed that under the direction of the facility's deputy superintendent, sadistic guards at the prison had forced black prisoners to torture white prisoners. In January 1929, inmates armed with table legs and other weapons had gone on a twenty-four-hour rampage sparked by the vile food served in the mess hall. The convicts overran sections of the prison and clubbed the guards. The guards fought back with tear gas bombs that produced choking fires. By the time Capone and Rio were imprisoned there the Holmesburg board of inspectors had been purged and the assistant superintendent forced out, but it remained a grim place to be incarcerated.[9] When Capone arrived at Holmesburg he was given a prison haircut, making the scars on his face more visible, which he detested. He was then given a shower, and his tailored suit was put in a prison locker, to be replaced by blue denim prison garb. "Not much like home here," was Capone's bitter remark to the assistant superintendent of the prison.[10]

When he was arrested he had been wearing an expensive diamond ring. That too was shut up in a locker with the tailored suit he had been wearing. At his trial a spectator asked Capone if it was worth $50,000. "Well, you made a good guess," Capone replied.[11] In newspaper reports and books ever after the ring was said to be worth $50,000. Capone had the ring in his possession when he was sent to Holmesburg, but reportedly he gave it to one of his lawyers who saw to it that it got to Ralph Capone in Chicago, perhaps a symbolic message that Ralph would run the Outfit until his brother Al came back home.[12]

Capone may have originally plotted to get into jail, but once in Holmesburg he did everything he could to get out. Perhaps he had anticipated receiving just ninety days in jail, the standard sentence for carrying a concealed weapon in the city of Brotherly Love, but, in recognition of his criminal notoriety, Judge Walsh gave him a full year, a long time for him to be removed from the leadership of the Chicago underworld. Rumors were circulating that a war would be waged to pick a successor to Capone;

one of the names mentioned was John Torrio. In Chicago Thomas D. Nash, Capone's longtime lawyer, spread the word that friends of the mob leader in the Windy City would seek to get him out of jail and that a war chest of $50,000 had been raised. Death threats were sent to police magistrate Edward P. Carney, who brushed them off: "Real gangsters never ring a fire alarm when they start out to get you."[13] There was a steady traffic of Capone's emissaries back and forth from Chicago to Philadelphia (sometimes with a stopover in Atlantic City) to assist with the arrangements for Capone's legal defense, including Jack Guzik, Frank Nitti, and Charles Fischetti.

Two Philadelphia lawyers, Benjamin Golder and Bernard Lemisch, both Jewish, assisted by the Irishman Cornelius Haggerty, represented Capone and, as a lower priority, Frankie Rio. Golder was a major figure in the city and at the time a Republican member of the U.S. House of Representatives from Philadelphia. Golder and his colleagues in the firm Golder, Felger & Lemisch faced a difficult assignment. Capone and Rio had pled guilty at their trial, which dimmed the chances of a successful appeal of the verdict. A reversal of the verdict and freedom for Capone, the city prosecutor argued, would expose the Philadelphia courts to ridicule. Golder pressed on nonetheless by filing multiple appeals over the next few months at the levels of the Philadelphia municipal court, the state Superior Court, and the state Supreme Court, each time looking for an angle that would get his clients out of prison. Capone and Rio were not permitted to leave prison to attend the appeal hearings. Golder's argument was that at the original trial, Capone and Rio had not been given sufficient time to prepare a defense, faced a chaotic courtroom with a circuslike atmosphere, and were coerced into entering a guilty plea by Judge Walsh, who was biased against the prisoners. Judge Walsh heard the appeal for a new trial, and, as might be expected, he turned it down flat. A request by Golder that Capone be released on bail while the appeal was considered by higher courts was subsequently denied by two superior court justices. In due course, both the Superior Court and the Supreme Court turned down the appeal for a new trial. Golder's next tactic was to argue that the time Capone spent in jail had the taught the gangster a lesson and that he had been punished enough; if released Capone and Rio would promptly leave Philadelphia. He also charged that the yearlong sentences violated the law and should be reduced. These pleas too were rejected.[14]

While Golder's doomed appeals were being turned down, life went on for Capone in Holmesburg. When approached to give a $250 contribution to a Children's Hospital he replied, "A mere $250 contribution to a hospital? Nothing doing. It'll be $1,000," which he paid. And he played on the Ward B baseball team at Holmesburg as a pitcher, demonstrating "speed and fair control" to strike out opposing batters.[15] But it was still a dreary place. Then came some good news. In August 1929 he was transferred to the more hospitable Eastern Penitentiary. The official reason for the transfer was that Holmesburg was overcrowded, but cynics pointed out that no other prisoners had been transferred out of Holmesburg and that prisoners like Capone who had been convicted of a misdemeanor were supposed to remain in county facilities, of which Holmesburg was one. Rumor had it that the real reason for the transfer was that Capone had been getting special privileges at Holmesburg, a development that angered other prisoners, some of whom made threats against him. It seems likely that Capone's team of lawyers had struck a backroom deal with the authorities to drop their appeals if their clients were transferred.

Compared to Holmesburg, the Eastern State Penitentiary was downright homey. Fred D. Pasley, Capone's first biographer, said that it provided the gang leader with peace of mind for the first time. "Whether or not he realized it, was the happiest period of his career."[16] One of the first things Capone did when he arrived was to buy $1,000 worth of knickknacks made by the prisoners, such as ship models and cigarette boxes, which he sent to friends on the outside. He donated $1,200 to a Philadelphia orphanage. He may have made some other less publicized donations (i.e., bribes) as well because he was provided with a deluxe cell, complete with comfortable furniture, abundant quantities of alcohol, a radio, and lighting. There was a bookshelf and even a book—about Napoleon—who, like Capone, had been imprisoned. The warden allowed Capone to use his office to greet visitors and make phone calls. Capone's job in the prison was lightweight—he was a file clerk in the library and handled magazine subscriptions. In October, Capone withdrew one of his legal appeals. No reason was given. Perhaps there was another backroom deal that his lawyers cooked up—in exchange for abandoning the appeal, Capone was guaranteed that he would be released two months early for good conduct.

Al's prison demeanor won over an admirer, Dr. Herbert M. Goddard, a doctor at the prison and vice president of the facility's Board of Trustees. Goddard had performed operations to fix a problem with Capone's nose and to remove his tonsils. "I have never seen a prisoner so kind, cheery, and accommodating," Goddard told reporters. "He does his work . . . with a high degree of intelligence. He has brains. He would have made good anywhere, at anything."[17]

Back to Chicago

The sentences of Capone and Rio came to an end on March 17, 1930. A crowd of reporters, movie cameramen, photographers, and the curious, estimated in the hundreds, gathered outside the Eastern Penitentiary to witness the historic release of the two men. But they were doomed to disappointment. The day before, the two former convicts had been spirited to Gratersford, a new prison located thirty miles away, from which on the 17th they were officially released and driven away in an automobile. Official word of this ruse was not made public until four hours later. Dr. Goddard and Warden Smith had been behind the trickery—one last favor to their celebrity inmate. Goddard told reporters that the whole thing was designed to thwart a hit from rival gang members. Another alleged aspect of the trick was that a fourteen-passenger airliner landed at Camden airport, ostensibly to take Capone and Rio back to Chicago, but this too may have been a ruse to deflect unwanted attention from the media.

Once out of custody, Capone dropped completely out of sight. There were conflicting claims that he was hiding in Chicago, or holed up in Indiana, or maybe Florida. Police were stationed outside his Prairie Avenue home and other locales frequented by the mob boss. The deputy police chief of Chicago, John Stege, said he would arrest Capone whenever he surfaced, although the legal grounds for such a move were unclear. Capone's actual arrival in Chicago was unpublicized. He reunited with his cronies, celebrated with a party at a hotel, and got wildly drunk—perhaps the result of unwinding after spending the past ten months in prison. Not until three days after his release did Capone finally reenter the public eye when, accompanied by his lawyer Thomas Nash, he casually sauntered into Stege's office. He told reporters that he and Frankie Rio had driven to the Windy City from Pennsylvania. Stege seems to have forgotten his threat to arrest Capone, but the deputy police chief ineptly took the gangster to federal and state law enforcement offices to see if there were any grounds for holding him. There were none.

Thus, Al was back with his customary saunter, but he would soon discover that the climate for organized crime had changed.

PART III

The Fall

"Please kill me, John—shoot me. I'm an old man and I'm through. Don't take me in for junk. How else can I live? Let me run, John, and then you shoot me."

—Waxey Gordon, after 1951 arrest by
Sgt. John Cottone of the NYC narcotics squad

CHAPTER 7

The Twilight of the Gangster?

The gangsters who attended the May 1929 conference in Atlantic City looked toward the future of their criminal enterprises. But they never anticipated a cataclysmic event that took place just five months later. In October 1929 the stock market crashed, killing the prosperity and high spirits that had characterized the Roaring Twenties. As historian William E. Leuchtenberg observed, "Never was a decade snuffed out so quickly as the 1920s."[1]

The crash morphed into the Great Depression of the 1930s, during which millions of Americans lost their jobs and "Hoovervilles," makeshift shanty towns set up by homeless men and women, sprang up in American cities. Decades later, historian Frederick Lewis Allen characterized the Depression as changing the psychological climate of the nation; for example, the short skirts and bobbed hair of the 1920s flapper became unfashionable in the 1930s. "The red-hot baby had gone out of style," said Allen, and with her went "that hysterical preoccupation with sex that preoccupied the Post-war Decade."[2] The 1920s party atmosphere of nightclubs, jazz bands, chorus girls, and champagne seemed out of place when compared to the needs of men and women forced to eke out a living in the world of the Depression. The *Ziegfeld Follies* gave its last performance in 1931.

In this atmosphere, gangsters became pariahs. The golden days of the 1920s—when Lucky Luciano hobnobbed with the governor of New York and Al Capone was selected to greet an Italian dignitary visiting Chicago—were over. In 1930 the Chicago Crime Commission invented the term "Public Enemy" to describe gangsters, and Al Capone became Public Enemy Number One. One can imagine a working man in 1920s Chicago who swilled Capone's beer, bet at Capone's casinos, and had sex with Capone's whores; suddenly in the 1930s he found himself out of a job and facing foreclosure, while the escapades of the millionaire Al Capone at his Florida mansion were covered in the press. To deflect criticism of this sort Capone opened a soup kitchen for the destitute in Depression Chicago, but, to give the devil his due, this boy from a poor Brooklyn family may have really wanted to help those people crushed by bad economic times. In October 1931, *Liberty* magazine published an angry article, "The Twilight of the Gangster: How Much Longer Are We Going to Put Up with Him?" The author, Edward Doherty, spoke of how, before the Depression, Americans had idolized their gangsters: "We've pampered and petted them. We've made them idols. We've cheered Alphonse 'Scarface' Capone every time he was acquitted. We've cried 'Persecution!' every time he went on trial. We've cheered Jack 'Legs' Diamond when he was acquitted of burning the feet of a man he was charged with kidnapping." But, said Dougherty, that all changed with the Depression:

> Hungry men know no jokes. And there are many hungry men in the nation today. Factories have been closed. Stores have gone out of business. Municipalities are broke. Chicago cannot pay its teachers or its policemen or its firemen. Men who were prosperous a few years ago are begging half dollars of their friends. . . . The glamour has been stripped from the gangsters. Even the most stupid of us see them now as they are, yellow louts, red-handed plunderers. We have begun to realize they have waged actual war upon us in this last red decade. Hunger has made us see the truth.[3]

There was public outrage in New York, when, on July 28, 1931, a carload of gangsters rolled up in front of an Italian American political club on East 107th Street in the Bronx and opened fire with one or more pistols and shotguns. The gangsters probably intended to hit people inside the building and a man in front who dashed away; instead, a five-year-old boy who had been playing on the sidewalk, Michael Vengali, was killed, and three other children were wounded. Nobody was convicted of the crime. This carnage, said a newspaper report, "has done more than anything to crystalize public sentiment behind an energetic campaign to drive gang killers from the streets of New York."[4]

The Attack on Immigrants

The anger against Prohibition gangsters actually extended back into the 1920s, well before the Great Depression. In the 1920s under the reign of the crime lords, people were alarmed that American respect for law and order was being corrupted and that evil gangsters were increasing in power and wealth. The rise of anti-immigrant sentiment helped to stoke resentment against the Jews and Italians who dominated organized crime. Historian John Higham refers to the period as the "Tribal Twenties," when many Americans feared the immigration tide. Prohibition played an important part in that resentment.[5] As dry White Anglo Saxon Protestants saw it, Prohibition would preserve the American way of life against the tide of immigrant groups, like the Jews and Catholics, who did not regard alcohol as immoral.

The Ku Klux Klan, founded in 1915 as a revival of the post–Civil War terrorist organization, lashed out against not only blacks but also Jews and Catholics. By the middle of the 1920s, the Klan, with an estimated four to five million members, offered the limitation of immigration as a major part of their platform. This sentiment was not confined to men and women in white bed sheets. Academic types in tweeds espoused the theory of eugenics, which depicted America as a "Nordic" nation being threatened by the influx of inferior groups. In 1920, Harry H. Laughlin, a leading eugenicist, told a congressional committee, "We want to prevent the deterioration of the American People due to the immigration of inferior human stock." He suggested that immigrants who committed crimes should be deported.[6] The Prohibitionists, nativists, Klansmen, and eugenicists triumphed with the adoption of the Immigration Act of 1924, which established quotas that sharply reduced the

number of Italians and Jews who could be admitted to the United States. Ironically, statistics assembled at the end of the 1920s showed that foreign-born
residents were far less likely to commit crime than the native born, but this fact
was drowned out by the anti-immigrant propaganda.[7]

There was a noticeable religious and ethnic divide between the gangsters and the top lawmen of the 1920s and 1930s who pursued them. Among
the latter were Protestants of Anglo-Saxon and Scandinavian descent such
as George E. Q. Johnson and Eliot Ness of Chicago, Tom Dewey of New
York, and Frank Wilson of the U.S. Treasury Department. Treasury agent
Wilson expressed his revulsion against aliens when he encountered Al
Capone at a race track in Florida, surrounded by bodyguards and sleazy
molls. "I looked on his pudgy olive face, his thick pursed lips, the rolls of
fat descending from his chin—and the scar, like a heavy pencil line across
his left cheek—and clenched my fists in frustration."[8]

It would be unfair, however, to regard the lawmen as totally bigoted.
Dewey had several Jews and a black woman on his legal staff in an era when
such minorities faced discrimination in being hired by law firms. Eliot
Ness was proud to have hired an Italian, Frank Brasile, for his Untouchables squad, although one reason he employed him was that Brasile did
not look Italian and so, undetected, he could overhear and understand the
conversations of gangsters who spoke Italian or Sicilian.[9]

Gangsters in Popular Culture from Movies to Comic Books

The anti-gangster sentiment unleashed by the Great Depression, coupled
with the anti-immigrant sentiment of the 1920s, spilled over into popular
culture. Prime examples were three movies from the early 1930s that created
the genre of the gangster film: *Little Caesar, The Public Enemy,* and *Scarface.*
All three depicted gangsters who viciously clawed their way to the top and
died violently at the end of the movie. The most caustic in depicting gangsters as a threat to the American way of life was *Scarface,* starring Paul Muni
as Tony Camonte, a figure clearly based on the real Scarface, Al Capone. The

movie was filmed in 1930, but its release was delayed for two years while the producer Howard Hughes and the director Howard Hawks revised it to make sure the Camonte character was depicted as sufficiently amoral, ruthless, and unworthy of emulation by the viewer. In its final version, the movie begins with the following successive notices on the screen:

> This picture is an indictment of gang rule in America and of the callous indifference of the government to this constantly increasing menace to our safety and our liberty.
>
> Every incident in this picture is the reproduction of an actual occurrence, and the purpose of this picture is to demand of the government: "What are you going to do about it?"
>
> The government is your government. What are YOU going to do about it?

In the original version of the movie Camonte dies in a furious shootout with police. Because this could be considered as an act of bravery, Hughes and Hawks changed the ending to show a stern judge sentence Camonte to the gallows.

The 1931 movie *Public Enemy,* starring James Cagney as gangster Tom Powers, had its own on-screen warning:

> It is the ambition of the authors of "The Public Enemy" to honestly depict an environment that exists today in a certain strata of American life, rather than glorify the hoodlum or the criminal.

In case any moviegoer missed the message, there was another one at the conclusion of the movie:

> The END of Tom Powers is the end of every hoodlum. "The Public Enemy" is not a man, nor is it a character—it is a problem that sooner or later WE, the public, must solve.

The 1930 movie *Little Caesar,* starring Edward G. Robinson as Enrico Bandello, began with a biblical warning:

"... for all they that take the sword shall perish with the sword"

(Matthew 26:52).

This same theme can be seen in other products of popular culture. In the 1939 science fiction serial *Buck Rogers,* starring Buster Crabbe, the hero wakes up in the year 2440. He learns that, because the people in the twentieth century could not control the criminal element, the world has been taken over by gangsters and in fact the "super-racketeer" Killer Kane with his army of gangster robots now rules the Earth. Of course, Buck Rogers wins and overthrows the evil Kane. One popular newspaper comic strip that captured the negative image of gangsters was the saga of the square-jawed police detective Dick Tracy, created in 1931 by cartoonist Chester Gould. Tracy battled a grotesque assembly of criminals such as Alphonse "Big Boy" Caprice, Broadway Bates, Dan "The Squealer" Mucelli, and Dippy McDoogan. Historian of popular culture Garyn G. Roberts observed that Gould "did not simply portray Gangsters as evil; he depicted the twisted social celebration of these rogues as evil also."[10]

A comic book launched in the early 1940s, *Crime Does Not Pay,* also sought to vilify gangsters. The first edition contained a letter to the reader from publisher Lev Gleason: "The object of the editors is to bring home sharply, to make crystal clear, that CRIME DOES NOT PAY! Crime never pays, it is a sucker's game. Criminals are not heroes, they are not even brave or 'nervy'—they are cowardly rats. Sooner or later they get their just reward. Their fate is prison and death."[11] But the formula used in the comics did not quite match those uncompromising words. A typical *Crime Does Not Pay* story would show the criminal in question leading the high life, with copious amounts of violence, scantily clad women, drinking, and piles of money. Invariably that main character would be depicted gleefully mowing down his enemies with bullets. This tone persisted in the story until the small last panel, which depicted a hangman's noose, or an electric chair, or a judge passing sentence, or a pretty girl holding the scales of justice, or the character "Mr. Crime" gloating at the bad guy's demise. An adolescent boy reading the comic book under his bed covers with a flashlight could reasonably conclude that 99 percent of a criminal's career was a pretty exciting adventure. The same boy who saw the movie *The Public Enemy* with the swaggering, wisecracking Jimmy Cagney character may not have gotten the official message that the criminal life was repugnant. *Crime Does Not Pay* was fantastically successful; at its height in the late 1940s it sold roughly a million copies of each issue.[12] It perished in 1955, the victim of the national campaign against violence and sex-drenched comics that were thought to corrupt children.

A level of seriousness above comic books, comic strips, and movies were popular magazines. In the early 1930s articles with titles like "Gangland's Challenge to Our Civilization," "High Cost of Racketeers Ruining Business," "Gangs, Bosses and Judges," "Graft: A Threat to Democracy," and "Business Can Whip the Racketeer" appeared frequently in periodicals such as *Literary Digest, Outlook, Review of Reviews, Nation's Business, Collier's Weekly,* the *New York Times Magazine,* and *Ladies' Home Journal.* In 1933, the Hearst newspaper chain launched a series of articles designed to rouse the public against gangsterism.

It is no surprise that the supporters of Prohibition hated gangsters for making a mockery of the Noble Experiment, but even those who campaigned for the repeal of Prohibition criticized gangsters. The influential Association Against the Prohibition Amendment charged that the war against bootleggers had cost the nation $310 billion in the 1920s and another $11 billion in the same period because of lost tax revenue from liquor. That money, the AAPA charged, should have been used to lift the nation out of the Depression.[13]

INVESTIGATIONS, REPORTS, AND AN ISLAND PRISON

Public opinion in America had obviously turned against gangsters, but, to paraphrase the on-screen message in *Scarface,* what was the government going to do about it? The government's response was predictable:

it established a commission to study the problem. On January 7, 1931, the National Commission on Law Observance and Enforcement, created in 1929 by President Hoover, issued its report. This eleven-member body, known as the Wickersham Commission after its chair, former attorney general George W. Wickersham, identified serious problems and made suggestions on their correction. Stating the obvious, the report warned that the nation's criminal justice system was plagued by the rampant corruption of gangsters and politicians. Criminals had spies in law enforcement agencies. "People of wealth, businessmen and professional men, and their families, and, perhaps, the higher paid workingmen and their families, are drinking in large numbers in quite frank disregard of the declared policy of the National Prohibition Act." Even college students—America's future leaders—were shockingly, becoming scofflaws.[14]

After cataloging these many drawbacks of Prohibition, the commission members nevertheless recommended that the Eighteenth Amendment should not be repealed and that legalized saloons should never be restored. And despite the ruinous decline of the nation's economy, the commission recommended an increase in the funds devoted to enforcement so that more agents and inspectors could be hired by the Prohibition Bureau to fight bootleggers. The fact that the commission clung to Prohibition despite its obvious failures reflected President Hoover's commitment to the Eighteenth Amendment. A popular columnist for the *New York World,* Franklin P. Adams, poked fun at the Wickersham Commission with the following ditty:

> Prohibition is an awful flop.
> We like it.
> It can't stop what it's meant to stop.
> We like it.
> It's left a trail of graft and slime,
> It don't prohibit worth a dime,
> It's filled our land with vice and crime.
> Nevertheless, we're for it.[15]

More productive than the Wickersham report was a series of investigations into corruption in New York City's judicial system conducted from 1930 to 1932 by the distinguished jurist Samuel Seabury. His probe disclosed that lawyers, judges, clerks, police, and political bosses conspired to squeeze money out of the system and dismiss charges against those with political connections. He found that court records were tampered with and judgeships were sold to the highest bidders. Innocent women picked up by the vice squad were subject to extortion. The city's district attorney was ineffectual in enforcing the law, and the popular mayor of New York, the genial Jimmy Walker, was forced to resign because of his ties to the underworld. Investigations into the gangster problem did not stop with the repeal of Prohibition. In 1933 the U.S. Senate Commerce Committee, chaired by U.S. Senator Royal Copeland, held hearings around the nation about the fact that, according to the New York Democrat Copeland, "The rats of the underworld have found ways to crawl through the meshes of the law to carry on their slimy business."[16] On October 12 of the same year, U.S. Attorney General Homer Cummings announced to the National Anti-Crime Conference of the United States Flag Association and simultaneously to a national radio audience that an "inaccessible prison island for dangerous, incorrigible federal convicts" was to be established on Alcatraz Island in San Francisco Bay. The purpose, said Cummings, fit with the Justice Department's battle against racketeers.[17]

The villains had been vilified and an island dungeon had been set aside for them. The hatred of gangsters that emerged in the 1930s was exemplified two days after the December 7, 1941, Japanese attack on Pearl Harbor, when in a radio talk to the American people President Franklin Delano Roosevelt angrily called the leaders of the Axis powers "powerful and resourceful gangsters" and rallied the nation to oppose "a world ruled by the principles of gangsterism."[18]

As it happened, organized crime as an industry survived the Depression and the repeal of Prohibition, but the same was not true of the 1920s crime lords, many of whom fell from grace through murder, suicide, deportation, and prison. A major factor in their destruction was the discovery of a new prosecutorial tool—the concept that gangsters were legally required to pay their taxes.

CHAPTER 8

Pay Your Taxes

Manley Sullivan was thirty-nine years old in 1921, a hard-working resident of Charleston, South Carolina. He sometimes sold cars and tractors, but his basic line of work was selling bootleg liquor to his fellow Carolinians. His 1921 estimated income for that activity was ten thousand dollars, handsome annual earnings for that era. Under the Federal Revenue Act of 1921, anybody who earned at least one thousand dollars a year (or two thousand dollars for a married couple) had to submit a tax form and pay a portion of their income. Sullivan failed to do that, and the District Court accordingly found him guilty of tax evasion. But Sullivan's lawyers took their case to the Circuit Court of Appeals. Their argument was based on the Fifth Amendment to the Constitution, which states that "no person . . . shall be compelled in any criminal case to be a witness against himself." The lawyers argued that if Sullivan were to submit a tax return stating that his income had come from violating the Volstead Act he would be incriminating himself big time. The appeals court agreed with that interpretation and added some Deep Southern sass by stating that Sullivan's acquittal was timely because "the legislative branch of the government, by innumerable laws, is steadily encroaching upon the individual liberties of the citizens of this country."

The U.S. Department of Justice disagreed with the decision of the appeals court and decided to fight back. In 1927 the case made its way to the U.S. Supreme Court. The government's position was handled by a remarkable woman, Assistant U.S. Attorney General Mabel Walker Willebrandt, whose authority extended to the enforcement of the Volstead Act and federal taxation, subjects not likely to endear her to a large percentage of the citizenry of the United States. In the Sullivan case, she argued before the Supreme Court that bootlegger Sullivan's Fifth Amendment defense was wrong on the grounds that it would have dire consequences for the nation. "The far-reaching effect of such a ruling upon the collection of taxes is apparent without argument. In effect, the Government's right to collect its taxes would be at the mercy of the law-breaker." The court agreed with Willebrandt. In his majority opinion, the esteemed eighty-six-year-old associate justice and Civil War veteran Oliver Wendell Holmes ruled that the Fifth Amendment had been stretched too far in this case and that an unlawful business should pay taxes just like a lawful enterprise.[1]

There was little mention of the case in the press, and the ruling didn't seem to bother Sullivan very much. He remained a man about town in Charleston, where in later years he competed in boat races and ran a boxing ring.[2] But his losing case provided the federal government with an enormously effective new weapon. Through bribery, intimidation, and lack of evidence, Prohibition gangsters had repeatedly been able to avoid murder convictions in the courts, but prosecutors, now armed with the Sullivan decision, had the power to put gangsters behind bars. In essence, the prosecution had only to prove two points to juries: the defendant (a) had earned money and (b) had not paid taxes on that money. This was the federal government's weapon of choice to bring down top mobsters. Three examples are Al Capone, Waxey Gordon, and Abner "Longie" Zwillman.

AL CAPONE

In 1929, the newly elected president of the United States, Herbert Hoover, committed himself and his government to bring down Capone. Hoover was inaugurated on March 4, less than four weeks after the Saint Valentine's Day massacre, and he devoted a portion of his inaugural address to

the crime problem. He warned his listeners that there had been a "dangerous expansion in the criminal elements who have found enlarged opportunities in dealing in illegal liquor," and Hoover went on to say "to those
of criminal mind there can be no appeal but vigorous enforcement of the
law. . . . Their activities must be stopped."[3]

Later that month Hoover met with a delegation of business leaders who
were members of the Chicago Crime Commission, a private organization of
civic-minded executives. The CCC members informed the president about
how gangsters had gone unchecked in the Windy City. Hoover recalled later,
"they gave me chapter and verse for their statement that Chicago was in
the hands of the gangsters, that the police and magistrates were completely
under their control, that the governor of the state was futile, that the federal
government was the only force by which the city's ability to govern itself
could be restored."[4] Hoover ordered his cabinet to come up with ways to put
Capone behind bars. The president, who believed in healthy living, would
gather with the members of his cabinet every morning except Sunday to
toss around a medicine ball on the White House lawn. At these gatherings,
he would make a point of asking his cabinet, and especially Secretary of the
Treasury Andrew Mellon, "Have you got Capone yet?" This would be followed up by a reminder: "Remember now, I want that Capone man in jail."[5]

In the end Capone was gotten, but it took two years, seven months, and
fourteen days from Hoover's inauguration until a jury convicted Capone
of evading the income tax. Crime writer Jonathan Eig has observed, "Not
since the manhunt for John Wilkes Booth, Abraham Lincoln's killer, had
so many resources been brought to bear in an attempt to jail one man."[6]
In all, an estimated one hundred government workers, mostly at the federal level, were involved in the attack on Al Capone. Collectively, they
did what gangsters like Hymie Weiss, Joey Aiello, and Bugs Moran with
their shotguns and tommy guns were unable to do—topple the Big Fellow. Because this was a federal government crime, the case was out of the
hands of corrupt and ineffective Chicago law enforcement, like the Illinois
State's Attorney for Chicago Robert E. Crowe and the bungling head of the

detective branch of the Chicago police John Stege. The federal jurisdiction meant that the case would be tried in a federal court, with a federal prosecutor and a federal judge.

A key figure in the effort was the U.S. Attorney for the Northern District of Illinois George E. Q. Johnson. A lawyer with a strong reputation for honesty, he was appointed by the Coolidge administration in 1927. The Special Investigative Unit (SIU) of the Internal Revenue Service in the U.S. Treasury Department provided the investigative force. The head of the SIU in Washington, D.C., was Elmer Irey, who was specifically assigned by Secretary Mellon to bring down Capone. Irey sent one of his best men, Frank Wilson, to the Chicago office where he worked with a team of agents who, like him, were tenacious in their effort to accumulate evidence.

But not all the law enforcement arms of the federal government entered the campaign against Capone. The ambitious empire builder J. Edgar Hoover, director of the Federal Bureau of Investigation, carefully kept his agency from messing with organized crime. Hoover felt that Prohibition mobsters were entrenched in their cities; therefore, sending FBI agents in to get them would risk those agents being caught up in bribes. "The Federal government," said Director Hoover, "can never be a satisfactory substitute for local self-government in the enforcement field."[7] The FBI chief preferred going after the likes of bandits like John Dillinger and Baby Face Nelson, pursuits which were more likely to be successful and win glory for the FBI. Capone biographer Bergreen has exposed the hatred that Hoover felt for U.S. Attorney Johnson, who won national attention for his prosecution of Capone. Hoover falsely claimed that the FBI had brought Capone down. Bergreen says this whole episode reveals J. Edgar Hoover's "pathological jealousy and reckless disregard for the truth."[8]

Another G-man who, like Hoover, craved the limelight of publicity and who claimed more credit than he deserved was Eliot Ness, an icon in the saga of Prohibition. The 1957 book *The Untouchables* coauthored by Ness and writer Oscar Fraley was a best-seller, and a highly successful 1959–1963 television series was based on the book and starred Robert Stack. An

Oscar-winning Hollywood 1987 movie starring Kevin Costner conveyed the Ness legend to new generations. Print, television, and movie versions picture Ness as a bold crime fighter who assembled a squad of agents to fight Capone. Unlike the corrupt world around them, Ness and his men are "untouchable"—they cannot be bribed. In the book, TV, and movie versions, Ness escapes assassination attempts, confronts the snarling Capone face to face, and in the end brings about the mobster's arrest and imprisonment.

There is a measure of truth to this legend. Ness was a University of Chicago graduate who in 1927 got a job with the Prohibition Bureau in Chicago. U.S. Attorney George E. Q. Johnson regarded Ness favorably, and in 1929 the young man was authorized to pull together a squad of elite law enforcement men that the newspapers later dubbed the Untouchables. With that squad he raided breweries and distilleries, frequently smashing through the doors with armored trucks, arresting the bootleggers, and destroying illegal liquor. He also put a telephone wiretap on Ralph Capone, Al's older brother. There were attempts on Ness's life, and at least one unsuccessful attempt was made to bribe him.[9] There is, however, no evidence that he ever met Capone or that Capone even knew his name, and, as we will see, the evidence that convicted Scarface did not come from Ness's activities; rather, Elmer Irey, Frank Wilson, and their SIU colleagues collected the pertinent evidence. Ness died in 1957, just before publication of the book that would make him famous.

While the SIU and the U.S. Attorney's office were gathering to bring down Capone, Scarface continued to operate as the crime lord of Chicago, and, as before, dead bodies appeared in the streets. On June 9, 1930, a staff member of the *Chicago Tribune*, Alfred "Jake" Lingle, was shot to death while he was making his way in a pedestrian tunnel toward an Illinois Central railroad station. On October 23, mobster Joseph Aiello was mowed down by sixty-two machine gun bullets as he walked out of a Chicago apartment building. At first Lingle was portrayed as a martyr—a crusading journalist struck down because of his exposés of crime. Further investigation into his life disclosed that he was thoroughly mobbed up and that he had been extorting his underworld friends. Capone knew Lingle, but Capone was only one of many criminals who might have wanted the reporter dead. It's much more probable that Capone ordered the death of Aiello, a longtime threat to Capone's dominance of Chicago. The Aiello hit—committed by a machine-gun nest manned by killers who patiently waited for days for their target to emerge—was similar to the Capone-ordered assassination of Hymie Weis four years before. As usual, nobody was ever convicted of the murders of Lingle or Aiello.

Whoever was responsible for the death of Aiello, it must have given Capone some satisfaction as he looked back over his career from the vantage point of 1930. The last of his major enemies was out of the way, he had finished his year behind bars in Philadelphia, and he had a fine home in Miami where he could enjoy life. But in that same year, the net around him began to close. In early 1930, Irey met with Wilson to discuss strategy. They concluded that the best course of action would be to get Capone's aides Frank Nitti and Jake Guzik behind bars because the evidence against them seemed stronger than what could be found on Capone; furthermore, putting away Guzik and Nitti would encourage others to cooperate with the Feds.[10]

The Internal Revenue Service's investigation of Ralph Capone actually began years before President Hoover vowed to crack down on gangsters and even before the Supreme Court decision in the Sullivan case. In 1926, an IRS agent in Chicago, Eddie Waters, convinced Ralph that it would be a good idea for him to fill out income tax reforms, and he assisted Ralph in completing the documents, which stated that his earned income since 1921 was $55,000, for which he owed the government $4,065. Waters was not trying to entrap Ralph; he was actually trying to do him a favor, as the agent had done for other criminals. But Ralph managed to turn this well-meant gesture into his own trap. For some unknown reason (probably his own stupidity) Ralph never got around to paying his tax bill. His nonpayment proved a stroke of luck for the Feds by supplying the hook to build a tax evasion case. As Ralph's lawyers were negotiating with the IRS about how much he owed, their position was that their client was essentially

broke.[11] Investigators in the Chicago office, Nels Tessem and Archie Martin, were assigned to look deeper into Ralph's finances. As luck would have
it, there had been a raid on a gambling parlor in Chicago known as "The
Subway," and some accounting books from the establishment were confiscated. The books led Tessem and Martin to a local bank, where they
minutely scrutinized deposit and withdrawal records and interviewed
bank employees. They concluded that Ralph Capone, under several aliases,
had maintained a hefty account in the hundreds-of-thousands-of-dollars
range. They felt they had enough evidence to arrest Ralph, which they did
when he was attending a boxing match on October 8, 1929. Ralph admitted that he had been squirreling money in the bank under aliases, and he
was duly indicted. Federal Judge Wilkerson presided over the trial, and
U.S. Attorney Johnson prosecuted Ralph Capone, who was convicted and,
on June 16, 1930, sentenced to three years in prison and a $10,000 fine; he
began serving his sentence in November 1931.

The SIU sleuths, emboldened by the conviction of Ralph Capone, now
focused on Guzik and Nitti. The case was initially made more difficult when
both men fled Chicago and had to be tracked down by SIU agents. Nitti was
ultimately sentenced to eighteen months in federal prison; Guzik's sentence
was five years. Al Capone fulminated at what was happening around him—
"the income tax law is a lot of bunk. The government can't collect taxes from
illegal money"; the Sullivan decision had already declared that position null
and void.[12] In these circumstances, Capone did what any sensible, well-to-do
individual would do; he hired a top-notch tax attorney, Lawrence P. Mattingly
of Washington, D.C., to negotiate a settlement. Mattingly had several meetings with the IRS agents, at least once with Capone in tow. To resolve the
matter of what Capone owed to the IRS, Mattingly sent a letter to the agent
in charge of the Chicago office on September 20, 1930. He began the letter
by stating that the information he was about to convey was "made without
prejudice to the rights of the above named taxpayer in any proceedings that
may be instituted against him."[13] In other words, Mattingly was asserting
that the data he was about to provide could not be used as evidence against

Capone. He then conceded that Capone had made between $26,000 and $100,000 in preceding years. The T-men now had sources, however underestimated, on the income for which Capone had not paid taxes, and, contrary to Mattingly's "without prejudice" plea, they would forcefully use that data to put Capone behind bars.

But the SIU agents needed to get more convincing figures on Capone's wealth. The paper trail was far thinner than what had been found about Ralph, Guzik, and Nitti. Now came a dramatic moment in the life of Frank J. Wilson, the head T-man on the Al Capone case. Wilson was a short, bespectacled government employee who favored cheap cigars and who was a workaholic who routinely put in eighteen hours a day. He was known for his steady coolness; "he sweats ice water," according to his colleagues.[14] But after two years he was discouraged that he lacked enough evidence to guarantee a guilty verdict for Capone. In his memoir Wilson wrote that one evening after midnight he was laboring over files in his cramped Chicago office. He picked up the files to put them away but bumped into the filing cabinet, accidentally locking it. He didn't have the key to open it so he went into a nearby storeroom where, bleary-eyed and tired, he found an old, unused file cabinet. He opened one of the drawers. "In the back was a heavy package covered in brown paper. Something prompted me to examine it, so I snipped the string and found myself holding three ledgers, black ones with red corners."[15] One ledger turned out to be the detailed financial records over an extended period of a large gambling operation, and the establishment was subsequently identified as Capone's Hawthorne Smoke Shop in Cicero. The ledgers had been confiscated in a police raid in the aftermath of the 1926 McSwiggen murder and had lain untouched since then in the file cabinet.

Wilson and his staff pursued the leads in the ledger and came up with the name of Leslie Shumway, a bookkeeper at the Cicero betting parlor. On a hunch, Wilson went to Florida to search horse tracks and dog tracks for Shumway and finally located him at the Miami Beach Kennel Club. Wilson confronted Shumway and asked him to provide information about Capone's finances, with the promise that he would be kept safe from retaliation by the mob. If he refused to cooperate Shumway was told that the Feds would let the Capone mob know that the bookkeeper was the subject of an investigation, which would probably result in his death. The terrified Shumway agreed to cooperate and was placed under federal protection.

The T-men had another informant they brought into play against Al Capone—one Frank Ries. In the course of their investigation into Ralph, Guzik, and Nitti, the SIU agents apprehended Ries, who had formerly been a head cashier in the Capone gambling enterprise in Cicero and knew the ins and outs of how profits from the casino were deposited in banks under assumed names and then distributed to the mob's top men. Ries was close-mouthed at first, but the Treasury agents knew he had a phobia about insects. After spending days in a bug-infested jail cell in Danville, Illinois, his resistance ended, and he agreed to testify for the prosecution.

Another witness came forward without the need for coercion—Edward O'Hare, a wealthy businessman in the dog-racing industry. O'Hare owned the patent for the mechanical rabbit that racing dogs pursued and owned several dog tracks. Capone had muscled in on a dog track O'Hare was building in Cicero, and O'Hare had thereafter borne a grudge against Scarface. O'Hare was eager to work with the SIU, and Wilson regarded the information he provided "the most important single factor resulting in the conviction of Al Capone"[16]

Another source was Michael Malone, a Treasury agent who volunteered to infiltrate the Capone mob at the Lexington Hotel. Malone, of Irish descent, could pass as an Italian. He checked into the Lexington for an extended period and spent much of his time in the lobby, chatting up Capone henchman. He used a made-up Italian name and let on that he was a mobster on the lam from Philadelphia. ("On the lam," by the way, is a phrase in vogue in the 1920s and 1930s to indicate a sudden flight, especially from the law. Word aficionados think it dates back at least to the 1880s, when pickpockets used the term to mean "to skedaddle." In the 1920s and 1930s lam's usage was expanded by referring to the people on the lam as "lamsters" or "lammisters.")[17] When Malone died in 1960, his obituary praised how he had provided "invaluable information at great personal risk" about Capone.[18] But there has been some skepticism about how dangerous it actually was or how vital the information turned out to be.[19] One of Malone's warnings was that Capone had hired out-of-town killers to eliminate U.S. Attorney Johnson, SIU investigator Wilson, and others. Then came word that Capone had changed his mind and the hit was off. Capone biographer Schoenberg suggests that Malone was not such a great spy and not really in danger; Capone claimed he knew Malone was a plant and made up the false assassination story just to confuse the authorities because Capone was far too smart to really intend to kill a federal official.[20] Perhaps Schoenberg is correct, but what good would this subterfuge do to help Capone? And as his career shows, Scarface was quite capable of unpredictable violence. For Malone to mingle with gangsters in the Lexington Hotel may not have been as risk-free an assignment as Schoenberg thinks.

Using the Mattingly letter, the gambling ledger, Shumway, Ries, O'Hare, Malone, and other sources, the SIU built its case against Capone. The task of using this evidence to prosecute the case rested with U.S. Attorney Johnson. Two charges were leveled against Capone: income tax evasion and violation of the Prohibition laws. Johnson decided that putting Capone on trial for both crimes made sense. Capone's two lawyers, Ahern and Nash, met twice with Johnson for some pretrial discussions, which lead to a plea bargain. Johnson agreed to request a prison sentence of two and one-half years for Capone if he (a) pled guilty to both charges, (b) went to prison immediately, (c) and did not appeal the conviction.[21] And so, on Tuesday, June 16, 1931, some judicial kabuki theater entitled *United States v. Alphonse Capone* was performed at the Federal Court House in Chicago when Al Capone, in the company of his lawyers, appeared before Judge Wilkerson to plead guilty to the charges against him. The judge announced that sentencing would take place two weeks later. The whole thing lasted a mere fifteen minutes. There was much praise in the national press for what appeared to be a victory for the prosecution, and President Herbert Hoover personally congratulated U.S. Attorney Johnson.

But word leaked out that the plea deal had included a short term behind bars, whereas without a plea he could have been sentenced thirty-two years on the income evasion charge alone. There has been a continuing debate about whether Johnson was wise to agree to that deal. In Johnson's favor is the argument that a full-scale trial might have failed to bring a conviction. Capone might have used the popular strategy of bribing jurors and threatening witnesses. Capone's lawyers might have been able to find legal loopholes to derail the prosecution's case—like getting the Mattingly letter declared inadmissible. Capone had a good record in escaping punishment; except for his stretch in Philadelphia, throughout his lengthy career of crime he had managed to avoid prison. Also, most income tax evasion cases in which the defendant had pled guilty had resulted in sharply reduced terms. Crime writer Jonathan Eig, in evaluating Johnson's decision, describes the inner debate he must have had: "His whole career as U.S. Attorney had led him to this moment, and now it had come down to a gut check for Johnson: Should he risk everything or hedge his bets?"[22] In the end, he chose to hedge.

This debate became academic when, on June 30, 1931, Judge Wilkerson presided over the sentencing of Capone at the Federal Court Building. Throwing a monkey wrench into the plea bargain, Wilkerson told the court that while the prosecution and defense could agree upon a recommendation for sentencing, the final decision rested with the judge, and in this case he was not buying the agreement. Said the uncompromising Wilkerson, "It is time for somebody to impress upon the defendant that it is utterly impossible to bargain with a Federal court."[23] Capone thereupon changed his plea to not guilty. The trial date was set to begin in October. And so on October 6 the trial that both the prosecution and the defense had tried to avoid began, again presided over by Judge Wilkerson. The judge opened the trial with another unexpected move. He announced that he was switching juries with another federal judge who was presiding over a case in the same courthouse. What lay behind this unprecedented decision was the fact that word had been received by the government side that the Capone Outfit was taking steps to bribe the jury members. U.S. Attorney

Johnson informed Judge Wilkerson of this threat, but Wilkerson was mum about what he would do. By switching juries at the last minute, Wilkinson was making sure that jurors who had been bribed were not the ones who would decide Capone's guilt or innocence.

One onlooker in the courtroom that day, and in fact on every day of the trial, was Damon Runyon, who was covering the case for the Hearst newspapers nationwide. In his dispatches Runyon provided descriptions of the principal actors. The star was, of course, Al Capone, whom Runyon described on the first day: "Al, being stout, is susceptible to the heat. Then too, he was in a hot spot. His soft collar was already crumpled. He frequently mopped his forehead with a white handkerchief. His swarthy jowls had been newly shaved. His black hair now getting sparse was plastered back on his skull." Runyon's portrait of the judge was more flattering: "Judge Wilkerson himself is a fine looking man with iron-gray hair. He is smooth shaved. His eyebrows are black and strong. He wears no flowing robes. . . . He was dressed in a quiet business suit of dark color and wears horn-rimmed glasses." Runyon thought that the chief prosecutor, U.S. Attorney Johnson, looked younger than his fifty-seven years, with, in Runyon's words, "a pink complexion, a rather beaming countenance, and a mop of gray hair, all mussed up." Capone's lead attorney, Michael Ahern, was described by Runyon as "a tall, good looking chap of perhaps middle age, who wore a gray suit and tan shoes." Ahern's associate was Albert Fink, "a ruddy-faced, baldish man given to easy attitudes."[24]

The prosecution began its case by bringing to the witness stand an employee of the Internal Revenue Service who confirmed that Capone had filed no tax returns for the years 1924 to 1929. During the course of the trial, other witnesses, among them the intimidated bean counters Shumway and Ries, established that Capone was the boss of gambling establishments that brought in great amounts of cash and that chunks of that cash had been turned over to him. Multiple witnesses from Florida—dubbed by Runyon as "the butcher, the baker, and the landscape maker, not to mention the dock builder, the telephone agent, and the chap who supplied the drapes"—testified to the vast amounts of money lavished by Capone on his Miami estate. The meat supplied by a local butcher over several seasons came to $6,500. Capone's expenses for clothing were discussed, including his silk underwear and the diamond-studded belt buckles he distributed to friends. When the Mattingly letter came up, Capone's defense attorneys argued it should be inadmissible, but Judge Wilkerson disagreed. An unexpected incident in the courtroom took place out of sight of the jurors. One of Capone's bodyguards, Philip D'Andrea, had been faithfully attending the trial. From his seat in the courtroom he would discreetly but menacingly display a gun he was carrying to prosecution witnesses on the stand. Once this antic came to the attention of the SIU agents, D'Andrea was arrested during a break in the proceedings and wound up serving six months in jail.

At the October 13 session, the prosecution suddenly rested its case; a shocker to Ahern and Fink who had not prepared their defense. They requested several days additional time; Judge Wilkerson gave them the next day. The best the defense could do was to bring to the stand bookies who testified that Capone had routinely lost tens of thousands of dollars in bad bets. The defense's point was that Capone's income was depleted by these losses, but the argument may well have backfired; it simply demonstrated that his vast wealth allowed him to squander it away on gambling. Capone himself was not called to the witness stand; his lawyers must have reckoned that he would have been subjected to a devastating cross-examination.

The last session took place on October 17. Judge Wilkerson turned the case to the jurors, who deliberated for eight hours. There was one last surprise—the jurors returned with a contradictory verdict, finding Capone guilty of only five of the twenty-three counts, even though there was little differentiation between some of the counts for which he was found guilty and those for which he was acquitted. But the five guilty counts were serious enough so that Judge Wilkerson could combine them into a single long term. At the sentencing on October 24, combine them he did: Capone received eleven years in prison and total fines and court costs of $80,000—the stiffest penalty ever handed out in a tax evasion case prior to 1931. One side effect of Capone's sentencing was that after the trial the Chicago Internal Revenue Service office received $1,136,588 more in payments by frightened taxpayers than in 1930.[25]

And so the fearsome Al Capone, the über gangster of the Prohibition era, was out of the picture. After his sentencing he served his time in the Cook County Jail, the Atlanta Federal Prison, and then the grim Alcatraz. As the years behind bars went on, his mental capacity was increasingly degraded by his chronic syphilis. The condition was so severe that in 1939 he was removed from Alcatraz and taken to the Federal Correctional Institution on Terminal Island and then to the prison medical center in Lewisburg, Pennsylvania. The prison doctors determined he was insane, and he was released to his family. He died on January 25, 1947, at his home in Miami, seriously debilitated. He was only forty-eight years old when he died, but it seemed like ages had passed since he dominated Chicago and symbolized lawlessness to the world. When he was sentenced to prison in 1931, Prohibition was still the law of the land, and Herbert Hoover was the president; the New Deal, Prohibition's repeal, World War II, and the Cold War lay in the unimaginable future. To people who read his obituary, Capone must have seemed like the relic of an ancient past.

Waxey Gordon

As Capone was being lead out of the courtroom, a reporter came up to Elmer Irey with a question: "When are you going after the New York mob, Mr. Irey?" The SIU chief replied, "I'm leaving for New York tonight." When he saw this statement in the newspapers, he realized it was melodramatic, as if with a major income tax evasion case finished in Chicago, another would immediately start on the East Coast. Irey was going to New York, but it was to get a progress report on an investigation that had been going on for some time by a determined lawman, Thomas E. Dewey.[26]

The target this time was Waxey Gordon (real name, Irving Wexler), the onetime Lower East Side pickpocket and labor shlammer whose association with Arnold Rothstein as a rum-runner opened up a whole new world of opportunity. His nickname "Waxey" has been said to reflect his skill at picking pockets as if they were greased with wax, but more likely "Waxey" was a corruption of his last name. By the late 1920s he was making lucrative investments in real estate, mostly hotels, besides his bootlegging activities. Rothstein regarded Gordon as a good investment and continued to provide him the capital needed to expand. For his part, Gordon, who was Jewish, had a taste for the high life, living with his wife and children in New York apartments on Central Park West and other upscale locations, plus a summer home on the Jersey Shore and a fleet of luxury cars, a library of classic books, and horseback riding lessons for his kids. One of Gordon's hobbies was investing in Broadway shows, and he was said to have often enjoyed the company of attractive chorus girls, despite being married. A story survives that while watching the rehearsal of a new production, he spotted an attractive young woman in the chorus line. "Whose gal is that?" he asked the director. "She ain't nobody's girl," the director replied. To which Waxey said, "If she ain't nobody's girl, how'n hell did she get in the show?"[27]

Where Gordon went, death and disappearance often seems to have followed. In 1913 he was a suspect in the murder of one Frederick Strauss outside a dance hall. In 1925, when he was a rising booze smuggler, a captain named Hans Fuhrman on one of his rum-running vessels volunteered to testify against Gordon in a court case brought by the Prohibition Bureau. But Fuhrman was found shot dead, and the case never came to trial. Five years later, Gordon sought to expand his bootlegging operations by buying up northern New Jersey breweries owned by an Irish gang that included James Culhane, James "Bugs" Donovan, Frank Dunn, and Fred Werther. Evidently the Irishmen did not wish to be bought out, and within a span of about six months Donovan and Dunn were shot to death, Werther wounded, and Culhane departed the state. Waxey had the breweries he desired.[28]

Then on April 12, 1933, by which time Gordon had established a presence in New Jersey, he was ensconced in the Hotel Carteret in the city of

Elizabeth. With him were two members of his gang, Max Greenberg and Max Hassel. At around 4:30 P.M. some person or persons unknown came to the hotel and murdered Greenberg and Hassel, while Gordon escaped. Like the Saint Valentine's Day massacre there are variants of the story. Some crime writers blame Meyer Lansky and Bugsy Siegel's Bug and Meyer gang; according to that theory Bug and Meyer provided protection to Gordon's breweries, but they lost that lucrative employment when beer was declared legal on April 1 and struck back at Gordon's gang. Another theory is that Dutch Schultz's mob did the killing in one of the Dutchman's fights over territory. Yet another theory is that the shootings were the work of brewery workers upset with their bosses; still another contends that the general sense of anxiety among mobsters about how they would survive repeal translated into shooting. One version adds a detail: Gordon was in another part of the hotel, bedded down with a prostitute named Nancy Presser when the shooting took place, and thus he escaped being murdered.[29] (As described chapter 9, Presser subsequently became involved in a criminal trial involving Lucky Luciano.) Not long after the hotel slayings, four other men thought to be members of his gang were killed and a fifth wounded in separate incidents in New Jersey and New York.[30] One incontrovertible fact is that the major players mentioned in this episode—Gordon, Schultz, Lansky, Siegel, Hassel, Greenberg, and the June victims—were all Jewish. The whole curious affair may have had something to do with what the turncoat gangster Joe Valachi puzzlingly referred to in his confessions as the "Jew War against Waxey Gordon."[31]

As if Gordon didn't have enough troubles, on April 27, 1933, Chief Assistant U.S. Attorney for the Southern District of New York Thomas E. Dewey obtained a grand jury indictment against him for income tax evasion. This was a major step in an investigation that took two years. In the last six months of the investigation, a joint task force consisting of six of Dewey's investigators and another twelve from the Special Investigative Unit of the Treasury Department cooperated in the effort to bring down Gordon—the same SIU that had brought down Capone. When he took on Gordon, Dewey was twenty-eight, half the age of George E. Q. Johnson when he battled Capone, but Dewey had at least twice as much ambition and determination, which led to some friction. The head of the SIU, Elmer Irey, complained that Dewey was "the perfectionist to end all perfectionists" and would drive the New York branch of the SIU crazy with demands for ever more evidence, "past all human endurance." Dewey has also been criticized for breaching the civil rights of defendants in order to win a conviction.[32] But whatever his flaws, he was unsurpassed among prosecutors in his ability to prepare a winning case.[33]

The investigators looked through large checks deposited in banks and compared those records with the handwriting of members of Gordon's gang on automobile license applications, insurance claims, property leases, and other written documents to match the gangsters with the checks deposited under aliases. According to Dewey himself, this patient comparison of handwriting was the most important factor in the prosecution's case against Gordon.[34] Investigators also ran wiretaps on Gordon's operations and examined the records of companies that supplied the trucks, plumbing, malt, hops, yeast, and much more needed to operate his beer business. Some one thousand witnesses were interviewed. Gordon fought back. He knew that he was being pursued for income tax evasion so he snatched away records that might convict him. In one instance a trucking firm that Gordon used came up with an utterly bogus set of accounting records to remove any mention of the mobster. On another occasion, Hoboken police arrested government investigators who had come to a local bank, and, while this was sorted out, crucial bank records disappeared from the bank's files. One of Gordon's important employees was in a New Jersey jail for ignoring a subpoena; but in the night the gang member was freed on five hundred dollars bail and promptly disappeared just like deposit slips and invoices.[35]

And there was another disappearance: at the time of the indictment, Gordon was nowhere to be found—he had gone into hiding after the Elizabeth hotel shootings. On a tip, SIU investigators found that dubious characters were living in a house on a lakeside in the Catskills region of New York; neighbors' suspicions were aroused because the occupants of the house only came out at night. The SIU, aided by police, raided the place and found it to be occupied by Gordon along with members of his gang. Gordon insisted that there had been a mistake; that his name was actually William Palinksi, to which SIU agent Michael Malone (the same sleuth who had infiltrated Capone's Chicago headquarters) wearily replied, "Look, Waxie, you're talking too much. You oughtn't to keep saying you're William Palinski and walk around in silk drawers that have I.W. embroidered on 'em. I.W. means Irving Wexler, Waxie."[36] Perhaps Gordon felt a bit of relief; being in police custody was safer than hiding from the rival gangsters who were out to kill him. In the book *The Last Testament of Lucky Luciano*, author Martin Gosch claims that Luciano and Meyer Lansky were quarrelling with Gordon. To get him out of the way they provided information on Gordon to the Internal Revenue Service that was used to convict him.[37] This is an unlikely scenario; Dewey and the SIU were perfectly able to dig up ample evidence to convict Gordon.

The trial of Irving Wexler for income tax evasion opened on November 20, 1933. It lasted for seven days, in session for ten hours a day, Sunday excepted. During this time, Dewey brought forth 131 witnesses to prove to the jury that Gordon had earned $2,365,403 in the years 1930 and 1931 but had paid only $2,618.76 in taxes. Among the prosecution witnesses was the executive of the trucking firm, who admitted he had cooked the books to exonerate Gordon. The supplier of malt and hops to Gordon's breweries revealed that he had been paid hundreds of thousands of dollars a year. Speakeasy owners testified how much they paid Gordon's salesmen for illegal beer shipments. Much of the prosecution's case was presented in the form of charts and diagrams that spelled out to the jury the maze of bank accounts, payments, supplies, telephone calls, workers, and operations.

In a trial where the lawyers, judge, defendants, and jurors were all male, there was one notable female: witness Helen Demback. She was a young Polish woman who owned a restaurant near one of Gordon's breweries.

On the stand she described how Gordon's men had made telephone calls from her establishment for which she had to pay the bills. She said that she had gone to see Gordon to complain, and he told her that he would cover the costs of "my men"—an indication that he owned the brewery. Part of her testimony concerned Bugs Donovan, the previous owner of the brewery, and on several occasions on the witness stand she talked about the time "before Bugs Donovan was murdered." Gordon's attorney vehemently protested this expression, and the judge said to the witness, "You must not say 'before Donovan was murdered.' Just say he didn't come around anymore." Helen innocently asked, "How could he come around, your honor? He was murdered!"[38] When the judge offered to strike these words from the record, the defense counsel wearily replied, "Apparently he's dead. So what's the use."[39] You can hear the echo of her accent and a bit of her determination when she described how she asked Gordon to let his employees eat at her establishment: "How about to give me a break and send your boys to my place."[40]

Another remark that caught public attention was an account given on the stand by Gordon's brewmaster, Oscar Brockert, about how the beer made its way from vats in one of Gordon's breweries to a garage in Paterson where it was poured into barrels loaded onto trucks. For this purpose a hose was secretly installed that ran through the city's sewers.[41] This information, undoubtedly disconcerting to customers who thought the beer they swigged was wholesome, suggested that quality control was not high on the priority list of bootleggers.

After the prosecution rested, defense lawyer Charles F. G. Wahle sought to convince the jury that Gordon was not a multimillionaire tax dodger, did not own breweries, and had only modest real estate holdings. He depicted Gordon as a devoted husband and father, whose ambition was to provide for his wife and children. When he took the stand, Gordon admitted that he had been a bootlegger but claimed that he was essentially was an employee of Greenberg and Hassel in the brewery and real estate businesses. In his cross-examination, Dewey was relentless, drilling down to the smallest details to put Gordon through the wringer. Dewey had another advantage—an extended background in vocal music. He had trained for some time to be an opera singer, and, although he never went into that profession, he was able to use his deep baritone voice to reach every corner of the courtroom.[42] Here is an excerpt from his dominating cross-examination of Gordon—the reader should imagine the prosecutor's booming voice and the slurred Lower East Side diction of the defendant:

> Q. Did you or did you not have insurance on your household furniture for $100,000 in the year 1931?
>
> A. I did.
>
> Q. How did you acquire $100,000 worth of furniture with an income of $6,000 a year?
>
> A. There was no $100,000 worth of furniture. That included everything.
>
> Q. What did it include?
>
> A. It included clothes, rugs and children's clothes, everything in the place—books.
>
> Q. How did you acquire $100,000 worth of property on an income of $6,000 a year?
>
> A. I had that since 1910.
>
> Q. You mean you were a wealthy man since 1910?
>
> A. In that year I lost $100,000 on a race track. Yes, I was a wealthy man in 1910.
>
> Q. Were you broke when you lost that, or did you have a lot left?
>
> A. Well, I had a little left.
>
> Q. What do you mean by a little?
>
> A. Well, I had enough to live on.[43]

The extent of Dewey's ability to marshal the evidence was demonstrated by the fact that it took the jury a mere fifty-one minutes to find Waxey Gordon guilty. The bootlegger was sentenced to ten years in federal prison and had to pay $20,000 in fines and $60,000 in court costs. *New York Times* reporter Meyer Berger described the scene when the jury rendered its verdict. "Gordon's jaws sagged and his dark eyes fixed in hatred on the men in the jury box as their verdict was pronounced." The judge directed Gordon to rise to hear the sentence. "Behind him a woman sobbed. It was Mrs. Leah Wexler, his wife. Her eyes and her face were red. She stifled the sound that came to her lips. She pressed her handkerchief against them."[44] Mr. and Mrs. Wexler were to have more to sorrow over. Their son, Teddy, a premed student at the University of North Carolina, was driving back to New York to be with his parents and to plead with the judge for a lighter sentence. Near Chester, Pennsylvania, the car he was in veered off the road in a fog, and Teddy was killed. Dewey permitted Gordon to attend his son's funeral, with the proviso that guards be stationed there to keep an eye on the convicted man.[45] Soon after, Gordon was taken to federal prison.

The Waxey Gordon story does not end here. Because of good behavior in federal prison, he was released after serving seven years of his ten-year sentence. Back in New York he was interviewed by reporters. He told them he was going to be a salesman. "Waxey Gordon is dead—that's all over. It's Wexler I'm interested in." Said one reporter, "He was a sort of underworld Rip Van Winkle, blinking in the new post Prohibition world."[46] He was broke and took a Pauper's Oath, a sworn statement that he was destitute and hence should be exempt from paying the $2,603,000 he owed. Before long he was back in the business of crime, selling black market sugar to an illegal distillery in violation of the World War II rationing laws, for which he was sentenced to a year in prison. After that he took up dealing in narcotics. In August 1951 he came to the end of the line. He was arrested on Sixth-eighth Street and York Avenue for selling heroin. This was not a nickel bag affair but a major deal to sell two pounds for $9,000. It was all an elaborate sting worked out by the Federal Bureau of Narcotics and the New York Police to bust a major smuggling operation. The sixty-three-year-old Gordon pleaded with the arresting officer, Detective Sergeant John Cottone of the New York Narcotics Squad: "Please kill me, John—shoot me. I'm an old man and I'm through. Don't take me in for junk. How else can I live? Let me run, John, and then you shoot me."[47] He was not shot; instead, he was sentenced to a term of twenty-five years to life. This was one sentence he was able to defy. On June 24, 1952, Gordon was in Alcatraz Prison when he died from a massive heart attack.[48]

ABNER "LONGIE" ZWILLMAN

For Ralph Capone, his error was to file income tax returns without sending a check. For his younger brother Alphonse, the Mattingly letter led to his downfall. In the case of Abner "Longie" Zwillman, the fatal mistake was to provide the IRS with a statement of his net worth. Zwillman was a Newark-born fruit-and-vegetable salesman who turned to bootlegging and became part of the inner circle of New York area mobsters that included Frank Costello, Meyer Lansky, and Louis Lepke Buchalter.

After the repeal of Prohibition, Zwillman invested in a vast number of enterprises that were mostly legal, among them real estate, movies, nightclubs, liquor stores and distributors, railroads, truck sales, parking garages, banks, commercial coin-operated laundry washing and drying machines, and scrap metal. Some of his investments lost money, like a company that marketed beer dispensers for saloons under the brand Harr-Kegtap; but some of his ventures were profitable, notably the Public Service Tobacco Company, which placed cigarette vending machines in bars and other venues. On the illegal side of his investments was a connection with illegal gambling casinos, the numbers racket, and bookmaking. A generous supporter of New Jersey politicians, he had a sweetheart deal with Newark politicians so that the city government's trucks were purchased from Zwillman's GMC and Diamond T Truck sales franchise. For many in Newark Zwillman was a hero. Starting in 1933, he had helped to rally the Jewish community against the home-grown supporters of Hitler and the Nazi party—the Friends of the New Germany and the German American Bund. In the Depression he subsidized a soup kitchen operated by Catholic charities.[49]

In 1947, Zwillman, accompanied by his accountant and lawyers, paid a visit to the IRS office in Newark to discuss his tax liabilities. IRS agents at the meeting advised Zwillman that, to begin the negotiations, he should put together a statement of net worth for himself and his wife Mary, which he duly did and signed. The statement set their net worth at $623,672.60.[50] But no settlement was ever worked out from this document.

Zwillman gained national notoriety on March 27, 1951, when he testified before the U.S. Senate Special Committee to Investigate Organized Crime in Interstate Commerce, presided over by Senator Estes Kefauver and broadcast to television sets around the nation. Forty-five times Zwillman refused to answer the committee's questions by invoking the Fifth Amendment. In its final report the committee called for further investigation of Zwillman; Kefauver himself described the man as America's top gangster.[51] In August and September of 1951, *Collier's Weekly* ran an expose of Zwillman that depicted him as the kingpin of crime in New Jersey. Trying to overcome this bad image, Zwillman justified himself to a reporter by talking about how he got into bootlegging as a poor young boy. "To understand me, you've got to understand my past. Sure I was a bootlegger and I'd be one again given the same setup; kid brothers and sisters hungry, no food, bills to be met. I might even do worse."[52]

Based on the recommendation of the Kefauver Committee, the IRS determined to go after several mobsters, including Zwillman, and in June 1952 he received a notification that he would be under investigation. On January 9, 1956, after years of furious legal maneuvering involving tax liens, grand jury probes, and failed indictments, the trial of Longie Zwillman opened in federal court in Newark. A key tool used by the government prosecutors was the net worth statement, which Zwillman's lawyers tried in vain to suppress. On March 4, after thirty hours of deliberations, the jury informed the judge that they could not reach a verdict, and Zwillman walked out of court a free man. But whatever satisfaction Zwillman may have felt was cut short by the fact that the IRS intelligence unit and the FBI investigated the possibility that some of the jurors had been bribed. Using microphone surveillance, informers, and interviews with jurors, the FBI arrested the men who had offered the bribes and the jurors who had taken that money. Zwillman was implicated in this crime by the fact that one of the bribers, Sam "Big Sue" Katz, was his aide and sometime chauffeur.

Zwillman now knew he was running out of options, and his family members found him increasingly morose and withdrawn. It was likely that he would be tried for both judicial tampering and income tax evasion. At the very least he would have to pay enormous legal bills and, if convicted, would be sentenced to a term in federal prison and have to pay his back taxes and penalties. He also knew that the U.S. Senate Rackets Committee wanted to have him testify as part of an investigation of corruption in the vending machine business. The fifty-four-year-old mobster was having chest pains too, and on February 25, 1959, he had gone to see his physician. He went out to dinner that evening with his wife and sister and drank heavily. Zwillman's wife Mary awoke around 2:00 A.M. to find her husband pacing the bedroom floor; he told her to go back to sleep and gave her a sleeping pill. Mary awoke next morning, and, not seeing her husband, she assumed he had gone to his office at the Public Service Tobacco Company. At 10:00 A.M. she went to the basement to get a box of tissues. She screamed when she saw her dead husband. A plastic extension cord looped over a ceiling rafter was wrapped around his neck. There were tranquilizers in his bathrobe pocket and nearby a half empty bottle of bourbon.[53]

There have been persistent rumors that Zwillman had actually been killed by mob hit men and trussed up to make it look like a suicide. It's more likely that he did himself in, an aging businessman with a bad heart and an unpromising future. Perhaps his final thoughts as he consumed the pills and booze were on the damnable net worth statement that had started his downhill slide.

CHAPTER 9

Lucky v. Dewey

TORTURE ON STATEN ISLAND

Early in the morning of October 17, 1929, Patrolman Blanke stationed in the Staten Island fishing village of Prince's Bay saw a disheveled man staggering down the road. Officer Blanke could see that the man had been savagely beaten, his eyes were swollen and bruised, and he had slash wounds on his face. "Get me a taxi," the man beseeched the policeman. "I'll give you fifty bucks if you do and let me go my way." But Blanke would have none of it. He took the man to Richmond Memorial Hospital for treatment. More wounds were found on the man's body. Detective Charles Schley arrived at the hospital to interrogate the man, who turned out to be Charles "Lucky" Luciano.

The gangster told Schley that at six o'clock the previous night he had been at the intersection of Fiftieth Street and Sixth Avenue in Manhattan, when a limousine with curtains covering the side windows pulled up. Three men with guns dragged him into the car and put adhesive tape over his mouth, after which he was beaten, kicked, and stabbed. The next thing Luciano recalled was waking up on a beach in great pain. He did not know his assailants. In the midst of the interrogation by police, Luciano clammed up. "Don't you cops lose any sleep over it. I'll attend to this thing myself, later." Instead, the policemen took him to police headquarters in

Manhattan, where he was jailed. His police file showed that he was wanted in a stolen automobile case, which enabled the judge to set bail at $25,000. It was paid, and Luciano left, leaving behind a mystery.[1] Twelve days after the incident, Luciano was called to testify about the episode to a Staten Island grand jury. He was as closed mouthed as criminals typically were in that age of *omerta.* He said that he could not identify his assailants because he had been unconscious the whole time. When asked if he had any enemies, he replied, "Not that I know of."[2]

In 1974, *The Last Testament of Lucky Luciano* by Martin A. Gosch and Richard Hammer was published. The book contained Luciano's own account of the incident, supposedly told in 1961. According to Luciano, he had driven his own car to a meeting with the Mafia boss Salvatore Maranzano on a Staten Island pier. Luciano at that time was a lieutenant of the rival Mafia figure Joe Masseria, he of the drooling spaghetti. Maranzano asked Luciano to switch allegiances and come to work with him, work that would include killing Masseria. Luciano refused, at which time he was knocked unconscious by one of Maranzano's henchman. He woke up to find that he had been tied up and dangled by the wrists from a beam. Six men with their faces covered by handkerchiefs began to beat him with belts, clubs, knives, and burning cigarettes. At one point he kicked Maranzano in the groin, for which the mob boss slashed Luciano's face with a knife. Finally, when a gun was aimed at Luciano, Maranzano called out, "No! Let him live. He'll do what has to be done or we will see him again." The assailants then dropped Luciano by the side of a road.[3] There are problems with this story. It does not seem logical that person A would beat and torture person B to induce him to kill person C. Quite the contrary, it would probably give person B a motive to kill person A. Moreover, being taken for a ride by mobsters invariably led to the subject's death so, if Luciano was allowed to walk away, it was unique in the annals of gangdom.

There have been many alternate theories offered for Luciano's ordeal. One speculation is that Legs Diamond, not Maranzano, administered the beatings, and the motive was to take over Luciano's prostitution racket.

Another theory is that Luciano had gotten a girl pregnant, and the girl's father (who happened to be a policeman) was taking revenge. Or maybe federal narcotics agents, who had gone to Staten Island to intercept a shipment of narcotics, found Luciano on the dock waiting for the same ship; knowing that he was a drug smuggler, they took the opportunity to teach him a lesson. Still another is that in a straight extortion effort, thugs demanded Luciano pay them $10,000 or else be killed.[4]

The most probable solution is one voiced by mobster Frank Costello, who years later told his lawyer, George Wolf, that the police (presumably from the New York City Police Department) assaulted Luciano. While he was on the floor of the car they stepped on his face, which caused the wounds. They wanted Luciano to reveal the whereabouts of Legs Diamond. Costello's statement makes ample sense. At the time of the Staten Island incident, Diamond was still in hiding as a result of shooting two customers at the Hotsy Totsy Club in Manhattan. Most likely Diamond spent part of his seclusion in a house that Luciano owned in upstate New York. Although gangsters would not have hesitated to kill their captive Luciano, policemen might have drawn the line at murder.[5]

Costello's version of the events is corroborated by the crime writer Joachim Joesten, who said in 1953 that he interviewed Luciano in Naples, Italy, and asked, "Do you know who did it?" Luciano replied "Sure—the cops. They were just trying to find out things." And an undercover U.S. narcotics agent, Sal Vizzini, encountered Luciano in Naples in June 1960, and in the course of the conversation the exiled mob leader said of the Staten Island incident, "It was the cops who really did it to me" to get information about Legs Diamond.[6]

The lasting legacy of this event was that Luciano's right eyelid always drooped. Another result might have been Luciano's feeling that the 1930s were going to be difficult times for those who earned their living in the underworld, but, if he could engineer it right, he might come out on top.

The Overthrow of the Mafia Chieftains

Luciano's survival fostered a reputation for being lucky, and for being a tough character to boot. Although at the time he was an underboss in the Manhattan mob ruled by Joe "the Boss" Masseria, his obedience was less than 100 percent, or, as crime writer Thomas Reppetto put it, "Lucky Luciano had already picked the eventual winner in the coming struggle—himself."[7]

If Luciano was becoming disenchanted with Masseria, the reverse was also true. Masseria distrusted his ambitious underling. According to traditional underworld accounts, Joe Adonis, another member of Masseria's gang, tipped off Luciano that the Boss wanted to have him killed. Luciano's response was to meet with Salvatore Maranzano. There is independent corroboration that the meeting took place because it was described in later years by mobster Joe Bonanno, a subordinate of Maranzano, who also attended. It was the first time that the fastidious Bonanno met Luciano, and he sized him up this way: "He was a thin man with a full head of black hair and a scarred and pockmarked face. He walked obliquely, lurching slightly from side to side. His Sicilian was scant, but what words he knew he used well. He usually expressed himself in American street slang. But he was not a big talker; he liked to get to the point without any flourishes. Luciano had an ardent, intelligent look about him."[8]

Luciano and Maranzano agreed that Masseria had to die and that Luciano would make it happen. On April 15, 1931, Luciano met with Massreria. Although Joe the Boss disliked going out in public, Luciano convinced him to go to lunch at Nuova Villa Tammaro, a Coney Island restaurant that the Boss favored. After a long lunch, Luciano and Masseria stayed at the table to chat and play cards. At some point Luciano excused himself to go to the men's room. A squad of hit men hired by Luciano then burst into the dining room and fired twenty shots, six of which penetrated Masseria's body and killed him. When the police arrived, Luciano told them he had been out of the room and had no information on the shooters.

The killing of Masseria has passed into the folklore of Prohibition crime and has often been depicted in movies. But there are some doubts about the details. For example, Bonanno says that the meeting between Luciano and Maranzano took place at a private house in Brooklyn; Luciano reportedly said it was at the Bronx Zoo.[9] There is also a difference of opinion about who constituted the hit squad. Valachi said it was Vito Genovese, Frank Livorsi, and Joseph Stracci; another crime writer says it was Albert Anastasia, Joe Adonis, and Bugsy Siegel, and still another reporter adds Ciro Terranova as the driver.[10] A more serious discrepancy is the fact that even though reporters swarmed over the restaurant after the shooting, none of the newspaper articles about the murder stated that Luciano had been there. Police reports also didn't mention him.[11] Ever since the Staten Island incident, Luciano was well known, and it is hard to imagine how he could have gone unnoticed if he had actually been present. Yet both Joseph Bonanno and Joseph Valachi, who were deep into the Mafia scene, affirmed that Luciano was with Masseria at the restaurant.[12]

However much the traditional story of the murder may vary from the truth, the death of Masseria did happen, and it did change the landscape of organized crime. With his rival dead, Maranzano exploited his position as the leading Mafia boss in New York. He called a meeting of Mafioso at a ballroom in the Bronx. Speaking in Italian, Maranzano declared himself to be the Capo di tutti Capi (boss of bosses), and he put his imprimatur on an existing structure of five families for New York and the bosses who headed each. Luciano took charge of the family that had formerly belonged to Masseria. The other four family heads were Tom Gagliano, Joseph Profaci, Joseph Bonanno, and Vincent Mangano.

The Five Families endured for generations, but Maranzano's leadership was short lived. At 3:45 P.M. on September 10, 1931—four months and twenty-six days after the assassination of Masseria—four men entered Maranzano's office suite in the Grand Central Station Building at 230 Park Avenue. The men identified themselves as Treasury agents who wanted to speak with the boss. This was not entirely unexpected because Maranzano was in trouble with the IRS. But the intruders' pose did not last long. One man pulled a gun and covered the people in the outer office while the other three forced Maranzano into his private office. From inside came the sound of gunshots and a ferocious struggle. All four intruders ran out of the suite and out of the building. Miss Frances Samuels, Maranzano's secretary, then entered her employer's office and found him dead from gunshots and knife wounds. It is likely that this hit was also arranged by Luciano. The traditional story is that Luciano had learned from an informer that Maranzano wanted to kill him and had hired a hit man from outside the Mafia, Vincent Coll, to do the job. Once again crime writers differ about who did the actual killing of Maranzano. Discrepancies aside, it says something about Luciano that both of his superiors—first Masseria and then Maranzano—independently came to the conclusion that he had to be murdered. Having struck first against Masseria and Maranzano, it was now Luciano's turn to be the most influential Mafioso in New York.

THE AMERICANIZATION DEBATE

Luciano's rise to power has helped to fuel an ongoing debate among crime writers over a topic that has come to be called "Americanization." Luciano was a decade younger than Masseria and Maranzano and, unlike them, had grown up in the United States. Luciano was different from the older men in other respects. He was more tolerant of Jews like Meyer Lansky and Bugsy Siegel, and he seemed more adept in the secular, pragmatic, and businesslike world of America. Some crime writers have seen this as evidence of a generational struggle between the younger "Americans" or "Young Turks" on one side and the "Mustache Petes" or "Greaseballs" that comprised the older leadership. The archtypical greaseball was caricatured by one crime writer as having "a fat belly, a flowing handlebar mustache, and a distinct aroma of garlic about him."[13]

This generational struggle has been depicted as violent. The years 1930 and 1931, when Luciano, Masseria, and Maranzano struggled for leadership, have been dubbed the "Castellamarese War," after the Sicilian town of Castellamarese del Golfo, from which Maranzano and his followers immigrated. Many crime writers have claimed that hundreds of mobsters took part in this struggle that radiated out of New York to the rest of the nation and that some sixty of them were killed. Writers have also reported that another bloodbath erupted immediately after Maranzano's death in which an additional thirty to ninety Mustache Pete–type Mafia figures were slaughtered by the Americans.

Some crime writers have steadily chipped away at this scenario depicting the bloody overthrow of an older generation in a one- or two-day period across the nation—a time known as the "Sicilian Vespers" or the "Purge." The war against the older generation, it is said, was carefully planned in advance by the younger Americans.[14] There was a Castellamarese War, the skeptics conclude, but the number of dead was small. Using newspapers as a main source, historian David Critchley tallied between nine and fourteen deaths, the difference being that some of those may have resulted from normal gang rivalries.[15] Critchley and others conclude that the Sicilian Vespers had no factual basis whatsoever.[16] Regarding the larger triumph of the Americans, Critchley finds that the Moustache Petes, far from being exterminated, continued to hold positions in the New York underworld. From all this, Critchley concludes that there was no vast, premeditated Americanization, at least as it has frequently been depicted. He is willing to grant that there was a difference in generations caused by the passing away of older mobsters, the restriction of immigration from Italy, and "the slowly acting acculturation process."[17]

One demonstration of that acculturation can be seen by comparing a gang leader who was raised in the United States and another whose formative years were spent in Italy. By 1931, Joseph Bonanno had spent only seven years in America, while Luciano had spent twenty-five. Bonanno had grown up in the traditional ways. In the memoir he wrote as an old man, Bonanno bemoaned the fact that American gang leaders were called "bosses," not "fathers" because the latter term implied a "paternal, kinship-oriented relationship between a leader and his followers," as opposed to a business approach. He thought of himself as a "squire in the service of a knight." Jews, he thought, could not be part of the Tradition (with a capital T) of the Mafia. He lamented that "American culture, with its marketplace values, made us rich for the most part, but at the same time it eroded our relationships, which had always been kinship-based."[18] Luciano, that child of the polyglot Lower East Side, had no such sentiment. Prohibition, with its large-scale bootlegging, gave a perspective to younger gangsters that the older generation did not have. If Bonanno was voicing his genuine sentiments in his autobiography, then it suggests there was an Americanization, but not in the violent and bloody way that it has sometimes been portrayed.

The five Mafia families of New York have sometimes been described as top-down operations, with strict lines of authority and defined job titles such as capo, underboss, consigliere, and soldier. Law enforcement agencies came up with elaborate organizational charts showing the different levels of authority and reporting relationships. Reppetto observes that these charts represent the mindset of government agents and prosecutors who themselves operated in a bureaucratic atmosphere of top-down management.[19] In real life, the families were far looser enterprises, where members received no set salaries and could pursue their own money-making endeavors.

It is revealing that an alternate term for "family" was "borgatta," which denoted a neighborhood, a loose collection of people who, within limits, were able to go their own ways. Mark A. Haller, whose analysis of the Capone gang as a diversified set of partnerships is discussed in chapter 2, sees the families as akin to a chamber of commerce or Rotary Club, through which men with independent business operations join to further their careers through contact with like-minded men and to "enjoy the prestige on the street from having been selected to join the elite of their professions."[20] Speaking of the Mafia, crime writer Virgil Peterson concludes that it was never "a highly formalized, rigidly structured, monolithic organization, but rather a collection of autonomous gangs."[21]

Some crime writers blame Joseph Valachi for creating a contrary picture. Valachi was a low-level criminal who was serving a life term in federal
prison for murdering a fellow prisoner. In 1963 he turned informer. He told
authorities, including a congressional committee, the FBI, and the Bureau
of Narcotics, that La Cosa Nostra was a tightly knit and rigidly organized
national criminal network that presented a threat to national security. From
Valachi's testimony an exaggerated image of the Mafia has emerged.

The position of Frank Costello in Luciano's family supports the idea
of a loosely organized Mafia. Costello has been described as Luciano's
underboss, but he was able to establish and conduct his own operations
and to make his own alliances with influential city politicians. Luciano's
Tammany connection was Albert C. Marinelli, while Costello's was James
Hines, and it's been said that in the election year of 1932, Luciano went
with Marinelli to the Democratic convention in Chicago to support former New York governor Al Smith for president, while Costello and Hines
went to the same convention as followers of the current governor, Franklin
Delano Roosevelt.[22]

INVESTIGATING THE PROSTITUTION RACKET

As it turned out, FDR won the nomination in Chicago and went on to win
the White House in a landslide defeat of Herbert Hoover. This was a ben-
eficial development for New York gangsters: the new Democratic administration replaced Thomas E. Dewey, the Republican Interim U.S. Attorney
for the Southern District of New York who had put away Waxey Gordon.
It must have cheered the New York underworld when Dewey went to work
for a private law firm. But any gloating was short-lived. There was a strong
reform movement afoot in the city, stoked by the revelations of the Seabury investigations into corruption in the courts. The reformers successfully lobbied Governor Herbert Lehman of New York to name a special
prosecutor—none other than Thomas E. Dewey, who was once again in a
position to crusade against gangsters. One of Dewey's staff of lawyers was

Eunice Hunton Carter, the rare black female in the gritty world of white, male prosecutors. Carter, who had experience in New York's municipal courts, became convinced that prostitution in the city was being taken over by the mob. She persuaded Dewey that prostitution should be a target of the special prosecutor. Dewey agreed, but in tackling this assignment he took pains to make clear that he was going after the "big wigs" in the racket and was not under the delusion that he could banish vice in the city. "I would be mad if I thought I could smash prostitution. I did not quit a good practice to chase prostitutes." The charge he leveled against those big wigs was "compulsory prostitution," that is, forcing women into brothels.[23]

Was Lucky Luciano the target of this investigation from the start? Once again the answers differ. In his book about his racket-busting years, *Twenty Against the Underworld*, Dewey implied that the role of Luciano was revealed only after the investigation had begun, when one of the figures in the prostitution racket, David Miller, blurted out the name "Charlie Lucky" when asked about the leaders of the prostitution racket. Said Dewey, "This was the thunderbolt. We now had testimony for the first time that Lucky Luciano, the top boss of the Mafia, was messing around with prostitution."[24] Dewey's biographer Mary M. Stollberg maintains that Dewey had his sights aimed at Luciano from the start, but he claimed otherwise in order to diffuse any criticism that the whole prostitution investigation was constructed in advance just to get a single criminal.[25] This makes sense; it would have been difficult to convict Luciano of any other crime. He had recently paid up his federal taxes so it would be hard to indict him for income tax evasion, and with the repeal of Prohibition Luciano could not be indicted for bootlegging.

Dewey felt he could pin on Luciano the crime of running the prostitution racket in New York on the grounds that the mobster was ultimately responsible for violating the law against forcing women into prostitution. In his autobiography Dewey painted a grim picture of whoredom, which was estimated to have two thousand prostitutes who worked at three hundred brothels in New York City at the time. At the top was a small group of mobsters who ran the racket, known as the "combine" or the "combination." Next were the major "bookers," who shuffled "strings" of prostitutes that moved from house to house, each house run by a madam, for a week or more in order to provide variety to customers. Dewey compared this to the vaudeville circuit, where acts were shuttled from theater to theater. The "girls" at the bottom of the pyramid were young women who became prostitutes to earn a living or because they were forced into it. They worked from ten to fourteen hours a day, six days a week. They kept records of how many customers they serviced at two to three dollars per trick. It was possible for a woman to earn three hundred dollars a week, but that was whittled down by payments to the bookers, to doctors who gave weekly medical examinations, and to the madams. According to Dewey, a new way to squeeze money was inaugurated around 1933 when the mob came into the racket. Each prostitute had to pay ten dollars a week into a "bonding fund" to pay bail if she was arrested. If the woman was convicted, she would be told to leave the city, and the bonds would be forfeited—in those cases her madam would have to pay 50 percent of the forfeited bonds. All of this took place in a sleazy environment where bail bondsmen, lawyers, magistrates, police, and court clerks were on the take.[26]

Nobody ever accused Thomas E. Dewey of half-measures. From his headquarters in the Woolworth skyscraper he planned two waves of police raids. The first was launched the evening of Friday, January 31, 1936, when police arrested bookers and their mob superiors, who were then jailed in local police stations. The next night the police raided thirty-nine whorehouses, rounding up roughly one hundred prostitutes and madams who were taken to the thirteenth floor of the Woolworth building and held as material witnesses. Dewey's staff members interviewed all those in custody, and from these interrogations Dewey assembled enough evidence to have a warrant issued for the arrest of Lucky Luciano, who was on the lam in Hot Springs, Arkansas, a favorite resort for mobsters. It required the direct intervention of the governor of Arkansas and a squad of state troopers to wrest Luciano out of Hot Springs and on April 18, 1936, deliver him in handcuffs to New York City, where he was jailed. His bail was set at an unreachable $350,000.

LUCIANO ON TRIAL

The criminal trial *People v. Charles Luciano, et al.* began on May 11. The contrast between the prosecutor and his target was dramatic. Dewey was a child of the Protestant Midwest, who had an outstanding school attendance record from kindergarten through high school in Oswego, Michigan; Luciano was the product of the immigrant Lower East Side whose schooling came mostly from the streets and back alleys. Dewey explained to the jury that Luciano could be found guilty of forcing women into prostitution; even if he did not do it himself, he had ordered underlings to do so. In reality his evidence against Luciano was thin; only three out of the dozens of prosecution witnesses he would put on the stand said anything that would incriminate the mob boss in the prostitution racket.

One of those witnesses was Florence "Cokey Flo" Brown, a cocaine-addicted prostitute and sometime madam. She testified that she had had been at meetings in a Chinese restaurant and a Manhattan garage where Luciano was present. On one occasion, she said, Luciano discussed franchising whorehouses "the same as the A & P," referring to a chain of supermarkets.[27] Another drug-addicted prostitute who testified for the prosecution was Nancy Presser (the former companion of Waxey Gordon), who claimed she had sex with Luciano and had heard him tell an underling to "wreck the joint"—referring to a whorehouse run by a madam who refused the combine's orders.[28] The defense attorneys did everything they could do discredit the disreputable prosecution witnesses like Cokey Flo and Nancy Presser. But Dewey had already inoculated the jury by telling them in his opening presentation that the prosecution's case would have to rely on the testimony of "prostitutes, madams, heels, pimps, and ex-convicts." He observed, "We can't get bishops to testify."[29]

When it was the defense's turn to present its case their witnesses were also non-bishops, including the dark lord himself, Lucky Luciano. In his cross-examination of the gangster, Dewey launched into the same persistent grilling he had applied to Waxey Gordon. Luciano denied any connection to prostitution, but Dewey dredged up every other suspicious crime or episode that the mob boss had been involved in, including narcotics smuggling, the Staten Island beating, a delay in paying back taxes, and a conviction for carrying unlicensed weapons in an automobile. Luciano said that the shotgun in the trunk of his car had been used to shoot game birds. Because he had done his shooting out of season, he had been fined. When discussing this episode from the witness stand, Luciano said he had been shooting "peasants" when he actually meant "pheasants," a slip of the tongue that produced a rare laugh in an otherwise grim and depressing trial. There was no humor when Dewey gave his fierce summation: "Convict him," Dewey told the jurors, "in the name of the safety of the people of this city."[30]

At the end of the four-week trial the jury spent the night of June 7 deliberating, and at 6:00 A.M. the next morning returned guilty verdicts for all the nine remaining defendants, including Luciano. (Originally there were thirteen defendants, but by the time the trial ended four had pled guilty.) Luciano was ultimately sentenced to a term of thirty-to-fifty years. This conviction was a tremendous victory for Dewey, and his reputation as a gangbuster helped him win election the following year as Manhattan district attorney and five years later as the governor of New York, a post he held for three terms. Meyer Lansky, however, was convinced that Luciano, his longtime friend and colleague, had gotten a bum rap. "Charlie had the same revulsion about running brothels that I did. He believed that no respectable man should ever make money out of women in that horrible way. I would never have anything to do with it, and I know perfectly well that neither did Charlie."[31] How important was Luciano in the New York underworld? It has been suggested that his influence has been mightily exaggerated, that in reality he was an ordinary mobster and not the mastermind figure as he is sometimes portrayed. One crime writer says

Luciano had no special status in the upper ranks of the Mafia, and another describes him as "a glorified pimp and drug pusher."[32] The theory here is that to advance his political career, Thomas E. Dewey deliberately exaggerated Luciano's importance, and that sensation-seeking crime writers swallowed the legend that had been created. At various times, Dewey pictured Luciano as "Public Enemy Number One in New York and the man who succeeded Al Capone in the West," "the absolute top boss of the Mafia in New York and, as far as we knew, in other cities as well," and "the Greatest gangster in America."[33]

So who is correct here? It is true that no one gangster dominated New York the way Capone dominated Chicago, but with its many centers of power New York was much more difficult for one man to rule. As much as anybody in the Big Apple, Luciano did cut a wide swath. On September 14, 1923, a championship boxing match was held at the Polo Grounds. Luciano, then only twenty-six, bought some twelve hundred tickets and entertained leading figures in business, politics, and crime.[34] This was not the kind of thing a common mobster would do. Further evidence of his prominence was the fact that the two rival Mafia bosses, Joseph Masseria and Slavatore Maranzano, each sought to hire Luciano as a top lieutenant and then plotted to have him killed because they saw him as a threat to their leadership. Perhaps the most succinct assessment of Luciano's place in the criminal underworld was a notation in the files of the New York City Police Department: "[Luciano] is the leading racketeer along Italian lines. Is very powerful and made considerable money in liquor."[35] At Luciano's prostitution trial, a low-level hood described a meeting at a Mulberry Street restaurant that Luciano attended: "It was funny. We were sitting down and when Charlie Lucky came in, all the Italians stood up."[36]

LUCIANO AND THE WAR EFFORT

After his sentencing Luciano was sent to the Clinton Correctional Facility in Dannemora. It was a chilly part of the state up against the Canadian border, remote from his New York City friends. While there he learned that his legal appeals failed. In May 1942 he was relocated to the Great Meadows Correctional Facility in Comstock, a better place, one hundred miles closer to New York, and reportedly had better-quality toilet paper and other amenities. In 1946, Luciano's nemesis Thomas E. Dewey, by then the governor of New York, gave him an early release. In his autobiography Dewey carefully specified that he had not pardoned Luciano but simply reduced his sentence, following a unanimous recommendation by the state's parole board. Because he was born in Sicily, Luciano was to be sent to Italy immediately following his release. He was forbidden to return to the United States; if he did so he would be treated like an escaped convict and returned to prison. Dewey justified his reduction in Luciano's sentence with the following statement he delivered to the state legislature, as required by the state constitution whenever a governor exercised executive clemency: "Upon the entry of the United States into the war, Luciano's aid was sought by the Armed Services in inducing others to provide information concerning possible enemy attack. It appears that he cooperated in such effort, although the actual value of the information produced is not clear. His record in prison is wholly satisfactory."[37]

Did Luciano actually serve the United States from behind bars? This question became a political hot potato in the postwar era when Republican Governor Dewey was a figure on the national scene. Democrats seeking to cast doubt on Dewey's reputation as a gangbuster charged that Luciano's supposed help with the war effort was simply a sham invented to justify the gangster's early release; some went further and alleged that Luciano gave Dewey a $75,000 bribe (sometimes stated as $250,000 or $350,000) to win his support. The investigative files of the 1950–1951 U.S. Senate Special Committee to Investigate Crime in Interstate Commerce (known familiarly as the Kefauver Committee) contain a staff report that contends the story of Luciano's war work was a myth. Some navy officials concurred with that view.[38]

The scenario presented by those who believe Luciano cooperated with the military is this: in the first six months of 1941 Nazi U-boats attacked the East Coast of the United States, torpedoing cargo ships and tankers. During this period the *Normandie,* an ocean liner being converted on the New York docks into a troop transport, caught fire and was burned into a useless hulk. The fire was suspected to be an act of enemy sabotage. U.S. Navy intelligence officials felt that dockworkers and seamen would follow the instruction of mob leaders to keep tabs on the Italian American fishing fleet, to spot enemy submarines, and to thwart sabotage attempts. Naval officers first contacted Socks Lanza, the mob czar of the Fulton Fish Market, who suggested that Luciano might be the best person. Luciano agreed to help the war effort and met regularly with officials. Later in the war when the Allies were planning to invade Sicily, Luciano reached out to Sicilian Mafia leaders to cooperate with the invading force and to provide map information. Several people have been singled out as dealing with Luciano in this capacity: Captain Roscoe McFall, a naval intelligence officer; Lieutenant Commander Charles Radcliffe Haffenden, a navy intelligence officer based in New York; Murray Gurfein, one of Dewey's staff who prosecuted Luciano; and Moses Polakoff, Luciano's lawyer at the trial.

The story has been endlessly debated. Governor Dewey asked the New York State Commissioner of Investigations, William Herland, to conduct a confidential examination of the whole issue. Herland produced a report that included 2,883 pages of testimony given under oath by fifty-seven major witnesses, including Luciano's former lawyers, U.S. Navy officers, and law enforcement personnel. The report took the better part of a year to complete. It supported the argument that Luciano did assist in the war effort. What Herland described as the "ruby nose"—his term for a "smoking gun" that he felt confirmed the veracity of the Luciano story—was a letter sent to him by Rear Admiral Carl F. Espe, the director of naval intelligence. The letter disclosed that the navy sought Luciano's assistance and that his transfer to Great Meadows prison was part of that effort. Said the admiral, carefully choosing his words, "We are advised that contacts were made with Luciano thereafter and that his influence on other criminal sources resulted in their cooperation with Naval Intelligence which was considered useful to the Navy."[39] FBI Director J. Edgar Hoover was skeptical, but one of his agents investigating the matter reported back to the FBI chief that the Office of Naval Operations had acknowledged that Luciano had served as an informant but that "the nature and extent of his assistance is not reflected in Navy records."[40] We can accept that Luciano was involved to some extent; whether that justified his release from prison is anybody's call.

There has even been controversy over the last days Luciano spent in the United States before he was deported. He had been removed from prison and locked up in Ellis Island, which by that time had been converted from a processing center for new immigrants to a holding tank for deportees. Several people came there to say goodbye, including his friends Frank Costello and Meyer Lansky. On February 9, 1946, Luciano was placed under guard on the cargo ship *Laura Keene,* docked at a Brooklyn pier. According to a Lansky biographer, a dozen mobsters and three Copacabana Club showgirls visited with Luciano on the ship.[41] But one guard on the ship, David Incarnato, painted a more mundane picture. He recalled that only five or six guests, all male, were in Luciano's room. They went down to the ship's mess hall in the evening. Greasy veal cutlets were being served, which Luciano could not eat, so some of his guests left and returned with spaghetti, lobsters, and wine. Luciano's stomach was bothering him so he just had some of the pasta.[42]

Life After Deportation

The *Laura Kean* set sail for Italy at 8:50 A.M. on Sunday, February 10, 1946. After seventeen days at sea Luciano disembarked in Naples where he was interviewed by the police. He then went on to Lercara Friddi, the Sicilian town where he was born. There he was treated like a celebrity and welcomed by relatives. He spent time in Naples and Rome, perhaps seeking out the excitement of big-city life he had known in New York, and began calling himself by his birth name, Salvatore Lucania. In late October he departed Italy, reportedly traveling to Caracas, Mexico City, and then to Havana where he stayed for a brief time at the Hotel Nacional before moving to a spacious home in the upscale neighborhood of Miramar. He was a major figure at a conference of American gangsters that took place at the Hotel Nacional from December 22 through December 26, 1947. The topics discussed included the development of gambling casinos in the Caribbean and in Las Vegas. Luciano stayed in Cuba after the meeting, enjoying days at the racetracks and making friends with influential politicians. He spent much time in the company of singer and Mafia favorite Frank Sinatra, who was vacationing in Havana.[43]

The fact that Luciano was living an enjoyable and possibly criminal life in Cuba, ninety miles from the United States, aroused the fury of segments of the American press and Washington officialdom. At the urging of Harry Anslinger, the director of the Federal Bureau of Narcotics, President Harry Truman authorized a ban on the shipment of legal medical drugs to Cuba until such time as Luciano was deported back to Italy. The Cuban authorities buckled under this pressure and, after incarcerating him at a detention camp, placed the gangster on a Turkish ship that departed for Italy on March 29, 1947.

It is clear from the FBI files that J. Edgar Hoover bore huge hatred for Luciano and kept voluminous files about the irregularities connected with Luciano's stay on Ellis Island, the party that allegedly took place aboard the *Laura Keene,* his claim of having helped the navy in World War II, his luxurious life in Cuba, and even his tattoos. Both the FBI and the FBN continued to keep tabs on Luciano once he was back in Italy. From time to time the Italian authorities subjected Luciano to restrictions like having his passport taken away, limiting his travel to only certain parts of the nation, and placing him under an early curfew. At other times these restrictions were lifted.

He invested some money in restaurants and was also getting regular payments from Costello and Lansky, although those payments declined as the position of Luciano's old friends deteriorated. When Fidel Castro came to power in Cuba and shut down the casinos, Luciano's income from mob activities declined even further. It did not help Luciano's position in Italy that America believed him to be a menace. The Kefauver Committee reported that Luciano was "the czar of a vast and secret underworld government" that could "easily become the basis of a subversive movement which could rock the nation."[44] This was simply wrong. By the early 1950s Luciano was an aging man with little power, authority, or wealth. He suffered a setback when, in October 1958, his longtime female companion, Igea Lissoni, died of breast cancer at age thirty-six. Luciano's death came on January 26, 1962, when the sixty-five-year-old mobster collapsed from a massive heart attack.

In light of the debate over the "Americanization" of gangsters, it is revealing that while in exile, Luciano requested that when he died his body should buried at Saint John's Cemetery in New York City. He was interred there in the family vault on February 7, 1962.

CHAPTER 10

Shot to Death

Prosecuting the crime lords for income tax evasion was an effective way for lawmen to put gangsters out of commission. But mobsters' more immediate and cheaper strategy for eliminating their rivals—shooting them to death—did not require any expenses for courts, judges, accountants, and lawyers.

The list of prominent criminals who never made it out of the 1920s is long and includes Arnold Rothstein, Dion O'Banion, Frank Yale, "Kid Dropper" Kaplan, and Hymie Weiss. At the start of the 1930s the most prominent murder victims were the feuding Joe Masseria and Salvatore Maranzano. More were to perish in that decade and beyond into the 1940s and 1950s. This chapter tells the story of some of the most notorious killings, when major criminals had their lives cut short in a burst of gunfire. Let us start with the feverish words of a dying mobster.

DUTCH SCHULTZ, 1935

"Oh, oh. Dog biscuit. And when he is happy, he doesn't get snappy. . . . the glove will fit what I say. . . . thinks he is grandpa again and he is jumping around. . . . get up your onions and we will throw up the truce flag. . . . he eats like a little sausage baloney maker . . . the sidewalk was in trouble and the bears were in trouble. . . . no payrolls, no walls, no coupons . . . a boy has never wept nor dashed a thousand kim . . . Sam,

you are a boiled man. . . . Mother is the best bet and don't let Satan draw
you too fast. . . . French Canadian bean soup."

The above are excerpts from a much longer text taken down by a Newark,
New Jersey, police stenographer who sat by the bedside of Dutch Schultz
in Newark City Hospital from four to six o'clock on the evening of October 24, 1935. Schultz had been shot the night before in a Newark restaurant.
The wound had become infected, producing a fever of 106 degrees, and
he lapsed into a ranting delirium. The police, thinking Schultz might say
something that would reveal who had attacked him, had the stenographer
take notes. But the transcribing effort was all in vain; he stopped talking, and at 8:35 P.M. he died. The two-hour transcript did not provide any
clues to who killed him, despite later efforts to make sense of his gibber-
ish. However, the stenographer's work did impress the American literary
avant-garde figure William S. Burroughs, who used it as the basis of a 1969
novel-screenplay entitled *The Last Words of Dutch Schultz*. The Dutchman's death symbolized not only stream-of-consciousness writing; it also
is a prime example of the long list of 1920s Prohibition era crime lords
who suffered violent deaths in the 1930s and beyond.

At the end of the 1920s, Dutch Schultz had emerged as the Beer Baron
of the Bronx, but he had the foresight to see that Prohibition might come
to an end so he aggressively pursued other rackets to replace bootlegging.
His partnership with political boss James Hines of Tammany Hall and his
ever-scheming attorney Richard "Dixie" Davis helped Schultz develop his
alternative pursuits. One of those rackets was labor extortion. He established a Metropolitan Restaurant and Cafeteria Association that owners
were compelled to join and took over management of two unions of restaurant workers, Local 16 of the Hotel and Restaurant Employee International Alliance and Local 13 of the Delicatessen Countermen and Cafeteria
Workers Union. He established another union for the men who washed
the windows of New York buildings; those who refused to join seemed to
get into accidents when their safety belts failed. Schultz also got into the

slot machine racket, installing peanut vending machines in speakeasies. Schultz realized that there was money well beyond peanuts in taking over the illegal betting industry known as "policy" or "numbers," which operated in Harlem and was run mostly by African Americans and immigrants from Cuba and the West Indies. Each of an estimated forty independent "banks," presided over by a boss, oversaw delivery of money and betting slips and payouts made to winners. Each bank had a "collector" who ran a network of people in the community, such as small merchants and apartment building superintendents, who took in the bets. A customer who plunked down ten cents to a dollar could get a payoff if he or she hit the right three-digit number. Each day's number was calculated on newspaper listings of racetrack betting or financial statistics.

The banks were sometimes subject to hijacking or police raids. Schultz and his gang offered to provide protection for five hundred dollars per week. Perhaps "offer" is not the way to describe the exchange; "demand" is more accurate because, if necessary, Schultz threatened to kill those bankers who did not join. At one point he pulled out a .45 handgun from his waistband and placed it on the table to convince a frightened bank boss of the benefits of being taken under Schultz's wing. Moreover, Schultz provided another vital service. By sheer bad luck, the banks sometimes faced the problem of not having collected enough money to pay off successful bets. In these instances Schultz provided loans to cover the deficits, for which he demanded a share of the business, typically 60 percent. A person who had once owned the bank now had only a 40 percent share. Schultz offered to pay former owners a salary, but after deducting exorbitant expenses there was surprisingly little left to give that former boss.[1]

Schultz worked long hours to run his many rackets. He typically started work at 8 A.M. at his headquarters in a speakeasy on Third Avenue and 168th Street in the Bronx and would not leave until late in the evening. Even so, he still had time for other escapades. On January 24, 1931, he was involved in a fierce fight with a rival mobster, Charles "Chink" Sherman, at the Abbey Club, a Manhattan nightspot. Sherman was beaten over the head with a chair and stabbed seven times with broken glass. Shots were fired. Chink survived the beating and thanks to the *omerta* tradition, Schultz walked away free.[2] On the night of June 18 in the same year, Schultz was in a Manhattan apartment when he and his bodyguard Danny Iamascia saw two suspicious men on the street below who seemed to be casing the dwelling. Schultz and Iamascia rushed out of the building and started firing. Those inquisitive men on the street were NYPD detectives, who fought back. Iamascia was shot dead by one detective. Schultz threw down his gun and tried to run away, but he was tackled by the other detective. Dixie Davis and James Hines made sure Schultz did not serve any time for this shootout.[3]

Schultz also found time to wage a violent war against mobster Vincent Coll, who had once worked for him but was now the Dutchman's mortal enemy. In the period from May 1931 through February 1932, according to one count, the death toll on the Coll side was five, and on the Schultz side the toll was six.[4] But Schultz could be considered the victor because the last person to die in this grubby conflict was Coll himself. His end has become one of the iconic events of the 1930s. As usual there are many different versions of what happened, but the basic facts are indisputable: on February 7, 1932, Coll went into the London Chemists drugstore on West Twenty-third Street to make a call from the phone booth. A hit man toting a machine gun entered the pharmacy and told the customers and clerk to be calm. He then fired into the booth, splintering wood and glass and killing Coll. It's been suspected that Bo Weinberg, a Schultz henchman, was the killer, but nobody was ever caught. There was no great mourning over Coll's death. He was much hated in the underworld because of his erratic nature and because he had engaged in kidnappings to get ransom money, one of his victims being a fellow gangster. He was hated even more in the overworld because, a year and a half before his death in the pharmacy, Coll had been in a Bronx gunfight in which a five-year-old boy was killed and three other children injured. Although acquitted of the murder, Coll was known afterward as the Baby Killer.

Trouble for Schultz now came from another quarter; on January 25, 1933, he was indicted by a federal grand jury in New York for failure to file income tax returns for 1929, 1930, and 1931, amounting to an unpaid tax bill of $92,103, which could lead to a sentence of up to forty-three years in prison and more than $100,000 in fines. He dropped out of sight for the next twenty-two months while his lawyers tried to negotiate a tax settlement. Even though some fifty thousand wanted notices with his photo were sent out by the New York police, and even though Schultz popped up in nightclubs, train stations, rented apartments, brothels, and gang haunts, he was not apprehended. His biographer, Paul Sann, believes Schultz was being shielded from capture by his political ally, James Hines.[5]

Schultz finally surrendered to federal authorities in Albany in November 1934. At one point while he was awaiting his date in court, Schultz and his entourage got rooms at a cheap, rundown hotel in a nearby town of Cohoes. Why not a classier hotel in Albany? It's been said that hotels in that city refused to register him; another possible factor was that Schultz, a notorious cheapskate, wanted to save money to pay his legal fees. Years after Schultz had passed from the scene, lawyer Dixie Davis, who was by then broke, disbarred, and in jail, wrote a series of articles for *Collier's Weekly* magazine about his association with the Dutchman. He claimed that during the Cohoes interval, Schultz had summoned one of his henchmen, Jules Martin, to come up to the hotel from New York City and to bring $21,000 with him. Martin (whose real last name was Modgilewsky) handled the restaurant racket for Schultz, so he withdrew the money from the Metropolitan Restaurant and Cafeteria Association. According to Davis, Schultz had been drinking heavily when Martin arrived, and the two men got in a shouting match over the charge that Martin had been stealing money. Davis said that at the height of this argument, Schultz pulled his pistol out of his waistband, shoved it in Martin's mouth, and pulled the trigger. Martin did not immediately die. As he collapsed on a chair blood dripped out of his mouth and he moaned loudly. (Episodes like this have lead crime writers, novelists, and filmmakers to conclude that Schultz had a problem with anger management.) After the shooting, Schultz directed two henchmen in the room to dispose of the body elsewhere. The corpse, with multiple stab wounds, was later found in a snow bank—the stabbing was presumably meant to stop the moaning noise. Schultz apologized to attorney Davis for the ruckus.[6] Ironically, the hostelry where this incident took place was named the Harmony Hotel. The murder was never pinned on Schultz, but his biographer Paul Sann believes Davis's story was true, though he notes for the record that a different account of the murder came from a convict in prison who claimed that Martin had been killed by Bo Weinberg.

A different kind of story about the Dutchman around this time comes from *New York Times* reporter Meyer Berger, who wrote a news item stating that the mobster was a "pushover for blondes." Schultz complained to Berger about the charge. The reporter started to defend his statement when Schultz interrupted him. "That's beside the pernt, I only remember it made me feel bad when I saw it in the *Times*. I don't think 'pushover for a blonde' is any kind of language to write for a newspaper like the *Times*." Bloodstained murderer or fussy newspaper critic—the Dutchman was a complex figure.[7]

His long-awaited trial began in Syracuse on April 16, 1935. The prosecution sought to demonstrate that Schultz was making ample amounts of money at the time he neglected to pay his taxes; the defense argued that Schultz had been misled by his financial and legal advisors who told him he did not have to pay taxes on revenue from illegal activities and that when they discovered the tax was in fact due they tried without success to reach a settlement with the government. The case went to the jury on April 27; after two days of deliberation the jurors found that they were hopelessly deadlocked. Schultz was released because of this hung jury, but the Feds did not relent; a second trial was arranged for the small New York village of Malone, 286 miles north of New York City on the Canadian border. Here Dutch Schultz went on a charm offensive to endear himself to the town's residents. He spent generously around the town, picked up the tab for alcohol, went to a baseball game, and generally appeared to be a nice guy. As the trial came to an end there were rumors afoot that once again the jury was deadlocked. But after deliberating for over twenty-eight hours, the jury announced that they found the defendant not guilty. Said a reporter, the judge "sat bolt upright in, disbelief written over his features." Schultz had a look of amazement on his face, too. Cheers and applause erupted from the audience in the courtroom. The angry judge gaveled them into silence and then turned to the jury: "Your verdict is such that it shakes the confidence of law abiding people in integrity and truth." He continued that the verdict had not been based on the evidence presented in court. Said the snobby *New York Times* headline: "SCHULTZ IS FREED; JUDGE EXCORIATES JURY OF FARMERS." It was clear that the residents of Malone had no love for the city of New York's imposition of the trial onto their community. The *New York Times* reporter summarized the attitude of the village: "If New York thinks he's so dangerous, why don't they get rid of him down there?"[8]

As a matter of fact, New York City lawmen, faced with the failures upstate, were seeking to make Schultz's life miserable. Mayor Fiorello LaGuardia announced that Schultz would not be permitted to return to the city; to back up the mayor, Police Commissioner Lewis Valentine restructured the Detective Bureau, members of which in the past had looked the other way when it came to the Dutchman. Presumably the authorities would have welcomed Schultz back to the city with open arms, providing he was in handcuffs and under arrest. Special Prosecutor Thomas Dewey was investigating Schultz's involvement in the Harlem numbers racket. The Feds were preparing to prosecute Schultz once again on income tax evasion. In the Malone trial, Schultz had been cleared of willfully evading the U.S. income tax, a felony. But the lawmen sought a new indictment on the charge of simply not sending in his taxes, which was a misdemeanor. Schultz also owed $36,937 in state taxes to New York.

After Malone, Schultz went first to Connecticut, then to New Jersey. He made arrangements to be arrested in Perth Amboy and released at

affordable bail. By October 1935 Schultz was in residence at the Robert
Treat Hotel in Newark. He hired a team of lawyers that included Dixie
Davis and a former governor of New Jersey, George S. Silzer, to fight off
demands from New York for his extradition. Schultz established a headquarters at the Palace Chop House in Newark where he oversaw his rackets.
On the night of October 23, 1935, Schultz was there with three long-standing
members of his gang: Abe Landau, Bernard "Lulu" Rosenkrantz, and Otto
"Abbadabba" Berman. It was after 10:00 P.M., and, as the only customers in
the place, they were going over some financial records in the dining room
at the rear of the building. At the front of the building, a lone bartender
saw two tough-looking hoods come through the front door, one holding
a pistol and the other a shotgun. The bartender, Jack Friedman, slid under
the bar as the gunmen made their way to the back. Friedman was a World
War I veteran who said later that the sound of gunshots from the back
room reminded him of his service on the Western Front.

Berman, Rosenkrantz, and Landau were shot by the intruders. But
where was Schultz? One of the gunmen walked to the rear of the room
where the men's lavatory was located. Kicking open the door he saw
Schultz inside and shot him in the stomach. One can imagine the Dutchman inside the men's room. He must have heard the gunshots start and
then stop and must have hoped against hope that the assassins would leave
and he would be safe, only to hear the steps coming closer. Astonishingly
enough, Schultz and his henchmen were still alive when they were taken by
ambulance to Newark City Hospital. But they could not be saved; Schultz
was the last to die. Curiously, while on his deathbed this Jewish gangster
asked for a Catholic priest to come and give him the last rites—an example
of the loose ethnic identity of the Prohibition generation.[9]

Around midnight on the same night that the Dutchman and his three
gang members were rubbed out in Newark, an attack took place across the
Hudson River in Manhattan when a gunman walked into a barbershop
located in a subway arcade at Broadway and Forty-seventh Street and fired
four shots into a customer who had just gotten up from the barber chair.

The target was Marty Krompier, a Schultz henchman who, like the late Jules Martin, had been taking care of the rackets during the Dutchman's New Jersey sojourn. Also wounded was Sammy Gold, a bookmaker friend of Marty's. Both men survived. The fact that the Newark and New York attacks took place on the same night suggests that there was a planned and coordinated effort to eliminate the Dutchman and his associates. But who had arranged it? The truth did not emerge until the early 1940s, when an investigation was being conducted into Murder Incorporated, a notorious Brooklyn mob whose specialty was killing (see chapter 11). Several of the Murder Incorporated mob had become informers to save their own skins. They talked to the police and district attorney's staff about unsolved killings that had been performed by their organization; one such job was the Dutch Schultz rubout.

The saga the informers provided began with the fact that Dutch Schultz hated the author of his woes, Thomas E. Dewey. The Dutchman decided that the only solution was for Dewey to be killed. The underworld was chary about going after prosecutors or other law enforcement officials; the killing of McSwiggin in Chicago demonstrated the backlash such a murder could create. So Schultz recognized that he needed to consult with other gang leaders first. Defying the warning of Mayor LaGuardia that he stay away from New York, Schultz went to the city to meet with top mobsters, who are thought to include Lucky Luciano, Meyer Lansky, Bugsy Siegel, Frank Costello, Abner Zwillman, Lepke Buchalter, and Gurrah Shapiro. This group has variously been called the Big Seven, or the Big Six, or the Seven Group, which met together from time to time.[10] To this board of directors Schultz proposed his plan. The group promised to think about the proposal and gave Albert Anastasia the assignment of determining whether Dewey was vulnerable. Anastasia spent a few days casing the area around Dewey's Fifth Avenue apartment building and found out that the special prosecutor would leave the building each workday morning and go with his assistant for coffee at a neighborhood drugstore while his bodyguards stood outside. Anastasia figured that a gunman could walk past the guards and use a gun equipped with a silencer to shoot Dewey, his assistant, and the manger of the drugstore and then stroll outside past the bodyguards. The gang leaders heard this assessment from Anastasia but decided not to give Schultz the green light. In fact, they come up with quite a different idea: Schultz himself should be eliminated because of not only his general reputation as a loose cannon but also their desire to divide up his rackets after he was gone.

So who did the shooting? When it came to the Schultz rubout, the informers said that the two triggermen were Mendy Weiss and Charles "the Bug" Workman (who took the long walk to the men's room). Weiss was already in prison for a different murder so there was no need to put him on trial for the Schultz killing, and he was electrocuted in Sing Sing prison in 1944. Workman had no such alibi so he was extradited to Newark for a trial in June 1941. Two of the stoolpigeons from the Murder Incorporated investigation testified against him. After serving a twenty-three-year sentence he was paroled and became a salesman in the New York's garment district.[11] This was the only murder of a mob boss for which the killers were brought to justice for the crime.

LEGS DIAMOND, 1931

No less an authority on violence than Dutch Schultz said of Legs Diamond that he was a "cowboy," in the sense of someone wild, reckless, and generally out of control.[12] Certainly the shootout at the Hotsy Totsy club in 1929 (see chapter 2) was a cowboy affair if ever there were one. After he avoided being charged for that crime, Diamond stayed in the headlines. In August 1930 he went to Europe, but the police in Germany determined that he was an undesirable alien and shipped him back to America in October. On his return to the United States, he told reporters that he had a stomach ailment and had been on vacation for his health, but the real purpose was probably to purchase narcotics that could be smuggled back into the United States.[13] A month after his return from Europe his stomach was stressed again, this time when he was shot in the abdomen by unknown enemies while staying in the Hotel Monticello on West Sixty-fourth Street in New York—the third time in his career he had been wounded in an attack. After Diamond recovered from his wounds he left the city for the rural upstate hamlet of Acra in the Catskill Mountains region where he owned a well-furnished, seven-room house several hundred yards from the country road and obscured by trees. He had acquired the property in 1928 as a summer home.

The repeated attempts on his life and the notoriety he achieved in Europe made Diamond an internationally known mob figure. Diamond thought that he could find a respite from the publicity in the tranquility in his Acra home, but relaxation was not in the cards. For one thing, there was the issue of his tangled domestic relationships. In 1917 he married an attractive waitress, Florence Williams, who left him after a few months because of his boozing and continued relationships with other women. His second wife, whom he married in 1926, was Alice Kenny, uncharitably described by one of Diamond's biographers as "a crass, nagging, beer guzzling ignoramus" and ugly to boot.[14] Now into the picture entered Kiki Roberts, a young, attractive performer in *The Ziegfeld Follies* and other Broadway shows where a fetching face and figure were prerequisites. Legs fell for Kiki (whose real name was Marion Strasmick), but he remained married to Alice. As might be expected, there was no love lost between Alice and Kiki, especially because, again according to Diamond's biographer, all three sometimes resided together in the Acra home. In addition, there were rumors of other girlfriends.[15] We can only imagine what happened when the lights went off at the Diamond residence.

One aspect of Diamond's life in Acra was bootlegging both beer and applejack—the latter a potent alcoholic beverage, favorite drink of the Catskills region, made by distilling cider. Just as he had done in New York City during the 1920s, Diamond's competitive instincts compelled him to drive out rival bootleggers. On April 16, 1931, one Grover Parks, a farmer from the town of Catskill, was driving his truck loaded with applejack near the Diamond estate. In the truck with Parks was a seventeen-year-old youth, James Duncan. According to testimony given later by Parks, his truck was stopped by a car carrying gun-wielding Legs Diamond, accompanied by Kiki Roberts and members of the Diamond gang. Parks and Duncan were taken to Diamond's garage and forced to lie on the floor. Parks was told to take off his shoes, after which the soles of his feet were burned by matches and lit paper tapers, torture to get him to reveal the location of a rival alcohol still. Diamond and company took Parks out of the garage, and they fastened a rope around his neck before throwing the rope over a tree branch and hoisting him upward until Parks fainted. When he woke up the gang put Duncan and him back in their truck. After driving for a while the truck stopped near a cemetery. The gang ripped out the transmission. Parks and Duncan were warned that they would be killed if they told the story to the police; Diamond then permitted the two to walk home. At least this was one version of what happened. In various accounts the details, including the date in April, change, but the rope and burning feet appear in all reports of the incident.

Diamond may have later regretted letting Parks live because the kidnap victim mustered up his courage and told his story to the chief of the Catskill Police, George Klein. Parks begged for protection: "Mr. Klein, you've got to let me have one of those .38s or I'm a dead man. That Diamond means business and if he catches me again he will blow my brains out without giving me a chance."[16] Based on Parks's testimony, Diamond was duly arrested and indicted for kidnapping and assault. But the gang leader did not seem particularly distressed. A few days after being released on bail, he paid an evening visit to the Aratoga Inn, a popular roadhouse in the Catskills. With him that night for some revelry were Kiki Roberts and other friends. At one point when Diamond was out on the front porch getting a breath of fresh air, two men outside dressed in hunter's garb blasted him with their shotguns and quickly drove away. The local hearse/ambulance rushed Diamond to the Albany Hospital, where doctors operated to stop the hemorrhaging of his lung; afterward he spent a month recuperating. This episode, along with the Parks kidnapping, motivated New York Governor Franklin Roosevelt and State Attorney General John J. Bennett to slam the door on what the *New York Times* called a "reign of terror" in the Catskills. A squad of twenty armed state policemen was sent to the area. Large-scale bootleg beer operations, allegedly run by Diamond, were shut down, and Diamond and some of his gang members (but not Kiki) were indicted by a federal grand jury for violation of the Prohibition laws.

Diamond went through three courtroom trials in quick succession. The first, a state indictment for the Parks abduction, took place in Troy, New York, in July 1931. The terrified Parks spoke directly to the jury: "They are going to kill me. You have got to put them away."[17] But after hearing from seven witnesses who said that Diamond was in Albany when the crime was committed and the argument of the defense that Parks was a hopeless liar, the jury returned a verdict of not guilty, which was followed by the judicial officials' and newspaper editorial writers' collective gnashing of teeth.

The second trial, which concerned the Prohibition law violation, took place in federal court in New York City. Diamond was not so lucky this time; on August 12 he was sentenced to a term of four years in the Atlanta federal prison. He was released on bail while his lawyers worked on his appeal.

The third trial was a state case held in Albany. Once again the case concerned the kidnapping episode, but this time Diamond was charged with abducting Park's passenger, young Duncan. "You know," said Diamond to reporters, "three trials in four months is too many for any man, even for a tough one like me."[18] At 9:00 P.M. on December 17, 1931, Diamond was acquitted once again. His wife Alice was in the courtroom, and when the not-guilty verdict was announced she climbed over the courthouse rail to kiss him ecstatically.

Diamond celebrated the victory by doing what he liked to do best—drinking himself into oblivion. That night he went to Young's Café, an Albany speakeasy, with Alice, and assorted relatives, lawyers, and friends.

At about 1:00 A.M., thoroughly soused, he announced that he was going to see some "newspaper pals." "I'll be gone about half an hour," he said. "Stick around till I get back."[19] He got into a car he had hired for the evening and directed the driver, Jack Storer, to take him, not to see any members of the press, but to Clinton Avenue and Tenbroeck Street where (surprise) Kiki Roberts had been waiting for him. It can be assumed that more ecstatic kisses were exchanged there. According to Storer, Diamond returned to the car after spending about three hours with Kiki and asked to be taken to 67 Dove Street, a rooming house where he had been living during the trial. Storer said the gangster was staggeringly drunk when he got out of the car. The landlady, Mrs. Laura Wood, and the driver agreed that Diamond arrived at the house around 4:45 A.M.; Wood heard him climbing the stairs to his room. She went back to sleep but was awakened by gunshots coming from the room above her and heard men clomp down the stairs and bolt out the front door. She and her sister looked out the window and saw a maroon car drive away.

When the police arrived they found the dead Legs Diamond sprawled out on the bed in his underwear, which reinforces the theory that he had been totally drunk when he returned. While he was sleeping some person or persons unknown entered his room and fired three shots into his head, killing him instantly. Four other times in his life he had survived being shot. But not this time.

Who did it? According to one theory his killers were two hoods, Salvatore Spitalie and Irving Bitz. The two, it was said, had loaned Diamond $200,000 to pay for his narcotics-buying expedition in Europe. Diamond had not only failed in that venture, but he also did not repay his two colleagues. The hoods had tried in vain to kill Diamond at the Hotel Monticello and, so goes this theory, tried again in Albany.

Another theory suggests that the Diamond murder was committed on the orders of Dutch Schultz, who was seeking vengeance for the killing of his partner Joey Noe. Or maybe it was Paul Quatrocchi and/or Gary Scaccio, members of Diamond's gang whom the boss had double-crossed.

Scaccio was in prison at the time, but he might have paid somebody to do the hit. And what about the women in his life? Crime writer Gary Levine suggests that Alice or Kiki might have had some connection to the crime. He thinks that Kiki could have given information on Diamond's Dove Street address to hired killers, or Alice, filled with hatred against her husband for his long-term affair with the dancer, might have done the same thing. Curiously, nobody has suggested that the culprit was the frightened truck driver, Grover Parks, who might have been seeking revenge. Perhaps Parks and an accomplice had first tried to kill Diamond at the Aratoga Inn. In trying to sort out who killed Legs Diamond, it is helpful to remember the rule that just because something *could* have happened does not mean that it *did* happen.[20]

JOHN LAZIA, 1934

The next major gangster to meet his maker was John Lazia, the genial, gum-chewing overseer of crime under the rule of Kansas City political boss Tom Pendergast. Lazia was noted for his personal charm. He mingled with respectable people of the city and was known affectionately as "Brother John." Nobody was more surprised than Lazia when he was fatally wounded. As his life ebbed away while he lay on a bed in Saint Joseph's Hospital, he said to the doctor, "Doc, what I can't understand is why anybody would do this to me. Why to me, to Johnny Lazia, who has been a friend of everybody?"[21]

On July 9 he had been out with his wife, Marie, and his second-in-command, Charles Carollo. It was a swelteringly hot night in the city, and the three had been at Lazia's lakeside home to catch some breezes in that era before home air conditioning. Returning to the city, they stopped for a meal and then drove to the Park Central Hotel where the Lazias had a suite. It was about 3:00 A.M. when they arrived in the car. John was in the back seat, and his wife was in the front; Carollo was driving. They stopped in front of the hotel, and John got out of the car to open the door for

Marie. At that moment John was hit by machine gun slugs. He shouted, "Get Marie out of here. Step on it, Charley!"[22] He died eleven hours later. Seven thousand mourners came to his funeral on July 13, thought to the largest ever in Kansas City.

Lazia's career shows that while he did put on a friendly face to the public, he was also capable of taking off the mask and using force on those who stood in his way. One such person was Harry D. Beach, an IRS agent in Kansas City who investigated Lazia's tax situation. He found that Lazia had not filed an income tax return for either 1929 or 1930, even though in those years he had amassed an estimated $100,000 from gambling operations and two companies with which he was affiliated—the North Side Distributing Company and the North Side Finance Company. Beach asked Lazia to come to the IRS office for a discussion; at that meeting Lazia denied that he made any money in those years because of his losses in gambling—the same lame excuse used by both Ralph Capone and Al Capone. On Sunday, March 13, 1932, four days after the interview with Lazia, two men knocked on Beach's apartment door. After Beach let them in the apartment, they brutally assaulted him with punches and kicks, leaving him with multiple fractures of the head and other injuries that contributed to his premature death several years later.[23] In retaliation, the Special Investigative Unit of the IRS sent agents to Kansas City to bring Lazia to justice by prosecuting him for income tax evasion. At that point Boss Tom Pendergast intervened by writing a May 12, 1933, "Dear Jim" letter to James Farley, postmaster general of the United States and close advisor to President Franklin Roosevelt. Pendergast's letter praised Lazia and asked Farley to "bring about a settlement of this matter," a veiled request to derail the investigation.[24] The letter seems to have worked, at least for a time; the federal government tried to negotiate a settlement that would benefit Lazia and delayed giving the U.S. Attorney in Kansas City the authorization to bring the case to trial. Finally the authorization was issued, and the tax evasion trial of John Lazia began on February 5, 1934. He was found guilty on the misdemeanor charge of neglecting to file tax returns, not the stiffer felony charge of willfully violating the tax law. His sentence was a fine and a year in jail, but he never received that punishment; at the time of his assassination he was out on bail while his case was being appealed.

Lazia also struck back at another enemy—Jewish rabbi Samuel S. Mayerberg of the B'nai Jehudah synagogue in Kansas City. Mayerberg was a "goo goo"—a good government reformer who was appalled at the corruption and open crime in the city. In 1932 he testified before the City Council and urged them to fire Boss Pendergast's flunky, city administrator Henry F. McElroy. The City Council responded by voting to strike the rabbi's statements from the council's records and issuing a tribute to McElroy's honest administration. Mayerberg encountered John Lazia for the first time at a council meeting: "Well, Rabbi," sneered Lazia, "you didn't get very far, did you?"[25] Mayerberg found that his telephone was tapped, he was shot at by a passing car, and his files were ransacked and stolen. The rabbi prudently kept a loaded pistol by his bed. His friends chipped in to provide bulletproof glass for his automobile.[26]

It does not take a Sherlock Holmes to conclude that neither Rabbi Mayerberg nor the Internal Revenue agents had a hand in killing John Lazia. His murder most likely resulted from the criminal element that infested Kansas City. Under Lazia's oversight and with the backing of Boss Pendergast, the city was known as a wide-open refuge for underworld figures. In the 1930s a lot of such criminals were roaming the Midwest. This was the golden age for bandits and robbers like John Dillinger, Ma Barker, and Bonnie and Clyde who made their living from sticking up banks, kidnapping, and other freelance activities. These desperadoes were not part of the organized crime empire of distilleries, gambling casinos, and brothels operated by big city gangsters like Al Capone, Lucky Luciano, Meyer Lansky, and yes, John Lazia.

Some have theorized that two of those desperadoes, Michael "Jimmy Needles" LaCapra and his partner Jack Griffin, may have been responsible for Lazia's death. Lazia was the man in Kansas City whose approval was needed to engage in racketeering and who collected protection money from the people who operated those rackets. For various reasons Lazia had a grudge against LaCapra and denied him permission either to open a casino or to compete with the established Kansas City mob in the labor union racket. For this reason, goes the theory, LaCapra decided to kill Lazia. This interpretation is reinforced by the fact that after his death, Lazia's Kansas City gang furiously sought to kill LaCapra and Griffin. Griffin went first. He was shot on a Kansas City sidewalk and taken to a hospital, from which he was mysteriously abducted and never seen again. One tradition is that mob killers put the wounded Griffin in a car. Griffin knew full well that they were going to kill him and asked for a last cigarette. After puffing on it, he suddenly smashed it into the eye of the abductor sitting next to him. For this act of defiance the killers threw Griffin, while still alive, into a burning furnace in an apartment building. Another version of Griffin's fate has him sealed in concrete and thrown into the Missouri River.[27] It's a grand guiginol scenario no matter how you slice it. As for La Capra, he was shot to death near New Paltz, New York, on August 21, 1935, a year after Lazia's assassination.

Incidentally, La Capra and Lazia are both thought to have had a connection with the most violent episode in the history of Kansas City crime—the Union Station Massacre that took place on the early morning of June 17, 1933, a year before Lazia's death. Four FBI agents, an Oklahoma police chief, and two Kansas City Police Department detectives were escorting a handcuffed prisoner, Frank "Jelly" Nash, out of the Union Railway Station and into a car scheduled to take him to the U.S. penetentiary in Leavenworth, Kansas. Somebody shouted "Up! Up! Get your hands up." A gunshot followed this directive, and then machine-gun blasts repeated at the car and the lawmen standing near it. The two, or maybe three, gunmen sped away in their car. The detectives, the police chief, and an FBI agent had been killed, as had the prisoner. Another FBI agent was seriously wounded. On September 1, 1934, FBI agents interrogated LaCapra, who at the time was in jail in Wichita. LaCapra claimed to know something about the massacre. He said that Verne Miller, a bank robber, who knew that his friend Nash would be under guard at Union Station in Kansas City the next morning, had organized the hit on short notice. Miller wanted to rescue Nash, but he knew he would need other men to carry this out so he went to see the Kansas City mob boss Lazia. According to LaCapra, Lazia recommended that Miller contact Charles "Pretty Boy" Floyd and Adam Richetti, both of whom Lazia knew to be holed up in Kansas City. Miller followed this advice, and he, along with Floyd and Richetti, were the assailants in the massacre the following morning. LaCapra's revelation became the standard narrative of that event.[28]

BUGSY SIEGEL, 1947

How did mobsters talk in private, as opposed to the way they bantered in public with reporters, or testified on the witness stand in courtroom trials, or babbled in delirium to a stenographer? We do know what the forty-year-old gangster Benjamin "Bugsy" Siegel said to his girlfriend Virginia Hill, twenty-nine, when they were alone together in room 601 of the Last Frontier Hotel in Las Vegas at 7:30 on the evening of July 20, 1946. Bugsy was outraged and profane. His anger was directed at the reporter and broadcaster Walter Winchell and FBI Director J. Edgar Hoover. On his popular national radio program the week before, Winchell had gossiped about an unnamed West Coast mobster who, according to the FBI, was planning to build a luxury hotel but had run into money problems. This was a thinly veiled reference to Siegel, who found out that Hoover had provided the information to Winchell.

Siegel flew into a rage as he explained all this to Virginia Hill in the hotel room. He described Hoover as a "dirty son of a bitch" and wanted to find out who had leaked this damaging information to the FBI director. "We'll make him [Winchell] bring Hoover in front of me and let that cocksucker tell me where he got it from." Of Winchell, Siegel said he would "knock his fucking eyes out." Siegel went on to tell Hill that as a result of all this bad publicity about his gangland connection and his money problems that he might not get a license for the hotel and would lose three million dollars, "every nickel we possess." "What kind of a license, honey?" Hill asked sympathetically. A gambling license he replied, and then he complained, "What am I gonna do with the hotel, stick it up my ass?" Siegel and Hill didn't know it, but the microphone device that had been installed by the FBI picked up every word they uttered in the hotel room; moreover, Siegel's phone was tapped, and his mail was read. The FBI agents who recorded the conversation regarded it as a threat to Director Hoover, and the full transcript was sent special delivery to Hoover at the Bureau headquarters in Washington, labeled "PERSONAL AND CONFIDENTIAL—OBSCENE."[29]

Siegel, the good-looking Jewish gangster who had been a partner of Meyer Lansky in the Bug and Meyer gang during Prohibition, is thought to have been a hit man in the slaying of Masseria, Maranzano, and others. He hated his nickname "Bugsy," which according to an internal FBI memo Siegel acquired because "many of the associates in the old days considered him as 'going bugs' when he got excited in that he acted in an irrational manner."[30] On one occasion he knocked down and kicked a man at a Florida casino who dared to address him by that nickname, which shows how apt it was.[31] In 1937, he left New York to explore business opportunities in California. He also explored Hollywood starlets and society girls, which led his wife to divorce him. Siegel's underworld specialty was the gambling racket, and he franchised the Los Angeles–based Trans-America News Service to bookies. Trans-America was a competitor of the Chicago-based Continental Wire Service, a successor to Moses Annenberg's racetrack telegraph empire.[32] Siegel made tens of thousands of dollars each month from the wire service.[33]

Then Siegel launched the greatest project of his life, a project that would ultimately lead to his death—the Flamingo Hotel in Las Vegas. It was a legitimate operation, because gambling had been legal in Nevada ever since 1931. Some maintain that at the time Las Vegas was just a spot in the desert and that Siegel is the man who deserves the credit for transforming it into the capital of glitz it is today. But that is not so. Several lodging and gambling establishments were already running when Siegel decided to build the Flamingo. The Flamingo would be a unique departure from the rustic cowboy boot, "howdy pardner" air of the existing Las Vegas tourist destinations; Siegel sought to produce something enormous, star-studded, luxurious, and sophisticated. But even this was not Siegel's own contribution. Billy Wilkerson, a Hollywood nightclub impresario and publisher of the *Hollywood Reporter* trade magazine, created that idea,[34] but Siegel deserves credit for bringing this concept to reality. Siegel brought together money for what came to be known as the Nevada Project Corporation. A major share came from the New York mob, including his longtime friend Meyer Lansky and reportedly Lucky Luciano and Frank Costello; the collective amount ran into millions. The Chicago mob reportedly put up $300,000. Siegel himself contributed $195,000—"every nickel" as he said in his recorded rant. There were local investors, too; Wilkerson, who owned the land on which the Flamingo was to be built, had a one-third share.

Construction workers broke ground for the Flamingo in December 1945, but the work did not go well. Delays and cost overruns plagued the already expensive construction project. Workers may have pilfered construction material to resell on the inflated post–World War II housing market. To bring in more cash, Siegel oversold shares by a reported 400 percent, making the shares owned by earlier investors worthless. There were rumors that he and Virginia Hill were skimming money, which they deposited in Swiss bank accounts. Siegel supervised the construction, although he knew next to nothing about it. Hill, who was equally ignorant, did the interior design. Investigators later found that $1.5 million in checks signed by Siegel and payable to the builder, the Dell E. Webb Company, had bounced. Originally estimated at $1 million, the cost of the project had skyrocketed to somewhere around $6 million.[35] Wilkerson quarreled bitterly with Siegel, and at one point the mobster threatened to have Wilkerson murdered. Because Wilkerson and J. Edgar Hoover were friends, it is not surprising that the FBI began to investigate Siegel.

Despite his concerns about the Walter Winchell expose, Siegel was able to get the necessary licenses, and, under increasing pressure from his investors, he picked December 26, 1946, for the opening, after which he hoped the investors could begin to make back some of their money. He hired expensive celebrities to provide entertainment, including Jimmy Durante, the Xavier Cugat orchestra, and George Jessel. By all accounts, the opening was a pathetic failure. Bad weather in Los Angeles prevented chartered planes bound for Las Vegas from taking off, which reduced the number of opening night attendees. There were also glitches in the operation of the casino so that gamblers came out ahead in their winnings. Although the casino and dining area had been built, the guest rooms were not yet completed so people at the opening had to find other Las Vegas hotels where they could sleep, further depriving the Flamingo of revenue. Alas for Siegel, the conference of gang leaders in Havana was in full swing at the time so that the news of the failed opening reached them and stoked their anger. Lucky Luciano was irate, while Meyer Lansky pushed to give Siegel another chance. Siegel shut down the Flamingo in late January so that the guest rooms could be completed and reopened the facility on March 1, 1947; this time the Andrews Sisters were the main act. Revenue now started coming in, but the investors were still unhappy.

All of which brings us to the evening of June 27, 1947. Siegel was at the Beverly Hills home of Virginia Hill. Virginia was in Paris at the time. The couple quarreled frequently, and they periodically separated in the course of their relationship. Siegel, on the sofa in the living room after dinner, was reading the *Los Angeles Times*. A friend, Allen Smiley, was in the same room; Virginia's brother was upstairs with his girlfriend. But then a succession of nine bullets came smashing through the window; two of them, striking Siegel in the head and neck, killed him. In the investigation that followed, detectives determined that the assassin had used a .30 caliber army-issue carbine and had steadied the weapon on an ornamental trellis near the window. Newspapers ran grisly photos of the dead Siegel fallen back on the sofa with blood from an empty eye socket spread over his once handsome face. The widely reported detail that one eyeball was found fifteen feet away from his body added to the ghastliness of the crime.

The killer was never found, and, as usual with gangland murders, there was ample speculation about who might have commissioned the rubout. One theory posits that Siegel had on several occasions beaten up Virginia Hill and that her many lovers in the underworld sought revenge. A related theory allows that Joseph Adonis, a rival for the affections of Hill, was responsible. Moving from affairs of the heart to those of the bank account, many crime writers have attributed the killing to his disgruntled investors, especially those from New York, and in particular Lucky Luciano, who is said to have arranged the killing through Los Angeles mob boss Jack Dragna.[36] It is probable that the murder had to do with Siegel's mismanagement of money from investors. In a normal business, if the stockholders are angry, then the CEO resigns, but the game was a lot rougher in the world of organized crime. One man who was pleased with the death of Siegel was FBI Director J. Edgar Hoover, the man Bugsy had called a cocksucker. Said Hoover, "The glamor that surrounded his life in all its vile implications was shockingly disgusting."[37]

ALBERT ANASTASIA, 1957

Albert Anastasia was the last of the Prohibition generation to be cut down by bullets. During the 1920s as a lower-level gun for hire, he did not command a syndicate in the manner of Luciano, Gordon, and Capone. By the 1930s, however, he was established in the waterfront longshoreman rackets and was an underboss in the Magnano family. But he was best known for his proclivities as an assassin. Not for nothing did the newspapers invent a nickname for him: "The Executioner." He was a principal figure in the blood-soaked Brooklyn mob of killers that came to be known as Murder

Incorporated and advised the top New York mobsters on the feasibility of killing Thomas E. Dewey.

At 10:20 A.M. on the morning of October 25, 1957, Anastasia went to a barbershop at the Park Sheraton Hotel at Seventh Avenue and Fifty-fifth Street. Was he aware that three decades before, when the hotel was known as the Park Central, the gambler Arnold Rothstein received his fatal gunshot wound there? Probably not. As he settled into the chair, he asked the barber to give him "the works," which referred to a shave and a haircut, but what he got was quite different from what he expected. Two gunmen entered the barbershop; Meyer Berger, the intrepid *New York Times* reporter, described what happened with a clean, admirable bit of prose: "The trigger-men fired ten shots. Five took effect. The first two caught Anastasia's left hand and left wrist. One tore into his right hip. The fourth got him in the back after he had come out of the chair and had stumbled into the mirror he had been facing as the barber worked. The fifth bullet caught him in the back of the head. Both killers had scarves over the lower part of their faces. They got away."[38] In the same article, Berger described how a squad of policemen and detectives swarmed over the barbershop, vainly seeking for clues to who had committed the murder. The NYPD Chief of Detectives James "Lefty" Leggett was asked, "Why do you think they killed him, Chief?" Leggett replied with a classic understatement: "Maybe somebody didn't like him."

Who was that somebody who didn't like Anastasia? At the time, informed opinion singled out Vito Genovese, and to this day he remains the most likely person who would have arranged for the execution. Genovese was every bit as vicious and brutal as Anastasia. An early associate of Luciano's from before Prohibition, Genovese was the main suspect in a string of murders. One oft-told tale is that after his first wife died, Genovese decided to marry her cousin, Anna Pertillo. The fact that Anna was married to someone else did not bother Genovese; he simply saw to it that the man was strangled to death, and then he married the widow a short time later.[39] Genovese is also thought to have been one of the men who killed the Mafia capo Joe Masseria in 1931; curiously enough Anastasia is said to have been in on that hit as well.[40]

In 1937, having sent Lucky Luciano to prison, Special Prosecutor Thomas E. Dewey went looking for another New York criminal to prosecute, and he set his sights on Genovese. Among other charges against Genovese was the murder a few years earlier of one of his former business partners, Ferdinand Boccia. Only seventeen years old when he arrived in New York from Italy, Genovese had returned to Italy in the intervening years for some drug smuggling so he concluded that fleeing to Italy would be a good way to avoid the wrath of Dewey. He seems to have done well in the old country, supported by $750,000 he reportedly brought with him.[41] He used some of that money to gain favor with the Fascist government. But in July 1943 the Allies invaded Sicily, and in September they fought their way to the Italian mainland. The wily Genovese then switched sides and became an interpreter and general advisor for the American invaders, for which he won a commendation. His real occupation, however, was in a black market operation, where he used stolen army trucks to transport pilfered supplies such as flour, sugar, and salt.

A young American sergeant with the odd name Orange C. Dickey who was assigned to the Criminal Investigation Division stumbled onto the double-dealing of Genovese and the fact that he was a fugitive from American justice. Nobody in the military seemed to care very much about this, but Dickey was finally allowed to bring Genovese back to the United States and deliver him to the district attorney of Brooklyn. Said Genovese to Dickey, "Kid, you are doing me the biggest favor anyone has ever done to me. You are taking me home."[42]

Genovese was put on trial for the murder of Boccia on June 10, 1946, but the evidence was thin; key witnesses had died under suspicious circumstances, leaving insufficient evidence to convict him. The disappointed judge remarked, "I cannot speak for the jury, but I believe that if there were even a shred of corroborating evidence, you would have been condemned to the chair."[43] Genovese was observed to be smiling as he left the courtroom. And so he rejoined the New York Mafia and gradually sought more power. As Joseph Valachi said, "Vito is like a fox. He takes his time."[44] The Fox finally made his move in 1957 with the killing of Anastasia. Twenty days later, a group of roughly sixty Mafia gangsters met in the little rural town of Apalachin, New York, two hundred or so miles from New York City. Crime writers think the meeting was called by Genovese to get approval for his ascension and mark the end of the Anastasia regime. But whatever the goal of the attendees, it was not realized; a squad of state police and federal agents swooped down on the conference, an entrance that caused mobsters to flee through the woods. They were not arrested because a simple gathering of like-minded men did not constitute a crime, but their names were publicized in newspapers. Two years later Genovese was convicted on a charge of dealing in narcotics, a reliable source of fall-back income for many mobsters, and sentenced to fifteen years in Atlanta Federal Prison. He continued his murderous ways and from his jail cell ordered the killings of many of his old enemies. He died in the Atlanta facility in 1969, his dream of Mafia dominance forever beyond his grasp.

CHAPTER 11

Lepke on the Hot Seat

Louis Lepke Buchalter was the "intelligent Hebrew" who became the master of the labor racket in New York, primarily in the city's garment industry (see chapter 3). By the 1930s he had branched out beyond the needle trades to bakeries and flour truckers. He was a leading crime figure; among the attendees at the bar mitzvah of his son were Lucky Luciano, Longie Zwillman, Meyer Lansky, and Bugsy Siegel.[1] He was making millions of dollars a year by ripping off unions and manufacturing establishments. With the death or imprisonment of most of his fellow crime lords, he was one of the last of the headline-grabbing New York bosses who had risen to power during Prohibition. He also has the distinction of being the only one of them to be executed in the electric chair for his crimes.

Lepke's path to the death chamber could be said to have begun with the pelt of the humble rabbit, *Oryctolagus cuniculus.* Fur was a popular fashion item in the 1930s, and, in the face of the Depression, rabbit fur predominated because it was cheaper than mink, fox, and sable. Lepke and his partner Gurrah Shapiro saw this as a business opportunity and took control of the Protective Fur Dressers' Corporation. They looted the dues of the organization and levied a ten-cent surcharge on every one hundred rabbit skins, not a bad deal considering that the furriers processed some twenty to thirty million skins a year.[2] Managers and owners in the fur industry who did not accept this arrangement either were beaten up or their property was destroyed. For example, one furrier had acid thrown in his face, and another was blown up by a car bomb.[3] Federal law enforcement officers realized that they could charge Lepke for violating the Sherman Anti-Trust Act, which made price fixing and restraint of trade illegal. As a side benefit, the U.S. Attorney for the Southern District of New York saw this as a way to grab the crime buster spotlight away from his rival, Special Prosecutor Thomas E. Dewey.

On November 13, 1936, Lepke and Shapiro were each sentenced in federal court to two-year prison terms and fined $10,000. A "slap on the wrist," said the presiding judge.[4] It was indeed a minor punishment, and it became even more ineffectual. Dewey, preparing his own case against the racketeers, went to see U.S. Court of Appeals Judge Martin T. Manton to request that bail be set at a level high enough so that Lepke and Shapiro would not be able to skip town while they appealed their antitrust conviction. Manton nodded sympathetically, but the next day he assigned bail at a measly $10,000 for each man, which they quickly paid and walked out of jail. In fact, Manton subsequently went even further by overturning Lepke's antitrust conviction! The furious Dewey launched an investigation that discovered Manton had been actively accepting bribes in exchange for favorable court decisions. When word of the investigation broke in the newspapers, Manton resigned in shame.[5] Crossing Tom Dewey from Owosso, Michigan, was clearly a losing proposition.

After being released on bail, Lepke's next hurdle was a retrial on the antitrust indictment. The new trial was scheduled for July 6, 1937, and Lepke must have been fretting for some time before the trial. Not only were the Feds after him, but Dewey was also building a case against him. Furthermore, Lepke must have known that he was being investigated by the Federal Bureau of Narcotics for smuggling drugs. Faced with all this, Lepke decided to go on the lam. When he did not show up for the trial he was officially regarded as a fugitive from the law, and in December 1937 he was indicted in absentia by a federal grand jury for narcotics smuggling, and a warrant was issued for his arrest.[6]

ON THE LAM

Lepke's disappearance turned into a long and notorious vanishing act. Dewey saw to it that a million "Wanted Dead or Alive" police circulars were sent out all over the nation. A five-thousand-dollar reward was offered by the state of New York, which eventually grew to fifty thousand dollars, half coming from the federal government and the other half from the state. The FBI designated Lepke Public Enemy Number One, and the New York City Police Department established a squad of detectives to track him down. Numerous rumors circulated about where he was hiding, and the police traveled as far as California and Europe looking for him. But they actually needn't have bothered with these excursions; the fugitive was right under their noses in the borough of Brooklyn, where he shuffled from one hideout to another. Part of his time was spent in an upstairs room at the Oriental Danceland, a name that conjures up exotic, sensual images of slinky Asian beauties, but was essentially an Italian catering hall. Other hiding places included the home of a mob widow. At another time he was allowed to use a first-floor apartment, where for three dollars a week he could meet with his wife.[7] Toward the end of his time in hiding he grew a moustache and wore dark glasses.

What happened to Gurrah Shapiro who, like Lepke, was enmeshed in the coils of the law and also went on the lam? Plagued with illness, he turned himself in on April 14, 1938.

During his time as a lamster, Lepke was looked after by gangsters associated with a gang based in the Brownsville section of Brooklyn. Although the members were mostly Jewish, Italian Albert Anastasia was a leader, and he devoted himself to finding hiding places for Lepke and moving him from place to place. In this he was assisted by one Abe Reles. If you wanted to see Lepke, you would find Reles on a Brooklyn street. Reles, whose nickname was "Kid Twist," would pass along your inquiry to Anastasia who might or might not permit you to visit Lepke. During his hiding, Lepke also made use of the gang's specialty: assassination. For this service the gang was known popularly as Murder Incorporated. Lepke was reported to have the gang on retainer of $12,000 a year,[8] and he used the organization to the hilt when he was undercover. He wanted to eliminate men who posed a danger to him as actual or potential informants to the government. This was not new for Lepke. In the years preceding his disappearance, three men had been killed, probably on his orders. The killing took on a faster pace when he was on the lam. The numbers are not entirely clear, but at least ten were killed and two wounded in this period by Murder Incorporated hit men, and one more killing took place after Lepke was back in custody.

Who were the victims? Virtually all were Jewish and had associated with Buchalter in the rackets. Because of what they knew about Lepke, they represented a threat to him. As Buchalter reportedly said, "All I know is that where there's no witness there's no case."[9] One victim was George Rudnick, a thug from the lower levels of Lepke's garment industry racket who was suspected of being a stool pigeon. Rudnick was lured to a garage where he was strangled, stabbed in the throat with an ice pick, and hit on the head with a meat chopper before he expired.[10] At a higher level on the totem pole was Max Rubin, a top lieutenant in the labor racket and a close confidant of Lepke. At the time Lepke went into hiding he instructed Rubin to leave the city. But Rubin was not happy about being away from his family so he disobeyed his instructions and came back home. For this disobedience Rubin had to be punished, and on October 1, 1937, Rubin was shot in the back of his head. He managed to survive this assault, although he spent more than a month in the hospital. He never fully recovered. Because muscles of his neck had been destroyed his head was permanently off-kilter. It was too bad for Lepke that Rubin survived because, as Lepke had feared, he became a vengeful and important informer. Another botched job was the attack on one Irving Penn, who was shot to death on the street as he was walking to his office at the G. Schirmer's music publishing business. Penn was described as "quiet, mannerly and man of regular habits."[11] It turned out that the Murder Incorporated killers mistook Penn for their actual target, a mobster named Philip Orlovsky, who resembled Penn.

By this time Lepke must have been stressed by life on the lam. He had a kidney ailment that required medical treatment, but police had been staking out the doctors' offices that he might visit. The reward on his head meant that he could not trust anybody he met, and he knew that other mobsters were lusting after his racketeering empire.

If he read the July 29, 1939, *New York Times*, his anxiety level must have increased. The paper carried an article about a press conference given by Dewey the day before. Said Dewey to the assembled reporters: "I am authorized to reveal that for many months the Federal Bureau of Investigation of the United States Department of Justice, the Narcotics Bureau of the United States Treasury Department, the Police Department of the City of New York and my office have been working in a single coordinated effort throughout the whole United States to apprehend Lepke, who is wanted by all of these agencies." Dewey went on to say that, as district attorney, he joined FBI Director J. Edgar Hoover, Federal Narcotics Bureau Director Harry Anslinger, and Chief of the New York Police Department Lewis Valentine in personally directing what the newspaper called a "get-Lepke-at-any-cost" campaign.

The article named the men reportedly murdered by Lepke and said that the D.A.'s office was grilling Philip Orlovsky and Max Rubin. Dewey announced the astonishing plan to have a policeman assigned as a bodyguard to every person in New York City who had been associated with Lepke—probably a move designed to help turn mobsters against the lamster. Perhaps Lepke came to the conclusion that turning himself over to the Feds would give him a better way to maneuver and plea bargain between the various charges of antitrust, dope smuggling, extortion, and murder.

LEPKE SURRENDERS

On August 7 the enormously popular New York City gossip columnist and radio personality Walter Winchell began his 9:00 P.M. program on the CBS radio network with a message directed at the fugitive: "Attention, Public Enemy Number One, Louis 'Lepke' Buchalter! I am authorized by John Edgar Hoover of the Federal Bureau of Investigation to guarantee you safe delivery to the FBI if you surrender to me or any agent for the FBI." Winchell then repeated what he had just said.[12] This was sent as a signal to Lepke. In his autobiography, Winchell said he had been approached two nights before on Broadway by an unnamed associate of gangsters. The unnamed person asked if Winchell could arrange for Lepke to surrender to some law enforcement officer who would not turn him over to Dewey. Winchell than made the arrangements with G-man Hoover. So it was that on the night of August 24, 1939, Lepke came out of hiding.

Several versions describe how the surrender was accomplished; the standard one is that Lepke was driven by the ever-faithful Albert Anastasia from Brooklyn to Twenty-eighth Street and Fifth Avenue in Manhattan. Anastasia parked behind another car. Lepke got out and walked to that car, where Winchell was waiting. J. Edgar Hoover, who had been watching nearby, then entered the car. Said Winchell, "Mr. Hoover, this is Lepke." To which Hoover replied, "How do you do?" Keeping up the polite tone, Lepke said, "Glad to meet you. Let's go." Hoover then directed the driver to proceed to the Federal Court House in Foley Square. As they drove along, it might have entered Lepke's head that he had made a terrible mistake. He had surrendered to Hoover in the belief that there was a deal in place that would have him tried only in a federal court and only on the narcotics charge, enabling him to avoid being prosecuted on state charges by Dewey. But what if there was no such deal?[13] If that's what he thought, then he was dead-on correct.

How had Lepke come to the false belief that such a deal had been struck? One theory suggests that the story was cooked up by the FBI to motivate the fugitive to come out of hiding. A different theory that has some authority came from Burton B. Turkus, an assistant Brooklyn D.A., who claimed his information came from an underworld informer. Turkus said that the impetus for the surrender came not from the FBI; rather, the mob itself cooked up the idea that a deal had been struck shielding Lepke from Dewey. Turkus stated further that when his underworld colleagues presented the idea to Lepke, Albert Anastasia was strongly against it and advised Lepke to remain in hiding. One flaw mars the Turkus theory—if Anastasia knew it was a trap, then why didn't he reveal that directly to Lepke?[14]

Winchell later offered an anecdote that sheds light on this issue. The columnist said that at Lepke's request, he went to visit him in jail. He was ushered into the cell where Lepke, his wife, and his attorney were waiting. The prisoner asked, "Did you ever tell my friends that if I came in I would only get ten years—and if I had a good behavior record, I'd get out in five or six?" Winchell replied, "I never told that to anybody. I said between twelve and fifteen." Lepke leaped up and banged his fist on the table, yelling, "That's what I thought! I knew it, I knew it!" Winchell left the cell, with the gangster's curses ringing in his ears.[15] Another unanswered question is whose idea it was to ask Walter Winchell to arrange the surrender. Anastasia? Costello? Zwillman? Whoever came up with the idea, Winchell turned out to be the right person. The columnist was close to Hoover. The two men dined together at the Stork Club, and in his newspaper column Winchell frequently praised the publicity-loving Hoover. If anybody could persuade the FBI chief to drive through Manhattan in the same car with Public Enemy Number One, it was Winchell. The idea of surrendering to Hoover and Winchell must have at first been reassuring to Lepke; it would ensure that he would not be killed in some kind of trumped-up "shot while trying to escape" execution.

On Trial Again

In late 1939, Lepke went on trial in a federal court on a drug smuggling charge. The case against him for that crime dated back to 1937, when the Federal Narcotics Bureau director Harry Anslinger received an unsigned letter from a female tipster, who subsequently called the Bureau to request a private meeting away from Anslinger's office. Anslinger agreed, and they met over drinks at the bar of a local Washington, D.C., hotel. The tipster turned out to be a woman in her mid-thirties whose boyfriend had been cheating on her; to get revenge she wanted to provide the Narcotics Bureau with information about the drug smuggling ring in which the boyfriend was involved. From this tip the details of a remarkable criminal narcotics enterprise emerged. The ring began operating in 1935, when some associates of Lepke's went to Shanghai to find a source of heroin that could be smuggled into the United States. The narcotic was shipped to France as bogus luggage that was loaded on the *Queen Mary* and other passenger ships bound for New York. By paying off government inspectors, official customs stamps were obtained for sticking on the luggage when it arrived at the New York piers. The luggage then made its way to a distributor. As the brains behind the ring, Lepke received half of the profits. From 1935 to 1937 there were six smuggling voyages, which were estimated in total to be worth ten million dollars in street value.[16] The part of all this that provided some minor titillation to newspaper readers was the fact that attractive young women were sometimes used as couriers by the smuggling ring.

The government was able to gather enough evidence on the smuggling charge to indict thirty-one mobsters, including Lepke, in December 1937. Because Lepke was on the lam at that time, his trial was postponed. When he was finally held in federal custody, his date in court began in December 1939, and as expected, he was found guilty and sentenced to fourteen years. Lepke now had to face a New York State trial for extortion. Manhattan District Attorney Thomas E. Dewey did not waste a minute. Two days after being sentenced in federal court, Lepke stood in another courtroom with eight codefendants to be arraigned before a state judge on a charge of extortion in the bakery and flour trucking industries. The start of his trial was delayed by legal maneuvering and finally opened on January 24, 1940, after the charge had been expanded to include the garment industry racket. A blow against Lepke came early on in the trial when his co-defendant William "Wolfie" Goldis pled guilty. According to the newspapers, Lepke became red in the face, once again pounded the table, and hissed "You dirty rat" to the turncoat.[17] Goldis became a major prosecution witness in the trial. Another damaging defense witness was Max Rubin, the former aide who had been shot in the neck for disobedience. On March 6 the jury found Lepke guilty; his sentence was thirty years to life. And so Lepke returned to federal prison to serve his fourteen-year narcotics sentence, after which his thirty-to-life term would kick in.

This was the last criminal case for Dewey, who now focused his attention on being elected governor of New York in 1942. For Lepke, his fate was about to be decided by a different prosecutor, William O'Dwyer, the district attorney of Kings County, known more commonly as the borough of Brooklyn. An Irish-born immigrant to New York, O'Dwyer had worked as a day laborer, a policeman, a lawyer, judge, and in 1939 was elected as a reforming D.A. O'Dwyer was a loyal Democrat, but he chose as his assistant D.A. for felony and homicide the Republican lawyer Burton Turkus, who O'Dwyer had come to know in the Brooklyn courts. Thanks to the depredations of Murder Incorporated, Brooklyn had a high homicide rate, especially in the Brownsville–East New York area. Turkus kept track of it on a map of the borough on his office wall, with pins sticking where killings had taken place. Under the previous D.A., painfully few convictions had been obtained. O'Dwyer had run on the promise to crack down on criminals, and right after he took office he got the police to arrest twenty-two known hoodlums, who were charged with vagrancy. It was a somewhat futile gesture because the hoods could only be held on that charge for a maximum of ninety days before they were back on the streets.

The Stool Pigeons of Murder Incorporated

But then came a break. An elderly criminal being held in the City Work-house on Rikers Island for another charge, one Harry Rudolph, offered to provide information to the DA on the murder of a friend of his, one Alex "Red" Alpert who had been killed some years before. Rudolph named Red's killers: Abe Reles, Buggsy Goldstein, and Anthony Maffatore. Assistant DA Turkus took this evidence to a grand jury and got indictments. Maffatore was the weakest of the trio, and to encourage him to talk he was placed in solitary confinement, which motivated him to identify another possible stool pigeon, Abe "Pretty" Levine, who at first refused to cooperate but changed his mind once Turkus put his wife in jail. This trickle of informing became a flood when the wife of Abe Reles came to tell the DA that her husband wanted to talk. Reles, a stumpy, shifty-eyed professional killer, was high in the Murder Incorporated hierarchy and literally knew where the bodies were buried. Reles spent twelve days in nonstop confessions about the inner workings of Murder Incorporated, unsolved murders, crime bosses, and other hitherto unknown information. His words were taken down by a team of weary stenographers who produced twenty-four notebooks in shorthand. "Reles's song," said Turkus, "was a full-length opera."[18] In exchange for this data dump, Reles was able to wring from the district attorney the promise that he would be immune from prosecution for the crimes he described. One high-level crime figure outed by Reles was Albert "Tick Tock" Tannenbaum, a hit man in the service of Lepke. He was interrogated by the Brooklyn D.A.'s office and added more information to supplement what Reles had spilled.

From this new information, the D.A.'s office felt confident enough to put Lepke on trial for murder. His codefendants were two Murder Incorporated figures, Mendy Weiss and Louis Capone. (Mendy was not related to Chicago's Hymie Weiss, and Louis was not related to Chicago's Al Capone.) A conviction was not a 100-percent certainty. The State of New York Criminal Code specified that "a conviction cannot be had upon the testimony of an accomplice, unless he is corroborated by such other evidence as tends to connect the defendant with the commission of the crime."[19] This set a high bar for the prosecution, and the D.A.'s office had to select a Brooklyn murder that could be convincingly tied to the defendants. The case they chose was the grisly 1936 murder of one Joseph Rosen, the owner of a small Brownsville candy store. Another hurdle the D.A. faced was to get Lepke into a Brooklyn courtroom. He was in the federal penitentiary in Leavenworth serving out his sentence for narcotics smuggling, and it was necessary to get the approval of both the federal director of prisons to turn him over and a federal judge to overrule the objections of Lepke's attorney. The next hurdle was to assemble a jury. It took an

nd two alternates, presumably hensive about sitting in judg-began on October 20, 1941, in

of Joe Rosen. The man had as a cog in Lepke's garment meeting one day where he his major customers because pping into Garfield Express, a nership. Rosen, realizing this ke for a break. There was an with some small-time jobs, vhat money he could find to make a living to support his

ate corporation that down-entered when word reached

was talking to Dewey. Lepke offered $200 to Rosen to go away for a while, but Rosen came back to Brooklyn and that angered the boss. Witness Max Rubin quoted Lepke as saying, "I stood enough of this crap. That son of a bitch Rosen, that bastard—he's around again, and shooting off his mouth about seeing Dewey. He and nobody else is going any place and do any talking. I'll take care of him."[20] An additional prosecution witness was Paul Berger, who had worked in Lepke's garment industry racket. He testified that Lepke had asked him to drive to Brooklyn with Mendy Weiss, another Murder Incorporated killer; Berger's job was to point out Rosen. Berger was asked if the purpose was for Rosen to be killed. He replied that he thought Rosen was just going to be beaten up.[21] Still another Murder Incorporated thug, Sholem Bernstein, testified for the prosecution that he had helped Louis Capone, Mendy Weiss, and Philip "Pep" Strauss with the arrangements for the Rosen murder and had driven the getaway car. At the time of the trial, Pep was behind bars, having been convicted of another murder.[22]

Turkus had to prove the connection between Lepke and the murderers of Rosen. It was not enough to say that Lepke had been furious at Rosen and that Rosen had subsequently been killed. There had to be some stronger link. For that reason Turkus, over the objection of the defense lawyers, brought Albert Tannenbaum to the witness stand. Tannenbaum described how, on the day after the murder, he was in Lepke's office when Mendy Weiss came in. "Was everything all right?" Lepke asked Weiss, to which Weiss replied that the murder went well, except for the fact that "after I shoot Rosen, and he is laying there, on the floor, Pep starts shooting him"—in other words, Pep had kept on firing his gun even after the victim was dead. According to Tannenbaum, what Lepke said next was, "All right, what's the difference? As long as everybody is clean and you got away all right."[23]

Turkus wrote later about Tannenbaum's dramatic courtroom statement, "For perhaps a dozen seconds, you could have heard a beetle blink its eyes in that courtroom."[24] Tannenbaum had provided the needed link between Lepke and Weiss in the killing of Rosen. But Louis Capone was still off the hook. Turkus addressed that issue when he brought Seymour "Blue Jaw" Magoon, another Murder Incorporated gunman, into court to discuss a conversation he had with Capone several years after the Rosen murder. Capone and Magoon had been talking about killing one Whitey Friedman and got into a discussion about whether Capone might be recognized because he lived in the neighborhood. According to Magoon, Capone said he wasn't worried. "Why, I worked on the Rosen thing, and it was right on Sutter Avenue, and I wasn't recognized."[25] Turkus wanted the jury to understand that Capone's alleged statement about the "Rosen thing" established his guilt.

In the defense stage of the trial, Lepke's lawyer argued that his client was being framed because of his notoriety and that Rosen's business was failing even before Lepke was supposed to have ruined him. The defense also disputed a key date when Max Rubin and Albert Tannenbaum were supposed to have met with Lepke about punishing Rosen. Mendy Weiss's attorney argued that on the night before the murder, when his client was allegedly casing the candy store neighborhood, he had actually been celebrating his brother's birthday with others at a dinner and show. Curiously, Capone's lawyer did not present any defense for his client, which surprised Turkus who thought that the skimpy evidence against Capone was the weakest part of the prosecution's case. After hearing from fifty-two witnesses, the trial ended. The case went to the jury on at 10:00 P.M. on November 30, 1941. Four and one-half hours later the jury filed back into the courtroom with a guilty verdicts for Lepke, Weiss, and Capone. At the sentencing, Judge Franklin Taylor took just nine minutes to sentence all three to be executed at Sing Sing Prison.

And what about Abe "Kid Twist" Reles, whose testimony had helped to bring down Murder Incorporated? Turkus was considering calling him as a prosecution witness, but that never happened.[26] The Kid died while the trial was in progress. On November 12, he either jumped or fell or was pushed out of a sixth-floor window at the Half Moon Hotel on Coney Island, where he was being held in protective custody by the NYPD. It is probable that he was murdered for being a stool pigeon. He earned fame in the history of the underworld as the canary who sang but couldn't fly. As with so many other aspects of mobster history, there has been speculation about who was responsible for the death of Reles. Maybe the cops who guarded him were bribed to kill him by mob bosses, or maybe one of the guards got into a fight with Reles and accidentally killed him, or maybe mob hit men snuck past the guards and did the job, or maybe the other gangsters who were under custody in the same hotel did it to protect themselves. Joe Valachi, another stool pigeon, made the caustic observation, "I never met anybody who thought Abe went out the window because he wanted to."[27]

There was an interesting incident from the time Reles was a living stool pigeon helping the authorities. On January 8, 1941, New York City detectives and FBI agents were interrogating one Lewis Martarello, the proprietor of the Oriental Danceland where for a time Lepke had been hiding. Martarello stated that he did not know Lepke, Anastasia, or Reles and went even further by denying that he had anything to do with the Danceland whatsoever, that the real owners were his brothers-in-law who had used Martarello's name on the license. This interrogation was taking place in the D.A.'s library room in the Brooklyn Municipal Building. The transcript records that there was an interruption when one of the detectives left the room and returned with none other than the stool pigeon Abe Reles himself, who was in custody in some other part of the building. Reles blithely told the interrogators that he had known Martarello for a decade and had often seen the man in the Oriental Danceland. The transcript concludes with a stern notation: "It was evident that Martarello was lying."[28]

To return to Lepke's murder trial, Judge Taylor had selected January 4, 1942, as the date for the executions of Lepke, Capone, and Weiss, but that date quickly came and went. Part of the delay was owing to appeals by the defense lawyers that twice reached all the way to the U.S. Supreme Court, only to be turned down. But much of the delay was due to the reluctance of federal lawmen to turn Lepke over to the New York authorities until he had completed his fourteen-year narcotics sentence. In fact, there had been tension between the Feds and the New York lawmen ever since Lepke had surrendered to the FBI back in August 1939 and Dewey's request to interview the prisoner was denied. In November 1943, by which time Dewey was governor, he charged that the president of the United States, Franklin Roosevelt, was protecting the mob boss from receiving the punishment that was due him. New York decided not to execute Capone and Weiss until Lepke could join them in Sing Sing.

As the months and years dragged on, accusations arose about the political aspect of this tangle. Franklin Roosevelt was seeking reelection in 1944; Governor Dewey was his likely Republican opponent. Labor unions were a major part of the liberal coalition that had kept Roosevelt in the White House for three terms, and Sidney Hillman, a noted force in the unionization of New York's garment industry, had been given high-level positions in the administration. Back in his tough union-building days in the 1920s, Hillman, like other labor leaders, had been involved with the rising labor racketeer Lepke Buchalter. For conspiracy buffs the implication was obvious: Roosevelt feared that if Lepke were released to New York, Dewey would set up a clemency hearing during which the dark deeds of Hillman would come to the surface and embarrass the president. This was the conclusion of Westbrook Pegler, a popular anti–New Deal newspaper columnist.[29]

Death Row

Finally, a deal was struck: the federal government turned Lepke over to New York on the condition that if Dewey commuted Lepke's sentence to life, the mob boss would have to be returned to federal custody to finish the remaining years of his narcotics sentence and then bounce back to a New York prison to live out the remainder of his life. Thus, Lepke finally wound up on death row in Sing Sing. But still the defense attorneys put forward appeals to keep their clients alive. At one point Lepke, Weiss, and Capone had eaten their last meals and were less than two hours away from execution. (They did not eat together, having been carefully kept apart in Sing Sing.) As the fatal hour approached, Governor Dewey ordered a two-day stay of execution because the U.S. Supreme Court wanted to consider a habeas corpus petition. Once the petition was turned down, the execution clock resumed. On March 4, 1944, the three once again ate their separate final meals. Then, one at a time, they were brought into the execution chamber, strapped into the electric chair, and killed with a jolt of 2,200 volts. The doctor confirmed each man's death, the room was tidied up, and the next convicted man was brought in. Capone was executed first, Weiss second, and Lepke third. The intelligent Hebrew offered no last words.

In his book *The Rise and Fall of the Jewish Gangster in America*, Albert Fried presented an interesting spin on Lepke Buchalter's life and death and how it all might have ended differently. Here is his scenario: During the New Deal of the 1930s the National Recovery Administration created industrywide cartels that brought together management and labor to set wages and prices. Garment industry labor unions flourished after the NRA, which helped bring about a measure of economic security. Fried says that Lepke's labor rackets sought to do something similar. Lepke might conceivably have survived as something of a respected pioneer of the labor movement, the crimes of his turbulent youth forgotten. What prevented that from happening, says Fried, was Thomas E. Dewey's resolute quest to bring down Lepke and so put pressure on his gang members and associates; Fried describes Dewey "calling them in repeatedly, threatening them with dire punishments, never ceasing to harass them, and when these failed, indicting then en masse." As a result, Lepke, driven underground, fought back with a campaign of murdering potential witnesses that brought him to the electric chair.[30] In accusing Dewey, Fried does not exonerate Lepke for his crimes, but Fried does point out how there might have been a different outcome. Perhaps so, but the image of Lepke eliminating people who annoyed him (like the pathetic Rosen), muscling in on legitimate and illegitimate business to demand a 50 percent share, and funneling dues designed to improve working conditions into his own wallet makes it difficult to imagine him as anything other than a murderous criminal and a chiseler.

CHAPTER 12

For Them, Crime Did Pay

Many members of the Prohibition generation passed from the scene prematurely: Al Capone, who died a syphilitic death; Longie Zwillman, a suicide in his basement; Lepke Buchalter, strapped into the electric chair; Albert Anastasia, shot to death in a barbershop; and the Lonardo and Porrello families of Cleveland, locked in a murderous feud. But some survived into old age, with a degree of dignity, at least some money to sustain them, and people who loved them. In a sense these survivors had achieved the best outcome we mortals can aspire to in our limited lifespans. For the fortunate men described in this chapter, crime actually paid off.

Meyer Lansky

Lansky was the longtime ally of Lucky Luciano, an alliance that endured beyond Prohibition to the palmy days in pre-Castro Cuba. With his head for numbers and reliability as a business partner, Lansky was valued in the world of organized crime and, especially after Prohibition, in both racetracks and the luxurious casinos known as "rug joints." He went into other, semilegitimate enterprises, among them a grocery store in Hoboken and a jukebox distribution business in New York bars.

One person who worked for him in the jukebox firm (circa 1945–1946) was Harriett Bloom, an attractive young woman in her mid-twenties. Bloom recalls Lansky as being soft-spoken, polite, businesslike, and much admired by the employees. Bloom also recalls that when she picked up the phone she heard clicking noises. She contacted the phone company about the problem and was blithely informed by an operator that the phone was being tapped. It was, of course, law enforcement, seeking incriminating information on Lansky that could be used to prosecute him--a fact hinted at in later FBI files.[1]

In 1951, Senator Estes Kefauver described Lansky as a top mobster, a leader of the "eastern crime syndicate."[2] When he was faced with similar government investigations, Longie Zwillman had committed suicide, but Lansky tried a different tactic. On July 27, 1970, he fled to Israel, a country with a "law of return," which enables a Jew to become an Israeli citizen. A provision of the law, however, specified that criminals who posed a threat to the public were not entitled to citizenship. Lansky spent two years, three months, and thirteen days in the country, much of it engaged in the legal campaign to admit him to citizenship on the grounds that the evidence of his criminal past was weak. Working against Lansky was the opposition of the U.S. government, which wanted him back in the States to stand trial. Ultimately, the Supreme Court of Israel turned down his citizenship request, a decision that forced him to leave the country. When his flight arrived in Miami, on November 7, 1972, he was arrested by the FBI. The situation was bleak. He was seventy years old and in poor health. He faced three charges that could bring him jail sentences: income tax evasion, contempt of court, and skimming casino profits. Lansky's talented attorney, David Rosen, used his considerable skill in the courtroom to get Lansky acquitted of all the charges.

Lansky spent his last years in Miami. Like any elderly man, he reflected on the good and the bad in his life. He was proud of his son Paul, who was a graduate of West Point, but saddened when his son divorced his wife and Lansky was cut off from contact with his grandchildren. Lansky also bore the burden of his elder son, Bernard, who was afflicted with steadily worsening paralysis. Money was another problem for the retired gangster. A best-selling 1971 accusatory biography of Lansky by Hank Messick claimed that the gangster had a personal fortune of $300 million—a claim that was firmly accepted by the media and the government. A second biography, written twenty years later by Robert Lacey, was much more sympathetic to the mobster and convincingly presents evidence that Messick was simply wrong. According to Lacey, Lansky lost a significant amount of money when Castro's revolution shut down the Cuban casino operations, and he incurred expenses from failed business ventures and continuing legal expenses. In his last years, Lansky was somewhat strapped for cash and lived in modest housing.

There were compensations. Lansky had divorced his first wife, Anna, in 1947, and in the following year married Thelma "Teddy" Schwartz, said to have been a hotel manicurist. Teddy gave him unwavering emotional support. Lansky also had longtime friends in Miami with whom he played gin rummy and kibitzed. On several occasions in 1981 he gathered with a group to watch the NBC television miniseries *The Gangster Chronicles*, in which actors played the parts of Luciano, Siegel, and Lansky. Lansky and his friends found the series hilarious.[3] He drew sustenance from his membership in a local synagogue.

His ailments finally overcame him, and the old mobster passed away on January 15, 1983. The cause of death was lung cancer, the result of years of smoking three packs of cigarettes a day. His family came to his bedside at the hospital. It was painful death; his last coherent words to Teddy were a heart-wrenching plea:"Let me go."[4] His death can be seen as the end of the long tradition of Jews in organized crime.

OWNEY MADDEN

The Irish bootlegger who carried the nickname "Killer" dropped out of the New York crime scene around 1935 and set up residence in Hot Springs, Arkansas. Crime writer T. J. English believes Madden realized that Irish gangsters were being eliminated and that it was a wise time for him to depart; another theory is that he was ill. But Hot Springs was not some isolated health resort far from the reach of the underworld. It was in fact a wide-open town, where a corrupt city government protected gambling and prostitution and where gangsters could go to evade the law and also play golf unmolested. (For example, Lucky Luciano went to Hot Springs in 1936 to fight a warrant from prosecutor Tom Dewey.) Madden ran criminal operations in Hot Springs with money invested by Frank Costello and Meyer Lansky, which indicates he had made his peace with the underworld.

He was a respected citizen in a disreputable town. He married the daughter of a former postmaster, and they lived in a rose-covered bungalow near Saint John's Catholic Church and contributed to local charities. He had a speedboat that he ran on the lake. Madden lived in the town for three decades, until his death from chronic emphysema in 1965 at age seventy-three. In a eulogy given by the side of Madden's coffin, a local dignitary proclaimed, "This community's prosperity and welfare were uppermost in the heart of this man, who for thirty years has given his all to Hot Springs. We know not and care not what they said about him in New York, Chicago, or Washington."[5]

Moe Dalitz

In Prohibition Cleveland, Dalitz was the senior partner in an ensemble that invested in legal and illegal businesses, leaving the blood feuds and violence to the Italian gangs in the city. After repeal, Dalitz branched out beyond Cleveland and opened illegal casinos in Kentucky and Ohio. After a stint in the army during the World War II, he moved to Las Vegas, where gambling was legal. Where Bugsy Siegel had crashed and burned, Dalitz built an empire. He was a partner in the Desert Inn casino in Vegas, the Rancho La Costa resort in Southern California, and other successful real estate development ventures. In the 1980s he was listed in *Forbes* magazine as one of the four hundred wealthiest Americans.

But all this was not without controversy. Continually dogged by his mob background, he was investigated in the early 1950s by the Kefauver Committee. The FBI kept tabs on Dalitz as part of its focus on criminal activities in Las Vegas, especially the practice of "skimming" casino profits to benefit underworld investors. He was later accused of both receiving money from the corrupt Teamsters Union pension fund and paying off national politicians. He was furious when a best-selling 1963 Las Vegas expose, *The Green Felt Jungle*, called him "the sanctimonious little mobster from Cleveland."[6] In 1975 he sued *Penthouse* magazine for libel when it ran an article entitled "La Costa: The Hundred-Million Dollar Resort with Criminal Clientele." The libel case ran for a decade before all parties agreed to bring it to a halt. In the course of the trial, the lawyers for *Penthouse* cited Dalitz's association with mobsters to prove that he himself was one. Dalitz dismissed this accusation with the remark, "If I shook hands with the Duke of Windsor, it didn't make me a duke."[7]

Whether out of a sincere charitable interest or as a way of striking back at his critics, Dalitz became a leading philanthropist, donating millions to the United Way, the American Cancer Research Center, the University of Nevada, the Anti-Defamation League of B'nai B'rith, and other civic and charitable organizations. His fund, to be divided among nonprofit charities when he died, provided the organizations $1.3 million.[8] For his generosity he won honorific titles from grateful recipients, like "Grand Patron of the Arts" and "Humanitarian of the Year"—quite different from the usual gangster nicknames.

Moe Dalitz died on August 31, 1989, from kidney failure and congestive heart disease. His age at death was uncertain; most likely he was eighty-nine or ninety.

Frank Costello

The statement "This is for you, Frank!" is one of the best-known lines in the history of twentieth-century American crime. The Frank in question was Frank Costello, the well-dressed and well-respected mobster who formed the basis of Damon Runyon's fictional character Dave the Dude and who became known as the "prime minister" of the underworld for his negotiating abilities.

The "this is for you" statement was uttered at about 10:55 P.M. on Thursday, May 24, 1957, in the lobby of the Majestic Apartments at 115 Central Park West in Manhattan where Costello lived. He was heading toward the elevator after a typical day of getting a haircut and shoeshine, cutting deals, and dining at elite eateries. The gunman in the lobby uttered the words and fired a shot at the gangster's head from a distance of six to ten feet. Costello was fortunate—he was just grazed by the bullet. But the wound produced a quantity of blood, and he was taken to Roosevelt Hospital. When detectives came to the hospital to interrogate him, Costello followed the code of silence by refusing to say who shot him and why. "I haven't an enemy in the world," he said, an obvious bald-faced lie, given the fact that a short time before someone had tried to kill him.[9]

He had other enemies, including the government of the United States. Like Lansky, Costello had become a nationally known figure after his inter-rogation by the Kefauver Committee in 1951. The hearing revealed the details of his investments, including a slot machine franchise he ran in Louisiana after the crusading Mayor Fiorello LaGuardia shut down the business in New York. The hearing also disclosed his vast influence over politicians in New York. One bombshell was the transcript of a wire tap on his phone, in which a candidate for a high-level judgeship said to Costello, "I want to assure you of my loyalty for all you have done; it's undying."[10] The Feds went after Costello for income tax evasion and contempt of Congress. They were able to pin an additional crime against the Italian-born Costello—that he should be stripped of his American citizenship and deported to Italy. The basis of the citizenship charge was the fact that in 1925, when Costello filled out his naturalization application, he did not reveal his bootlegging opera-tions. All of these charges resulted in numerous trials and appeals that went all the way to the U.S. Supreme Court. During this time he received various prison sentences, including eighteen months on the contempt of Congress charge, five years for income tax evasion, and thirty days for contempt of a New York grand jury. The deportation attempt was abandoned when the government of Italy stated it would refuse to admit Costello.

In the midst of all this legal turmoil came the murder attempt in the lobby of the Majestic Apartments. The consensus among crime writers is that Vito Genovese, who was seeking to eliminate rivals to his rise in the Mafia, arranged the Costello shooting during the same campaign that lead to the deaths of Willie Moretti and Albert Anastasia. Costello was a powerful figure who had taken over Lucky Luciano's crime family after Lucky went to prison, and it made sense for the ambitious Genovese to move up the ladder by having Costello killed. What happened next? Crime writer Selwyn Raab says that Costello simply went to Genovese and told his rival that he was going to relinquish power and retire.[11] Costello's power was on the decline anyway, and the shooting gave him the excuse to step down.

In the search for the lobby shooter, the doorman at the Majestic Apartments was shown photos of criminals and identified Vincent "the Chin" Gigante, a henchman of Vito Genovese, as the man in the lobby who fired the shot. Gigante went on trial for attempted murder. Costello was called as a witness but stoutly refused to corroborate the doorman's story. Crime writer Fred J. Cook feels that this was a sign of Costello's obeisance to Genovese. When Gigante was acquitted by the jury on May 27, 1958, according to an observer, he came over and shook Costello's hand with a heartfelt "Thanks, Frank."[12] The same observer said that at a later date he saw the Chin cheerfully enjoying a dinner party thrown by Costello.[13] In the world of organized crime an attempted murder did not prevent bygones from being bygones.

Costello finally finished his last prison sentence in 1961 and spent the rest of his life in retirement. Like Dalitz, but on a lesser scale, he donated money to charities. He had a loving relationship with his wife Bobbie, so loving in fact that Bobbie overlooked the fact that her husband had a long-term relationship with a mistress. He continued to stroll down Central Park West, dined with his friends at the best restaurants, and wore the finest clothes. He and Bobbie spent weekends at a home they maintained in Sands Point, Long Island, where he enjoyed gardening. He died at Doctor's Hospital on February 19, 1973, from a coronary.

JOSEPH BONANNO

The last of the Prohibition crime lords to die was Joseph Bonanno. The only mobster to make it into the twenty-first century, he passed away in 2002 in the ninety-seventh year of his life. There is some irony here: he outlasted Luciano, Costello, Lansky, and his other gangster colleagues. Of all the Prohibition gangsters, he was the one who seems to have been most wedded to the long-ago traditions of the Sicilian Mafia, a tradition that to him meant "family ties, trust, loyalty, obedience."[14] Bonanno felt that those noble traditions had been bastardized in money-grubbing America.

In the early 1930s, Bonanno had been named the boss of one of the five New York crime families, although he much preferred the term "father" because it was more paternal and less mercenary than "boss." He maintained his leadership for more than three decades, longer than any of the other four leaders. He may have attributed this to his benevolent leadership, but crime writer Selwyn Raab paints a darker picture of Bonanno—an ambitious gangster whose cunning enabled him to stay on top. In the 1960s, says Raab, Bonanno had set out contracts on the lives of his rivals. But when the plan backfired, he became the target of a revolt.[15] This started a power struggle that became known as the "Bananas War." During this period Bonanno, under investigation by New York lawmen, had received a subpoena to testify before a New York grand jury on October 20, 1964, but he never showed up. The night before, he later claimed, two men grabbed him off the Park Avenue sidewalk in Manhattan and hustled him face down on the floor of an automobile. His version of what happened next is that his kidnappers drove him to a farmhouse in rural upstate New York, where he discovered his captor was his cousin, mobster Stefano Magaddino. After six weeks of captivity he was let go. He decided to stay out of the limelight and secretly went to a home he maintained in Tucson, Arizona. He then grew a beard and disguised himself with an eye patch and cane so he could go to Brooklyn to meet quietly with his supporters. He also traveled to safe houses in Long Island and upstate New York. There was much speculation about where was hiding, and rumors circulated that he had gone back to Sicily or maybe to Canada or California. After being out of the public eye for nineteen months he appeared in New York to answer the charges against him for avoiding his grand jury subpoena.

There is doubt that a kidnapping actually took place. Even the wanted posters issued by the New York City police expressed uncertainty: "WANTED AS AN ALLEGED VICTIM OF A KIDNAPPING." Skeptics believe that the abduction story was false and that he went into hiding to save his skin from the police, the FBI, and rival mobsters. A friend of Bonanno in his later years said that the gangster had told her he faked the abduction.[16] Whether he was really kidnapped or went into hiding under his own steam, it is likely that at some point he met with other Mafia bosses to negotiate his retirement from the leadership. Bonanno contended that, if he were killed, a full-scale gang war would erupt so he proposed that the other bosses should simply allow him to step down and quietly retire in Arizona. He promised, under threat of death, to stay away from the New York mob, and he abided by the terms.[17]

He was sixty-three years old when he retired, but tumultuous times lay ahead. At various times his home phone and nearby payphones were tapped by lawmen, his garbage was stolen for analysis, his house was searched, he was befriended by people who were secret informers for the FBI, his two grown sons were imprisoned for their own illegal activities, his house was bombed, his wife died, and he developed a serious heart condition. When he was in his seventies he served a year in prison for conspiracy to obstruct justice; in his early eighties he served fourteen months for refusing to be a witness in a federal racketeering case.

But it was not all bad. Bonanno found that prominent Arizona businessmen and politicians sought his company, and he observed that they did so to tell others that they were friends with the underworld celebrity and to get funding for business deals. In his seventies the widower Bonanno had a passionate sexual relationship with a widow, Theresa D'Antonio.[18] In 1995 he celebrated his ninetieth birthday. Three hundred guests attended the celebration, and Bonanno spoke at length about his life. He died seven years later and was given a prominent funeral at the local Catholic church.

Proud of his education in Italy Bonanno was known to launch into issues of philosophy and ethics. To satisfy that side of his life, he wrote an autobiography—the only top American gangster from the Prohibition generation to do so. In 1983 he published the story of his life, *A Man of Honor*, written with journalist Sergio Lalli. Among other things, he praised his own character and stated that he had refused to be involved in immoral activity such as narcotics smuggling. (A gangster who heard about that boast said into his wiretapped phone, "Like he says he ain't never been in narcotics, he's full of shit. . . . He was making piles of money.")[19]

Much of his book was devoted to his belief in the purity of the Mafia tradition he had come from and how he regretted the decline of that tradition in not only the United States but also Italy. But he offered a chilling sort of hope: "If society breaks down in the future, however, who knows if the pure Mafioso spirit will blaze again?"[20]

ORGANIZED CRIME IN PERSPECTIVE

The generation of Capone, Costello, Lansky, Luciano, Madden, and their contemporaries is long gone. They were the sons of immigrants in a world different from what their fathers had known. On a scale never before seen in America, they used ingenuity and initiative to build large and complex criminal organizations. Their universe included transatlantic smuggling, alliances with politicians, infiltration of unions, and massive bribery of law enforcement. Underlying it all was a calculated willingness to kill those who got in their way.

What has happened in the criminal world since Prohibition? One important development has been that local judges, juries, and police departments, which were once so easily manipulated, have now been replaced by the agencies of the federal government as the main force in the prosecution of organized crime.[21] Federal prosecutors now have tools beyond what Thomas E. Dewey could employ, notably the Racketeer Influenced and Corrupt Organizations (RICO) laws and the Witness Protection Program.

The Italian and Jewish makeup of organized crime has given way to gangsters from Africa, Asia, and Latin America. The fear of a centrally controlled American organized crime syndicate has been replaced by the fear of international criminal cartels in the financial industry that can move money from continent to continent; money usable for narcotics, weapons, and other illegal purposes.[22] The ancient battle between law enforcers and law breakers continues to evolve, like the unending arms race between predators and prey in the natural world.

Cast of Characters

Bonanno, Joseph "Joe Bananas" (1905–2002): New York Mafia leader who was a follower of Salvatore Maranzano; became the capo of one of New York's five families in 1931, later forced out by rivals.

Buchalter, Louis Lepke (1897–1944): New York labor racketeer; the only major gangster to be executed in the electric chair; for many years a partner of Jacob "Gurrah" Shapiro.

Burke, Fred (1893–1940): Gangster who got his start in St. Louis; later became a member of the Capone Outfit in Chicago; suspect in the Saint Valentine's Day massacre.

Capone, Alphonse "Scarface" (1899–1947): The most famous gangster in American history who brought his older brothers Frank and Ralph into the gang; grew up in Brooklyn and relocated to Chicago where he became the dominant figure in the Chicago underworld; first man to be named Public Enemy Number One; went to prison for income tax evasion.

Cohen, Louis (d. 1939): Also known as Louis Kushner; minor New York criminal known mainly for assassinating Nathan "Kid Dropper" Orgen outside a Manhattan courthouse in 1923; probably put up to the job by Louis Lepke Buchalter and Gurrah Shapiro.

Coll, Vincent (1908–1932): New York crime figure noted for his independence from the established gangs and for his erratic and violent behavior; known as "Baby Killer" for accidentally killing a five-year-old child in a shootout; shot to death in a Manhattan phone booth.

Costello, Frank (1891–1973): Birth name Francisco Castiglia; major New York City gangster who took over Luciano's Mafia family; got his start in bootlegging and slot machines and developed strong political connections with Tammany Hall; known as the "Prime Minister" for his skill at negotiation.

Dalitz, Moe (1899–1989): Originally a member of the Detroit Purple gang before going to Cleveland where he became the chief partner of a syndicate that engaged in both legal and illegal investments; spent his last years in Las Vegas as a philanthropic casino magnate.

Diamond, Jack "Legs" (1897–1931): Major New York criminal regarded as an unstable outsider who preyed on other gangs; accused of drug smuggling and kidnapping; survived multiple shooting attacks before his enemies finally killed him.

Donovan, James "Bugs" (d. 1929): Member of a gang that manufactured beer in northern New Jersey; probably killed on the order of Waxey Gordon who sought to take over the gang's breweries.

Drucci, Vincent "Schemer" (1901–1927): Member of the Dion O'Banion gang in Chicago that opposed Capone; shot to death in a tussle with police, much to Capone's satisfaction.

Dwyer, William "Big Bill" (1883–1946): New York dockworker at the start of Prohibition who became a pioneer in smuggling liquor from Europe; served a thirteen-month term in prison for bribing Coast Guard members; invested in sports teams and established the Phoenix Brewery in Manhattan.

Entratta, Charles (d. 1931): New York crime figure; partner of Legs Diamond in the Hotsy Totsy nightclub; with Diamond, killed two rowdy customers in the establishment; tried for the killing but acquitted; later shot to death in Brooklyn by unknown assailants.

Erickson, Frank (1896–1968): New York–based racketeer whose specialty was operating sports gambling operations using a telegraph service.

Gagliano, Gaetano "Tom" or "Tommy" (1884–1951): Became the capo of one of New York's Five Families when they were reorganized in 1931.

Genovese, Vito (1897–1969): New York Mafia figure; fled to Italy to avoid a murder trial and spent World War II there; back in the United States he fought to become the capo of the Luciano-Costello family by having his rivals killed.

Gordon, Waxey (1889–1952): Birth name Gordon Wexler; New York pickpocket and labor slammer who rose during Prohibition to become a wealthy bootlegger and narcotics smuggler; convicted of income tax evasion and other charges; died in Alcatraz prison.

Greenberg, Max "Big Maxie" (1883–1933): St. Louis gangster who moved to New York where he became a bootlegging partner of Waxey Gordon; died in a hotel shootout along with gang member Max Hassel.

Guzik, John "Jack" or "Jake" (1887–1956): High-ranking member of the Capone Outfit who managed the gang's finances.

Holtz, Hyman "Curly" (c. 1896–1939): Labor racketeer associated with Louis Lepke Buchalter and Gurrah Shapiro.

Howard, Joseph (d. 1924): Chicago criminal who was shot to death by Al Capone during an argument at a saloon.

Johnson, Enoch "Nucky" (1884–1969): Political boss of Atlantic City in the 1920s and 1930s; known for keeping the resort town a center of vice.

Kaplan, Nathan Lewis "Kid Dropper" (1895–1923): Early New York City labor racketeer and rival of "Little Augie"; killed in a spectacular gangland hit outside a Manhattan court building while in the custody of police.

Lansky, Meyer (1902?–1983): Birth name Maier Suchowljansky; New York City gangster who became a nationally known mob figure; associate of Lucky Luciano, with exceptional financial ability and experience in gambling operations.

Lanza, Joseph "Socks" (1904–1968): New York racketeer who dominated the Fulton Fish Market through extortion and labor racketeering.

Lazia, John (1897–1934): Italian gangster and politician who worked for Tom Pendergast, the boss of Kansas City, Missouri; shot to death by unknown triggermen.

Lombardo, Anthony (1892–1928): Chicago crime figure; installed as president of Chicago branch of the Unione Sicilione; assassinated in broad daylight on the busy Chicago intersection of Madison and State streets.

Lonardo, Joseph "Big Joe" (d. 1927): Major Cleveland gangster murdered in an ambush while playing cards in the backroom of a barbershop; probably murdered by his former employee Salvatore Todaro, who had joined the rival gang of Joseph Porrello.

Luciano, Charles "Lucky' (1897–1962): Birth name Salvatore Lucania; regarded as the most powerful of the New York Mafia leadership; oversaw many rackets, including bootlegging, prostitution, and narcotics; became capo of one of the city's five Mafia families; convicted of running a prostitution network for which he received a prison sentence; later deported to Italy.

Madden, Vincent Owen "Owney" (1891–1965): New York City mobster of Irish descent; arrested forty-four times before Prohibition; operated bootlegging and nightclubs; departed from the New York crime scene and moved to Hot Springs, Arkansas.

Magnano, Vincent (1888–1951): In 1931 became a capo of one of New York City's five Mafia families.

Maranzano, Salvatore (1886–1931): Charismatic New York City Mafia leader who immigrated to America as an adult; involved in setting up the five New York families that dominated the underworld; assassinated, probably on the orders of Charles Luciano.

Marlow, Frank (d. 1929): Birth name, Gandolfo Curto; New York figure known as a "Broadway racketeer"; invested in boxing, nightclubs, and horseracing; Ciro Terranova suspected in his murder.

Martin, Jules "Julie" (d. 1935): Birth name, Julius Modgilewsky; member of the Dutch Schultz gang who handled restaurant rackets; said to have been shot to death by Schultz in the course of an argument at the Harmony Hotel near Albany.

Masseria, Giuseppe (1879–1931): New York City Mafia figure; began as a minor criminal but gained power in clashes with rival gangs; final enemy was Salvatore Maranzano, who had him killed.

McErlane, Frank (1894–1932): Chicago member first of the McErlane-Saltis gang and subsequently the Torrio-Capone Outfit; early adopter of the Thompson machine gun; said to have killed more than fifteen men in his career.

McGurn, Jack (c. 1902–1936): Birth name, Vincenzo Antonio Gibaldi; bodyguard for Al Capone; suspected of involvement in the Saint Valentine's Day Massacre, but had an alibi in the person of his girlfriend, who said she had been with McGurn in the hotel on that day.

Moran, George "Bugs" (1891–1957): Chicago mobster who, after the death of Dion O'Banion, inherited the Northside gang that was decimated by the Saint Valentine's Day Massacre.

Morello, Guiseppe "Clutch Hand" (1867–1930): New York Mafia figure whose criminal career began prior to Prohibition; engaged in extortion, counterfeiting, and murder; allied with Joseph Masseria and related by marriage to Terranova brothers; nicknamed for his malformed arm and hand.

Moretti, Guarano "Willie" (1894–1951): New York area mobster, best known as a bootlegger and overseer of gambling operations in New Jersey; killed by his criminal colleagues who felt he was mentally failing.

Nitti, Frank "the Enforcer" (1884–1943): Birth name, Francesco Raffele Nitto; former barber who became a leading figure in Al Capone's Outfit; committed suicide rather than face prosecution for extortion.

Noe, Joseph "Joey Noey" (d. 1929): Business partner of Dutch Schultz; fatally wounded at the Chateau Madrid Hotel shootout.

O'Banion, Dion (1892–1924): Chicago gang leader of Irish descent who warred with Al Capone over bootlegging; killed in his flower shop.

O'Donnell brothers: 1920s bootlegging gang that included Myles, Bernard, and William O'Donnell; Myles in the car with Assistant State's Attorney William McSwiggen on a night in 1926 when McSwiggen was killed.

Orgen, Jacob "Little Augie" (1894–1927): Early New York labor racketeer noted for his extreme violence; battled "Kid Dropper" for dominance; murdered by Lepke Buchalter and Gurrah Shapiro.

Profaci, Joseph (1897–1962): Brooklyn Mafia chieftain who in 1931 became the head of one of New York's five Mafia families.

Rio, Frank (1895–1935): Also known as Frank Cline; member of Capone's Outfit who served as bodyguard; arrested with Capone in 1929 for carrying concealed weapon in Philadelphia.

Rothstein, Arnold (1882–1928): New York gambler and investor known as "The Brain" and "the Big Bankroll"; notorious for his involvement in fixing the 1919 World Series; provided loans for bootlegging operations and served as mentor for many up-and-coming gangsters in the 1920s.

Schultz, Dutch (1902–1935): Birth name, Arthur Flegenheimer; major New York regional gang leader who started in bootlegging and expanded to numbers racket, nightclubs, and labor racketeering; killed with members of his gang in a shootout at a Newark, New Jersey, restaurant.

Shapiro, Jacob "Gurrah" (1899–1947): Longtime partner with Louis "Lepke" Buchalter in New York labor racketeering.

Siegel, Benjamin "Bugsy" (1906–1947): New York gangster associated with Meyer Lansky and Lucky Luciano; suspected of several murders; oversaw construction of the Flamingo casino in Las Vegas; killed, reputedly for mismanagement of the property.

Solomon, Charles "King" (1884–1933): Boston mobster leader who was part of the inner circle of East Coast bootleggers associated with Lucky Luciano.

Terranova, Ciro "The Artichoke King" (1881–1938): New York racketeer; controlled market for artichokes and other produce; worked for Giuseppe Masseria; survived his two brothers Nick and Vincenzo, who were murdered in gang conflicts.

Torrio, John (1882–1957): Brooklyn gangster who moved to Chicago as an aide to "Big Jim" Colosimo; took over the rackets from Colosimo and brought Al Capone to Chicago as his lieutenant; after an attempt on his life, returned to New York and turned the operation over to Capone; regarded as a mediator between warring gangs.

Valachi, Joseph Michael (1904–1971): Small-time Mafia hoodlum in New York; while serving time in federal prison turned informer, providing information on what he called La Cosa Nostra, and influenced the government's view of organized crime.

Valenti, Umberto (1891–1922): Immigrant from Sicily who became a New York crime figure; battled for leadership rival Joseph Masseria who had him killed.

Weinberg, Abraham "Bo" (1897–1935): New York mobster, member of Dutch Schultz's gang, not related to Louis Weinberg; suspect in several murders; vanished in 1935 possibly for trying to double-cross Schultz.

Weinberg, Louis (d. 1929): Birth name, Benjamin Greenberg; New York mobster, thought to be a member of Legs Diamond gang; involved in the Chateau Madrid shootout, in which he was fatally wounded but also killed one of his attackers.

Weiss, Earl "Hymie" (1896–1926): Birth name, Earl Wajcieckowski; Chicago gang member and enemy of Al Capone; member of the Northside gang of Dion O'Banion; after O'Banion's death allied with George "Bugs" Moran; murdered while walking down a Chicago street, probably on the orders of Capone.

Yale, Frank (1885–1927): Birth name, Francesco Ioele; last name also given as Uale; Brooklyn gangster who was leader of the national Unione Sicilione; thought to have been murdered on the orders of Al Capone.

Zwillman, Abner "Longie" (1899–1959): Prohibition gangster from Newark who became a well-known figure in New York region crime; after Prohibition's repeal invested in both legal and illegal projects; committed suicide when faced with multiple prosecutions.

A Note on Sources

The first sentence in the first chapter in this book has waiter Al Capone say to Lena Gallucio, a female customer at a Brooklyn restaurant, "'You got a nice ass, honey, and I mean it as a compliment. Believe me.'" This quote comes from William Balsamo's interview with Lena's brother Frank, which appeared in an article in the March 1990 issue of *Chicago* magazine—a valid enough source to justify using it in this book. But in the 2011 book *Young Al Capone* by the same William Balsamo, this time coauthored with his son John, Capone says to Lena, "'Do you like ragtime?'" to which she answers, "'Really fellow, I'm not going to sit here and recite my musical preferences to you so please leave.'" The same passage describes minute things that Capone did, like staring at the girl, "his eyes aware of every delicate movement of tender flesh beneath her soft-yellow dress as she danced." What Balsamo reported in the 1990 magazine article changes dramatically in the 2011 book. The book's authors admit that the dialogue in the book "is written with the hopeful intention of providing a plausible discourse to the events as defined by the historical record."[1] In other words, the authors are making it up.

Many other so-called "true crime" books about gangsters contain made-up dialogue without any warning to the reader. For example, a 1985 biography of Longie Zwillman purports to relate bedroom talk between Longie and his girlfriend, actress Jean Harlow. The author, in unintentionally ridiculous imagery describes how Harlow was wearing a skimpy dress when she met Zwillman: "Her large nipples seemed to be forcing their way through the cheap fabric as if gulping for air." Later the two lovers are alone together in a luxury suite at the Waldorf Astoria Hotel in New York. Longie looks out at the city lights. "'Come here,'" he says, "'I want you to see real beauty. Look at the way the lights shine from the windows, like diamonds. Play your cards right and you can have as many diamonds as you see from this window,'" after which Harlow "felt Longy's fingers brush against her bare back. She leaned back against him." Zwillman and Harlow were long dead by the time the book was published. This leads the reader to assume that the book's author must have been taking notes from underneath the bed.[2]

Similarly, many true crime books lack the scholarly apparatus of footnotes, bibliography, and index. Furthermore, many books make assertions that can be called into question—for example, that Lucky Luciano hid in a restaurant men's room while his boss was assassinated in the dining room. These writers do not present to the reader alternate interpretations. Even worse, one prolific crime writer, Jay Robert Nash, informs readers that he has inserted falsehoods in his books to trap those who violate his copyrights—a tactic that certainly violates the basic principles of scholarship.

Perhaps the most notorious book in this genre is *The Last Testament of Lucky Luciano* by Martin A. Gosch and Richard Hammer. Published in 1975, the book sparked a major controversy about its reliability by focusing on whether the quotes attributed to Luciano were made up and whether incidents described were invented. Alan A. Block, a professor at Pennsylvania State University, accurately describes the situation when he says that much crime writing is a "subject plagued by unreliable works based on unsubstantiated sources."[3] In this book I have sought to use the tools of the historian to question whether the author of a source was in a position to know what he or she was describing, whether the author had a bias that might color his or her presentation, and whether other sources lend support to that description. For all their faults, true crime books do contain some valuable information. I have sought to act on behalf of the reader by sorting out controversies and presenting the most probable interpretation.

Readers who want to find out more about the history of organized crime can find many secondary sources that focus on facts rather than sensationalism. Among the best analyses of the history of organized crime are David Critchley's work on the rise of the Mafia in New York and Mark Haller on the inner workings of criminal gangs. Among the best biographies of crime figures are Robert Lacey on Meyer Lansky and Laurence Bergreen on Al Capone.

Regarding primary sources, Internet technology has made it possible to retrieve digital versions of newspapers from around the country in seconds. In earlier days, a researcher would have to spend vast amounts of time of eye-straining and mind-numbing work scrolling through reels of microfilm. Now, a researcher seeking information about, say, the Saint Valentine's Day Massacre can find what wire services and newspapers had to say at the time. The standards of journalism in the Prohibition era were not what they are now, but newspapers from that era provide information that cannot be found elsewhere and give the researcher a sense of what people who were alive at the time knew.

Acknowledgments

The task of doing research has been vastly improved by digital age tools such as ProQuest, Google Archives, and WorldCat. But people still make the difference, and I want to thank the library and agency staff members who assisted me: at the Library of Congress, Kristi L. Finefield; National Archives, Richard W. Peuser, Gregory J. Plunges, Maryellen Trautman, Rodney Ross, and William H. Davis; Atlantic City Free Public Library, Heather Halpin Pérez; Walter P. Reuther Library, Elizabeth Murray Clemens; Newark Public Library, James Lewis; Boston Public Library, Linda B. MacIver; New York City Municipal Archives, Michael Lorenzini and the legendary Leonora A. Gidlund; New Jersey State Library, Deborah Mercer: Rutgers University Libraries, Linda Langschied, James Hartstein, Tom Glynn, Ron Becker, and Glenn Sandberg; New Jersey State Archives, Betty Epstein and Joseph Klett; New Jersey State Museum, Margaret O'Reilly; Robert Lesser Foundation, Robert Lesser and Bryan Lautz. I also offer a shoutout to the Microforms Reading Room of the majestic New York Public Library.

Debra Burns, a masterly editor, kindly took the time to read the entire manuscript and provided invaluable suggestions, for which her compensation was an occasional biscotti at the local coffee shop. Other people who provided assistance and advice were Jon Blackwell, Harriet Bloom, Gordon Bond, David Critchley, Monica Devanas, Robert Frank, Alan Gottlieb, Mary Hartman, Ann and Carl Kessler, Vicki Gold Levy, Claire McInerney, Sandra Moss, and Helen Pike.

Special thanks to Marlie Wasserman, the director of the Rutgers University Press and to her staff, as well as to Lisa Nowak Jerry, the wise copyeditor assigned to this project.

Thanks also to my children Benjamin and Rebecca for their unwavering belief that their dad was not off his rocker. And finally, my beloved wife Ellen helped in countless ways with her loving support and keen insights. I cannot express how much her encouragement has meant to me to me during our lives together. I know she is glad that those gangsters who have metaphorically been a part of our daily lives finally took their feet off the sofa and cigar butts off the floor and departed our house so that we can get some privacy.

Notes

PROLOGUE

1. *Chicago Tribune,* May 28 and May 30, 1992; Roemer, *Accardo,* 429–430.

2. Bergreen, *Capone,* 332–333.

3. *Pittsburgh Press,* July 15, 1958.

4. Elkins and McKitrick, "Founding Fathers," 799–816.

5. Bell, *End of Ideology,* 142–143.

6. Reppetto, *American Mafia,* 97.

7. Bergreen, *Capone,* 284; Gosch and Hammer, *Last Testament,* 57.

8. Kavieff, *Purple Gang,* 203.

9. Talese, *Honor,* 355.

10. Kobler, *Capone,* 130–131; Pasley, *Self-Made Man,* 58.

11. Dash, *First Family,* 268.

CHAPTER 1 — THE BIG FELLOW IN THE WINDY CITY

1. Balsamo and Balsamo, *Young Al Capone,* 116–118; Bergreen, *Capone,* 49; Helmer, "Dillinger's Brain," 112–113; Schoenberg, *Mr. Capone,* 33. There are different versions of what Capone said, but they all amount to the same thing.

2. Pasley, *Al Capone,* 11.

3. McPhaul, *Johnny Torrio,* 15, 42–43.

4. Russo, *The Outfit,* 18.

5. Eig, *Get Capone,* 5–6.

6. McPhaul, *Johnny Torrio,* 31.

7. Kobler, *Capone,* 77

8. Brandt, *No Magic Bullet,* 119.

9. An example of the city map can be seen in Allsop, *Bootleggers,* 40.

10. Allsop, *Bootleggers*, 77.

11. Bergreen, *Capone*, 129; English, *Paddy Whacked*, 149–154: Kobler, *Capone*, 105.

12. Bergreen, *Capone*, 98ff.

13. *New York Times*, April 2, 1924.

14. Haller, "Illegal Enterprise," 217–226.

15. McPhaul, *Johnny Torrio*, 185–188.

16. Kobler, *Capone*, 129.

17. McPhaul, *Johnny Torrio*, 213–214.

18. Bergreen, *Capone*, 111.

19. *Chicago Tribune*, May 10, 1924.

20. Nash, *Encyclopedia*, 84.

21. *Chicago Daily News*, April 28, 1926.

22. *Chicago Tribune*, April 29, 1926; Pasley, *Self-Made Man*, 133.

23. *Chicago Tribune*, April 28, 1926.

24. Bergreen, *Capone*, 169.

25. Kobler, *Capone*, 181–182.

26. Ibid., 178.

27. Bergreen, *Capone*, 210.

28. Allsop, *Bootleggers*, 117.

29. *Chicago Tribune*, September 20, 1926.

30. Maas, *Valachi*, 77.

31. Kobler, *Capone*, 208.

32. May, "Unione Siciliana."

33. *Chicago Daily News*, February 14, 1929.

34. Eig, *Get Capone*, 199; Russo, *Outfit*, 39–40.

35. Bergreen, *Capone*, 215.

36. Eig, *Get Capone*, 191, 199, 250–253.

37. AP newswire in the *Evening News of Providence* [RI], March 1, 1929.

38. Pasley, *Al Capone*, 331.

39. Eig, *Get Capone*, 223–225.

40. Pasley, *Al Capone*, 329.

41. Bergreen, *Capone*, 45.

42. Fox, *Blood and Power*, 45; Lyle, *Dry and Lawless*, 40; Nash, *Encyclopedia*, 78; Reppetto, *American Mafia*, 99; Pasley, *Al Capone*, 11.

43. Schoenberg, *Mr. Capone*, 257–258.

44. Bergreen, *Capone*, 262.

45. Russo, *Outfit*, 25.

46. Schoenberg, *Mr. Capone*, 192.

g Bankroll, 55–56.

omy of a Gangster, 64; New York
etrusza, Rothstein, 321.

ke Buchalter files, part 3 of 4,

igation, Louis Lepke Buchalter

of a Gangster, 56; Sann, Kill the

nd Raymond, Gang Rule, 16.
.

156.

54. Ibid., 92.

35. Ibid., 70.

36. Feder and Joesten, *Luciano Story*, 55; Newark, *Lucky Luciano*, 36; Reppetto, *American Mafia*, 134.

37. Wolf, *Frank Costello*, 31–32.

38. Senate Special Committee to Investigate Organized Crime in Interstate Commerce, Memorandum from Thomas Cahill to Rudolph Halley, March 1, 1951. Record Group 46, box 77.

39. Critchley, *Origin*, 76–79.

40. Nash, *Encyclopedia*, 237–238; Thompson and Raymond, *Gang Rule*, 263–271.

41. Dash, *First Family*, 150.

42. Maas, *Valachi*, 69–70.

43. Thompson and Raymond, *Gang Rule*, 5–7.

44. *New York Times*, June 25 and July 11, 1929; Thompson and Raymond, *Gang Rule*, 106.

45. *New York Times*, December 13, 1929; Thompson and Raymond, *Gang Rule*, 200.

46. *New York Times*, December 27, 1929.

47. *New York Times*, December 18, 1929.

48. *New York Times*, December 28, 1929.

49. Dash, *First Family*, 276.

50. Gosch and Hammer, *Last Testament*, 132.

51. Dash, *First Family*, 310.

52. O'Grady, *Irish*, 70; Casey, "Irish," 598–602.

53. Thompson and Raymond, *Gang Rule*, 80–99.

54. *New York Times*, December 4, 1925.

55. *New York Times*, January 27, 1926; Thompson and Raymond, *Gang Rule*, 96.

56. Wolf, *Frank Costello*, 65.

57. Levine, *Anatomy*, 28.

58. English, *Paddy Whacked*, 184.

59. Levine, *Anatomy*, 59–61.

60. *New York Times*, July 20, 1929.

61. Levine, *Anatomy of a Gangster*, 60.

62. English, *Paddy Whacked*, 185.

CHAPTER 3 — SMALLER CITIES

1. "Detroit" Jewish Virtual Library. http://www.jewishvirtuallibrary.org/jsource/judaica/ejud_0002_0005_0_05142.html.

2. Paul R. Kavieff, interview by author, April 25, 2012.

3. *Detroit News*, November 28, 1937.

4. Okrent, *Last Call*, 107.

5. Mason, *Rumrunning*, 39, 43–44.

6. Okrent, *Last Call*, 129.

7. Porrello, *Cleveland Mafia*, 34.

8. *Detroit News*, November 28, 1937; *New York Times*, March 9, 1968.

9. Kavieff, *Purple Gang*, 4.

10. Newton, *Mr. Mob*, 18, 24.

11. Federal Bureau of Investigation files, "Purple Gang" file, part 2 of 4, 37–48.

12. Reppetto, *American Mafia*, 144.

13. Hayde, *Mafia and Machine*, 8–9.

14. Reddig, *Tom's Town*, 82–85.

15. Mayerberg, *Chronicle*, 109.

16. Ibid., 110.

17. Fox, *Blood and Power*, 249–251.

18. Reddig, *Tom's Town*, 252.

19. Dorsett, *Pendergast Machine*, 88.

20. Newton, *Mr. Mob*, 17–18.

21. Ibid., 35.

22. Ibid.; Porrello, *Cleveland Mafia*, 126–127.

23. Newton, *Mr. Mob*, 36–38.

24. *Cleveland Plain Dealer*, October 7, 1927; Messick, *Silent Syndicate*, 35–36; Porrello, *Cleveland Mafia*, 55–59.

25. Gentile, *Unpublished English Translations*, 63.

26. Porrello, *Cleveland Mafia*, 67–72.

27. Ibid., 97–121.

28. *New York Times*, January 29, 1931.

29. *Chicago Tribune*, December 6, 1928; Messick, *Silent Syndicate*, 39; Porrello, *Cleveland Mafia*, 84–96; Reppetto, *American Mafia*, 149–150.

CHAPTER 4 — GANGSTERS IN THE SURF

1. Johnson, *Boardwalk Empire*, vii.

2. Ibid., 79–102.

3. Gosch and Hammer, *Last Testament*, 100.

4. Bergreen, *Capone*, 331; Messick, *Lansky*, 37; Nelli, *Business of Crime*, 178; *Newark Evening News*, May 17, 1929; Stuart, *Gangster*, 72.

5. Katcher, *Big Bankroll*, 352–353.

6. Bergreen, *Capone*, 332.

7. English, *Paddy Whacked*, 171.

8. Nash, *Encyclopedia*, 42.

9. English, *Paddy Whacked*, 171–175.

10. Gosch and Hammer, *Last Testament*, 105–106.

11. *Atlantic City Daily Press*, May 20, 1929; Decter and Martens, *Other Promised Land*, 51–53.

12. Gosch and Hammer, *Last Testament*, 106.

13. *Atlantic City Daily Press*, May 16, 1929.

14. Thrasher, *Gang*, 235.

15. Bergreen, *Capone*, 116.

16. Johnson, *Boardwalk Empire*, 79.

17. Messick, *Lansky*, 35.

18. Gosch and Hammer, *Last Testament*, 106.

19. Eisenberg, Dann, and Landau, *Lansky*, 144.

20. Gosch and Hammer, *Last Testament*, 50.

21. Newark, *Lucky Luciano*, 118, Smith, *Dewey*, 198; Poulson, *Case Against Luciano*, 142.

22. Gosch and Hammer, *Last Testament*, 49–50.

23. *North Adams [MA] Transcript*, August 2, 1941, reprinted at www.myalcaponemuseum.com/id27.htm.

24. Nash, *Encyclopedia*, 178.

25. *Atlantic City Daily Press*, May 16, 1929.

26. Gosch and Hammer, *Last Testament*, 106.

27. Wolf, *Frank Costello*, 89–90.

28. *New York Times* and *Press of Atlantic City*, May 16, 1929.

29. Nash, *Encyclopedia*, 177–178.

30. Ogden, *Legacy*, 106–107, 220–221.

31. Ibid., 102; May, "Race Wire."

32. Nelli, *Business of Crime*, 215.

33. Eisenberg, Dann, and Landau, *Lansky*, 144; Nelli, *Business of Crime*, 215, 217.

34. Nash, *Encyclopedia*, 42.

35. "Philadelphia Justice," *Literary Digest*, 39.

36. *Philadelphia Inquirer*, May 18, 1929.

37. Pasley, *Al Capone*, 326.

38. Powell, *Lucky Luciano*, 65, 68.

39. Katcher, *Big Bankroll*, 352–353.

40. Cook, *Mafia*, 68.

41. Wolf, *Frank Costello*, 87.

42. "Philadelphia Justice," *Literary Digest*, 34.

43. Bergreen, *Capone*, 355.

44. "Philadelphia Justice," *Literary Digest*, 39.

45. *Chicago Tribune*, May 18, 1929.

46. "Philadelphia Justice," *Literary Digest*, 32.

47. *Atlantic City Daily Press*, May 20, 1929.

CHAPTER 5 — THE CONFERENCE AS COMEDY

1. The story is reprinted in Damon Runyon, *The Bloodhounds of Broadway and Other Stories*, 43–60.

2. Breslin, *Damon Runyon*, 26.

3. Ibid., 292.

4. For information on the movie, see Maslon, *Some Like it Hot*, and Kimmel, *I'll Have What She's Having*, 127–146.

CHAPTER 6 — CAPONE'S LONG TRIP HOME

1. *Philadelphia Inquirer*, May 17, 1929.

2. *New York Evening Journal*, May 20, 1929.

3. *Philadelphia Inquirer*, May 18, 1929.

4. *Chicago Tribune*, May 20, 1929.

5. *Newark Evening News* morgue file, June 4, 1929; *Philadelphia Inquirer*, May 19, 1929; Schoenberg, *Mr. Capone*, 236.

6. "Philadelphia Justice," *Literary Digest*, 33–34.

7. *Philadelphia Inquirer*, May 18, 1929.

8. *New York Times*, May 18, 1929.

9. *New York Times*, January 13 and February 10, 1929

10. *New York Times*, May 18, 1929.

11. Schoenberg, *Mr. Capone*, 238.

12. Bergreen, *Capone*, 338.

13. *Newark Evening News* morgue files, May 21, 1929.

14. *New York Times*, June 30, July 2, September 22, November 7, 1929.

15. *Newark Evening News*, June 4, 1929; *New York Times*, June 7, 1929.

16. Pasley, *Al Capone*, 334.

17. Bergreen, *Capone*, 353.

CHAPTER 7 — THE TWILIGHT OF THE GANGSTER?

1. Leuchtenburg, *Perils of Prosperity*, 265.

2. Allen, *Only Yesterday*, 348.

3. Dougherty, "Twilight of the Gangster," October 24, 1931: http://www.liberty magazine.com/crime_doherty.htm.

4. Associated Press dispatch in the *Reading [PA] Eagle*, August 1, 1931.

5. Higham, *Strangers in the Land*, 164.

6. U.S. Congress, "Biological Aspects of Immigration," *Hearings Before the Committee on Immigration and Naturalization. H.R. 66th Congress, 2nd Session*, April 16, 1930, 3–4.

7. U.S. National Commission on Law Observance and Enforcement, *Report on Crime and the Foreign Born* (Washington, D.C.: U.S. Government Printing Office, 1931), 195.

8. Wilson and Day, *Special Agent,* 38.

9. Ness and Fraley, *Untouchables,* 47–48.

10. Roberts, *Dick Tracy,* 5.

11. *Crime Does Not Pay,* 10.

12. Hajdu, *Ten-Cent Plague,* 87.

13. Kyvig, *Repealing National Prohibition,* 129, 132; Okrent, *Last Call,* 332–333.

14. National Commission on Law Observance and Enforcement, *Report on the Enforcement of the Prohibition Laws of the United States,* January 7, 1931: http://www.druglibrary.org/schaffer/library/studies/wick/index.html.

15. Kyvig, *Repealing National Prohibition,* 114.

16. Fox, *Blood and Power,* 146–149.

17. *New York Times,* October 13, 1933.

18. "On the Declaration of War with Japan—December 9, 1941," Franklin D. Roosevelt Presidential Library and Museum, http://docs.fdrlibrary.marist.edu/120941.html.

CHAPTER 8 — PAY YOUR TAXES

1. *New York Times,* May 17, 1927; *United States v. Sullivan,* 274 U.S. 259 (1927).

2. *Charleston News & Courier,* February 2, 1946.

3. "Inaugural Address of Herbert Hoover, March 4, 1929," Herbert Hoover Presidential Library and Museum. http://www.hoover.archives.gov/info/inauguralspeech.html.

4. Hoover, *Memoirs,* 277.

5. Irey and Slocum, *Tax Dodgers,* 36.

6. Eig, *Get Capone,* 210.

7. Fox, *Blood & Power,* 297.

8. Bergreen, *Capone,* 420–421.

9. Ibid., 346–353, 358; Schoenberg, *Mr. Capone,* 252, 295, 297–298.

10. Irey and Slocum, *Tax Dodgers,* 45.

11. Schoenberg, *Mr. Capone,* 230–231.

12. Kobler, *Capone,* 274.

13. Schoenberg, *Mr. Capone,* 259.

14. Wilson and Day, *Special Agent,* 35.

15. Ibid., 36–37.

16. Ibid., 32.

17. *New York Times,* March 1, 1998.

18. *Toledo Blade*, November 18, 1960.

19. Eig, *Get Capone*, 300; Irey and Slocum, *Tax Dodgers*, 36–60; Wilson and Day, *Special Agent*, 33.

20. Schoenberg, *Mr. Capone*, 296–297.

21. Eig, *Get Capone*, 324–325, 331–332.

22. Ibid., 332.

23. Kobler, *Capone*, 330.

24. Runyon, *Trials*, 228.

25. Guy Helvering, "Organization, Functions and Activities: A Narrative Briefly Descriptive of the Period 1919 to 1936," Intelligence Unit, Bureau of Investigation, n.d., Unpublished document in files of the Senate Committee on Organized Crime in Interstate Commerce, National Archives and Records Administration.

26. Irey and Slocum, *Tax Dodgers*, 134.

27. Thompson and Raymond, *Gang Rule*, 30.

28. Downey, *Gangster City*, 102–103.

29. Thompson and Raymond, *Gang Rule*, 387.

30. Downey, *Gangster City*, 107–108.

31. Maas, *Valachi*, 113; *Pittsburgh Press*, April 13, 1933; Thompson and Raymond, *Gang Rule*, 387.

32. Fried, *Jewish Gangster*, 178–179.

33. Irey and Slocum, *Tax Dodgers*, 135–136; Wolf, *Frank Costello*, 112.

34. Dewey, *Twenty*, 120.

35. Ibid., 119.

36. Irey and Slocum, *Tax Dodgers*, 146–147.

37. Gosch and Hammer, *Last Testament*, 140–141.

38. Irey and Slocum, *Tax Dodgers*, 149.

39. Downey, *Gangster City*, 109.

40. Dewey, *Twenty*, 123.

41. Ibid., 124–125.

42. Powell, *Ninety Times*, 46.

43. Dewey, *Twenty*, 133.

44. *New York Times*, December 2, 1933.

45. Downey, *Gangster City*, 110; *New York Times*, December 6, 1933.

46. *New York Times*, January 4, 1942.

47. *New York Times*, August 4, 1951.

48. May, "Waxey Gordon," *Crime Magazine*, 285–287; *New York Times*, August 4, 1951.

49. Grover, *Nazis*, 39–46.

50. Messick, *Secret File*, 276; Stuart, *Gangster*, 191–193.

51. Stuart, *Gangster*, 184.

52. Undated *World Telegram* news clip in the *Newark Evening News* morgue file, Newark Public Library.

53. *Newark Evening News*, February 26, 1959; Stuart, *Gangster*, 223–225.

CHAPTER 9 — LUCKY V. DEWEY

1. Feder and Joesten, *Luciano Story*, 64–68; *New York Times,* October 18, 1929.

2. Newark, *Lucky Luciano*, 59–61.

3. Gosch and Hammer, *Last Testament*, 115–120.

4. Feder and Joesten, *Luciano Story*, 64–72; Gosch and Hammer, *Last Testament,* 118–119; Nash, *Encyclopedia*, 252.

5. Wolf, *Frank Costello*, 84.

6. Feder and Joesten, *Luciano Story*, 71; Vizzini, Fraley, and Smith, *Undercover Agent*, 166–167.

7. Reppetto, *American Mafia*, 136.

8. Bonanno, *Man of Honor*, 121–122.

9. Ibid., 121; Gosch and Hammer, *Last Testament*, 129.

10. Eisenberg, Dann, and Landau, *Lansky*, 134; Feder and Joesten, *Luciano Story,* 78; Maas, *Valachi Papers*, 104.

11. Lacey, *Little Man*, 462–463n65.

12. Bonanno, *Man of Honor*, 122; Maas, *Valachi Papers*, 103.

13. Maas, *Valachi Papers*, 87.

14. Ibid., 98; Peterson, *Mob*, 365; Reppetto, *American Mafia*, 139.

15. Critchley, *Origin*, 180.

16. Block, *East Side—West Side*, 3–4; Critchley, *Origin*, 199–200.

17. Critchley, *Origin*, 233.

18. Bonanno, *Man of* Honor, 76, 404.

19. Reppetto, *American Mafia*, 141.

20. Haller, "Illegal Enterprise," 226–227.

21. Peterson, *Mob*, 443.

22. Gosch and Hammer, *Last Testament*, 162–163.

23. Allhoff, "Tracking," *Liberty Magazine;* Dewey, *Twenty*, 193.

24. Dewey, *Twenty*, 198; Newark, *Lucky Luciano*, 144.

25. Stolberg, *Fighting Organized Crime*, 127.

26. Dewey, *Twenty*, 188–190.

27. Smith, *Dewey*, 197.

28. Ibid., 198–199.

29. Newark, *Lucky Luciano*, 128; Smith, *Dewey*, 194.

30. Smith, *Dewey*, 205.

31. Eisenberg, Dann, and Landau, *Lansky*, 163.

32. English, *Paddy Whacked*, 114; Critchley, *Origin*, 206.

33. Dewey, *Twenty*, 185, 261; Nash, *Encyclopedia*, 254.

34. Gosch and Hammer, *Last Testament*, 55–58.

35. FBI FOIA Files Luciano 1A, p. 4.

36. Dewey, *Twenty*, 201.

37. Campbell, *Luciano Project*, 2.

38. Kefauver Committee files, Staff memo January 1, 1951, Records Group 46, box 97.

39. Campbell, *Luciano Project*, 150.

40. Newark, *Lucky Luciano*, 156.

41. Eisenberg, Dann, and Landau, *Lansky*, 224–225.

42. Kefauver Committee, March 19, 1951 memo, Record Group 46, box 97.

43. English, *Havana Nocturne*, 30–50.

44. Associated Press dispatch in the *Geneva [NY] Daily Times*, March 1, 1951; Newark, *Lucky Luciano*, 230.

CHAPTER 10 — SHOT TO DEATH

1. Sann, *Kill the Dutchman*, 121–126.

2. Downey, *Gangster City*, 313–314.

3. Ibid., 211–222.

4. Ibid.

5. Sann, *Kill the Dutchman*, 206–210.

6. Davis, "Things I Couldn't Tell," 10, 38.

7. Sann, *Kill the Dutchman*, 238.

8. *New York Times*, August 2, 1935.

9. *New York Times*, October 25, 1935.

10. Sann, *Kill the Dutchman*, 19-20; Thompson and Raymond, *Gang Rule*, 358.

11. *New York Times*, October 25, 1935.

12. Sann, *Kill the Dutchman*, 303-337.

13. Ibid., 78.

14. Newark, *Lucky Luciano*, 17-18; Levine, *Anatomy of a Gangster*, 122.

15. Levine, *Anatomy of a Gangster*, 71.

16. Ibid., 69-72.

17. Ibid., 126.

18. Ibid., 151.

19. Downey, *Legs Diamond*, 201.

20. *New York Times*, December 19, 1931.

21. Downey, *Legs Diamond*, 211-213, 185-189; Levine, *Anatomy of a Gangster*, 171ff.

22. Reddig, *Tom's Town*, 262.

23. Messick, *Secret File*, 123-125; Ouseley, *Open City*, 112-113.

24. Ouseley, *Open City*, 114.

25. Mayerberg, *Chronicle*, 121.

26. Ibid., 131.

27. Waugh, *Gangs of St. Louis*, 232-233.

28. Associated Press dispatch in *Ellensburg [NY] Daily Record*, October 12, 1934; Messick, *Secret File*, 127; Burrough, *Public Enemies*, 428-429, 446-447.

29. Federal Bureau of Investigation, "Bugsy Siegel" file, part 1, 23-24, 60-61; Westbrook Pegler clipping in same file.

30. Federal Bureau of Investigation, "Bugsy Siegel" file, part 1, 40.

31. Lacey, *Little Man*, 155.

32. Records of the Senate Special Committee to Investigate Organized Crime in Interstate Commerce, 1950-1951, Vol. 10, 713-716; Russo, *The Outfit*, 205.

33. Russo, *The Outfit*, 292.

34. Lacey, *Little Man*, 152.

35. Eisenberg, Dann, and Landau, *Lansky*, 235; Wilkerson, *Las Vegas*, 113.

36. For a summary of theories, see Eisenberg, Dann, and Landau, *Lansky*, 240-241; Lacey, *Little Man*, 158; International News Service dispatch in *Milwaukee Sentinel*, January 22, 1947; *New York Times*, February 28, 1951.

37. Westbrook Pegler column, *Toledo Blade*, October 6, 1947.

38. *New York Times*, October 26, 1957.

39. Raab, *Five Families*, 61.

40. Gosch and Hammer, *Last Testament*, 131.

41. Maas, *Valachi Papers*, 151.

42. Ibid., 194-195; Newark, "Hunting Down Vito Genovese in WWII Italy," *Crime Magazine*, June 1, 2007.

43. Maas, *Valachi Papers*, 195.

44. Ibid., 210.

CHAPTER 11 — LEPKE ON THE HOT SEAT

1. Kavieff, *Lepke*, 83.

2. Ibid., 93–94.

3. Downey, *Gangster City*, 241–242.

4. *New York Times*, November 13, 1936.

5. Dewey, *Twenty*, 453–460.

6. *New York Times*, December 1, 1937.

7. Turkus, *Murder*, 354–355.

8. Ibid., 104.

9. *New York Times*, November 20, 1941.

10. Fried, *Jewish Gangster*, 206.

11. *New York Times*, July 26, 1939.

12. Winchell, *Exclusive*, 136.

13. Kavieff, *Lepke*, 131–132; Turkus, *Murder*, 359–360; Winchell, *Exclusive*, 142–147.

14. Turkus, *Murder*, 355–359.

15. Winchell, *Exclusive*, 147.

16. Tully, *Treasury Agent*, 55–57.

17. Kavieff, *Lepke*, 148.

18. Turkus, *Murder*, 64.

19. Ibid., 61.

20. Ibid., 375.

21. Ibid., 376–377.

22. *New York Times*, September 21, 1940.

23. Turkus, *Murder*, 393.

24. Ibid., 394.

25. Kavieff, *Lepke*, 184–185; Turkus, *Murder*, 398.

26. Kavieff, *Lepke*, 178.

27. Elmaleh, *Canary*, 177–185.

28. Testimony Taken in the District Attorney's Library, January 8, 1941. Kings County D.A. Murder Inc. case files, M.N.# 22178, Roll 7. New York City Municipal Archives.

29. Kavieff, *Lepke*, 199–200.

30. Fried, *Jewish Gangster*, 200–201.

CHAPTER 12 — FOR THEM, CRIME DID PAY

1. A 1958 FBI report called for using a "highly confidential source" on Lansky, FBI jargon for a wiretap or other eavesdropping device. Federal Bureau of Investigation, "Meyer Lansky" files, part 5, 70.

2. Lacey, *Little Man*, 299.

3. Ibid., 406–407.

4. Ibid., 421.

5. Abbott, *Bookmaker's Daughter*, 111–112, 273.

6. Fried, *Jewish Gangster*, 65.

7. Newton, *Mr. Mob*, 272.

8. Smith, "Double Life of Moe Dalitz," http://www.1st100.com/part2/dalitz.html.

9. Katz, *Uncle Frank*, 205.

10. Ibid., 126.

11. Raab, *Five Families*, 110.

12. *New York Times*, May 28, 1958; Wolf, *Frank Costello*, 257.

13. Wolf, *Frank Costello*, 257.

14. Bonanno, *Man of Honor*, 404.

15. Raab, *Five Families*, 162–163.

16. Talese, *Honor Thy Father*, 528.

17. Raab, *Five Families*, 167; Talese, *Honor Thy Father*, 529.

18. Talese, *Honor Thy Father*, 529.

19. Davis, *Mafia Dynasty*, 232.

20. Bonanno, *Man of Honor*, 404.

21. Reppetto, *Bringing Down the Mob*, 288-289.

22. Ibid., 292.

A NOTE ON SOURCES

1. Balsamo, *Young Al Capone*, 115–118; Helmer, "The Man Who Stole Dillinger's Brain," 112–113.

2. Stuart, *Gangster*, 83, 86.

3. Block, *East Side—West Side*, 12.

Selected Bibliography

GOVERNMENT DOCUMENT COLLECTIONS

Federal Bureau of Investigation Files, Washington, D.C. www.fbi.gov/. Freedom of Information Act Files on Albert Anastasia, Al Capone, Louis Lepke Buchalter, Meyer Lansky, Mafia, George "Bugs" Moran, Eliot Ness, Purple Gang, Dutch Schultz, Bugsy Siegel, Abner Zwillman.

Library of Congress, Washington, D.C., Prints and Photograph Division

National Archives and Records Administration (New York City and Washington, D.C.)

National Commission on Law Observance and Enforcement (aka the Wickersham Commission); Records of the Senate Special Committee to Investigate Organized Crime in Interstate Commerce, 1950–1951 (aka the Kefauver Committee); *United States v. Irving Wexler.*

New York City Municipal Archives, District Attorney files on Murder Incorporated, Louis Lepke Buchalter, and Charles Luciano.

NEWSPAPERS

Asbury Park Evening Press
Atlantic City Press
Boston Daily Globe
Boston Post
Chicago Daily News
Chicago Herald & Examiner
Chicago Sun
Chicago Tribune
Cleveland Plain Dealer

Detroit News
Ellensburg [NY] Daily Record
Evening Independent [St. Petersburg, FL]
Evening News of Providence [RI]
Geneva [NY] Daily Times
Lewiston [ME] Daily Sun
Miami News
Milwaukee Journal
Milwaukee Sentinel
Newburgh [NY] News
New York American
New York Evening World
New York Herald Tribune
New York Journal and New York Evening Journal
New York Mirror
New York Times
North Adams [MA] Transcript
Philadelphia Evening Bulletin
Philadelphia Inquirer
Philadelphia Public Ledger
Pittsburgh Post-Gazette
Pittsburgh Press
Reading [PA] Eagle
[Rochester, Indiana] News-Sentinel
Schenectady Gazette
Spokane Daily Chronicle
Telegraph-Herald [Dubuque]
Toledo Blade

BOOKS AND ARTICLES

Abbott, Edith, et al. *Report on Crime and Criminal Justice in Relation to the Foreign Born.* National Commission on Law Observance and Enforcement. Washington, D.C.: Government Printing Office, 1931.

Abbott, Shirley. *The Bookmaker's Daughter.* Boston: Ticknor & Fields, 1991.

Albini, Joseph. *The American Mafia: Genesis of a Legend.* New York: Appleton Century Crofts, 1971.

Allen, William Frederick. *Only Yesterday: An Informal History of the Nineteen-Twenties.* New York: Harper & Row, 1931.

Allhoff, Fred. "Tracking New York Crime Barons." *Liberty Magazine,* October 31, 1936. http://www.libertymagazine.com/crime_allhoff.htm.

Allsop, Kenneth. *The Bootleggers: The Story of Chicago's Prohibition Era.* London: Hutchinson, 1961.

Anslinger, Harry, and Will Oursler. *The Murderers: The Story of the Narcotics Gangs.* New York: Farrar, Straus and Cudahy, 1961.

Asbury, Herbert. "Frank Costello: America's Number One Mystery Man." *Collier's Weekly,* April 19 and 27, 1947.

Balsamo, William, and John Balsamo. *Young Al Capone: The Untold Story of Scarface in New York, 1899–1925.* New York: Skyhorse Publishing, 2011.

Bell, Daniel. *The End of Ideology.* Cambridge, Mass.: Harvard University Press, 1988.

Berger, Meyer. *The Eight Million: Journal of a New York Correspondent.* New York: Simon & Schuster, 1942.

Bergreen, Laurence. *Capone: The Man and the Era.* New York: Simon & Schuster, 1994.

Block, Alan. *East Side, West Side: Organizing Crime in New York, 1930–1950.* New Brunswick, N.J.: Transaction Books, 1983.

Bonanno, Joseph, with Sergio Lalli. *A Man of Honor: The Autobiography of Joseph Bonanno.* New York: Simon and Schuster, 1983.

Brandt, Allan. *No Magic Bullet: A Social History of Venereal Disease in the United States since 1880.* New York: Oxford University Press, 1987.

Breslin, Jimmy. *Damon Runyon: A Life.* Boston: Ticknor & Fields, 1991.

Brown, Dorothy. *Mabel Walker Willebrandt: A Study of Power, Loyalty, and Law.* Knoxville: University of Tennessee Press, 1984.

Burrough, Bryan. *Public Enemies: America's Greatest Crime Wave and the Birth of the FBI, 1933–34.* New York: Penguin Books, 2004.

Campbell, Rodney. *The Luciano Project: The Secret Wartime Collaboration of the Mafia and the U.S. Navy.* New York: McGraw-Hill, 1977.

Carr, Charlie, ed. *New York Police Files on the Mafia: A Collection of New York's Five Families' Files, Arrest Records and Mug Shots from the 1940s and 1950s.* N.p.: Hosehead Productions, 2012.

Casey, Marion. "Irish." In *The Encyclopedia of New York,* ed. Kenneth Jackson. New Haven: Yale University Press, 1991. 598–602.

Clark, Tom. *The World of Damon Runyon.* New York: Harper & Row, 1978.

Clarke, Donald Henderson. *In the Reign of Rothstein.* New York: Vanguard Press, 1929.

Cohen, Rich. *Tough Jews: Fathers, Sons, and Gangster Dreams.* New York: Simon & Schuster, 1998.

Cook, Fred. *Mafia!* Greenwich, Conn.: Fawcett Gold Medal Book, 1973.

Cressey, Donald R. *Theft of the Nation: The Structure and Operations of Organized Crime in America.* New York: Harper & Row, 1969.

Crime Does Not Pay, vol. 1. Milwaukie, Ore.: Dark Horse Books, 2012.

Critchley, David. *The Origin of Organized Crime in America: The New York City Mafia, 1891–1931.* New York: Routledge, 2009.

Dash, Mike. *The First Family: Terror, Extortion, Revenge, Murder, and the Birth of the American Mafia.* New York: Random House, 2009.

Davis, John H. *Mafia Dynasty: The Rise and Fall of the Gambino Crime Family.* New York: HarperCollins, 1993.

Davis, J. Richard "Dixie." "Things I Couldn't Tell Till Now." *Collier's Weekly,* July 22 and 29, 1939; August 12, 19, and 26, 1939.

Decter, Avi Y., and Melissa Martens. *The Other Promised Land: Vacationing, Identity, and the Jewish American Dream.* Baltimore: Jewish Museum of Maryland, 2005.

Dewey, Thomas. *Twenty against the Underworld.* Garden City, N.Y.: Doubleday & Company, 1974.

Dickie, John. *Cosa Nostra: A History of the Sicilian Mafia.* New York: Palgrave Macmillan, 2004.

Dorsett, Lyle. *The Pendergast Machine.* New York: Oxford University Press, 1968.

Dougherty, Edward. "The Twilight of the Gangster: How Much Longer Are We Going to Put Up with Him?" *Liberty Magazine,* October 24, 1931: http://www .libertymagazine.com/crime_doherty.htm.

Downey, Patrick. *Gangster City: The History of the New York Underworld 1900–1936.* Fort Lee, N.J.: Barricade Books, 2004.

———. *Legs Diamond: Gangster.* N.p.: Createspace, 2011.

Eig, Jonathan. *Get Capone: The Secret Plot That Captured America's Most Wanted Gangster.* New York: Simon & Schuster, 2010.

Eisenberg, Dennis, Uri Dann, and Eli Landau. *Meyer Lansky: Mogul of the Mob.* New York: Paddington Press, 1979.

Elkins, Stanley, and Eric McKitrick. *The Founding Fathers: Young Men of the Revolution.* Washington, D.C.: Service Center for Teachers, 1962. This article also appeared in *Political Science Quarterly* 76 (June 1961): 799–816.

Elmaleh, Edmund. *The Canary Sang But Couldn't Fly: The Fatal Fall of Abe Reles, the Mobster Who Shattered Murder, Inc.'s Code of Silence.* New York: Union Square Press, 2009.

English, T. J. *Havana Nocturne: How the Mob Owned Cuba . . . and Then Lost It to the Revolution.* New York: William Morrow, 2007.

———. *Paddy Whacked: The Untold Story of the Irish American Gangster.* New York: HarperCollins, 2006.

Feder, Sid, and Joachim Joesten. *The Luciano Story.* New York: Da Capo Press, 1994.

Fried, Albert. *The Rise and Fall of the Jewish Gangster in America.* Rev. ed. New York: Columbia University Press, 1993.

Fentress, James. *Eminent Mobsters: Immigrants and the Birth of Organized Crime in America.* New York: University Press of America, 2010.

Fox, Stephen. *Blood and Power: Organized Crime in Twentieth-Century America.* New York: William Morrow, 1989.

Gage, Nicholas. *The Mafia Is Not an Equal Opportunity Employer.* New York: McGraw-Hill, 1971.

————, ed. *Mafia, USA.* New York: Playboy Press, 1972.

Gentile, Nicolo. Unpublished English translations of autobiographical information in Italian circa 1947 and 1963. Author's collection.

Gosch, Martin, and Richard Hammer. *The Last Testament of Lucky Luciano.* Boston: Little, Brown, 1975.

Grover, Warren. *Nazis in Newark.* New Brunswick, N.J.: Transaction Publishers, 2003.

Hajdu, David. *The Ten-Cent Plague: The Great Comic Book Scare and How It Changed America.* New York: Farrar Strauss Giroux, 2008.

Haller, Mark. "Illegal Enterprise: A Theoretical and Historical Interpretation." *Criminology* 28 (May 1990): 217–226.

Hayde, Frank R. *The Mafia and the Machine: The Story of the Kansas City Mob.* Fort Lee, N.J.: Barricade Books, 2007.

Helmer, William. "The Man Who Stole Dillinger's Brain!!!: and Other Torrid True Confessions from the Golden Age of Gangsters." *Chicago,* March 1990, 112–113.

Helmer, William, and Rick Mattix. *The Complete Public Enemy Almanac.* Nashville: Cumberland House, 2007.

Helvering, Guy. "Organization, Functions and Activities: A Narrative Briefly Descriptive of the Period 1919 to 1936." Intelligence Unit, Bureau of Investigation, n.d. Unpublished document in files of the Senate Committee on Organized Crime in Interstate Commerce, National Archives and Records Administration.

Higham, John. *Strangers in the Land: Patterns of American Nativism, 1860–1925.* 2d ed. New Brunswick, N.J.: Rutgers University Press, 1988.

Hoffman, Dennis. *Scarface Al and the Crime Crusaders: Chicago's Private War against Capone.* Carbondale: Southern Illinois University Press, 1993.

Hoover, Herbert. *The Memoirs of Herbert Hoover.* New York: Macmillan, 1952.

Irey, Elmer, and William J. Slocum. *The Tax Dodgers: The Inside Story of the T-Men's War with America's Political and Underworld Hoodlums.* New York: Greenberg Publisher, 1948.

Jennings, Dean. *We Only Kill Each Other: The Life and Bad Times of Bugsy Siegel.* Greenwich, Conn.: Fawcett Publications, 1967.

Johnson, Curt. *Wicked City Chicago: From Kenna to Capone.* Chicago: December Press, 1994.

Johnson, Nelson. *Boardwalk Empire: The Birth, High Times, and Corruption of Atlantic City.* Medford, N.J.: Plexus Publishing, 2003.

Katcher, Leo. *The Big Bankroll: The Life and Times of Arnold Rothstein.* New York: Harper & Brothers, 1958.

Katz, Leonard. *Uncle Frank: The Biography of Frank Costello.* New York: Drake Publishers, 1973.

Kavieff, Paul R. *The Life and Times of Lepke Buchalter: America's Most Ruthless Labor Racketeer.* Fort Lee, N.J.: Barricade Books, 2006.

————. *The Purple Gang: Organized Crime in Detroit, 1910–1945.* Fort Lee, N.J.: Barricade Books, 2000.

Kefauver, Estes. *Crime in America.* Garden City, N.Y.: Doubleday & Company, 1951.

Kimmel, Daniel. *I'll Have What She's Having: Behind the Scenes of the Great Romantic Comedies.* Chicago: Ivan R. Dee, 2008.

King, Rufus. *Gambling and Organized Crime.* Washington, D.C.: Public Affairs Press, 1969.

Kobler, John. *Capone: The Life and World of Al Capone.* Cambridge, Mass.: Da Capo Press, 1992.

Kyvig, David. *Repealing National Prohibition.* Kent, Ohio: Kent State University Press, 2000.

Lacey, Robert. *Little Man: Meyer Lansky and the Gangster Life.* Boston: Little, Brown, 1991.

Lavine, Emanuel. *"Gimme" or How Politicians Get Rich.* New York: Vanguard Press, 1931.

Lerner, Michael A. *Dry Manhattan: Prohibition in New York City.* Cambridge, Mass.: Harvard University Press, 2007.

Lesy, Michael. *Murder City: The Bloody History of Chicago in the Twenties.* New York: W. W. Norton, 2007.

Leuchtenburg, William E. *Herbert Hoover.* The American President's Series. New York: Henry Holt, 2009.

————. *The Perils of Prosperity, 1914–1932.* Chicago: University of Chicago Press, 1958.

Levine, Gary. *Anatomy of a Gangster: Jack "Legs" Diamond.* New York: A. S. Barnes, 1979.

Lyle, John H. *The Dry and Lawless Years.* Englewood Cliffs, N.J.: Prentice-Hall, 1960.

Maas, Peter. *The Valachi Papers.* New York: G. P. Putnam's Sons, 1968.

Maran, A.G.D. *Mafia: Inside the Dark Heart.* New York: Thomas Dunne Books—St. Martin's Press, 2008.

Maslon, Laurence. *Some Like it Hot: The Official 50th Anniversary Companion.* New York: Collins Design, 2009.

Mason, Philip. *Rumrunning and the Roaring Twenties: Prohibition on the Michigan-Ontario Waterway.* Detroit: Wayne State University Press, 1995.

May, Allen. "Chicago's Unione Siciliana 1920—A Decade of Slaughter." American Mafia, http://americanmafia.com/Allan_May_11–13–00.html.

———. "The History of the Race Wire Service Part II." *Crime Magazine,* n.d. http://crimemagazine.com/history-race-wire-service-part-ii 8, 2012.

Mayerberg, Samuel. *Chronicle of an American Crusader.* New York: Bloch Publishing Company, 1944.

McCulloch, David. *Truman.* New York: Simon & Schuster, 1992.

McPhaul, Jack. *Johnny Torrio: First of the Gang Lords.* New Rochelle, N.Y.: Arlington House, 1970.

Messick, Hank. *Lansky.* New York: Berkley Publishing, 1971.

———. *Secret File.* New York: G. P. Putnam's Sons, 1969.

Moore, Lucy. *Anything Goes: A Biography of the Roaring Twenties.* New York: Overlook Press, 2010.

Morello, Celeste A. *The History of the Philadelphia Mafia: Before Bruno,* Book 1: *1880–1931.* Philadelphia: Jefferies & Manz, 1999.

Nash, Jay Robert. *World Encyclopedia of Organized Crime.* New York: Da Capo Press, 1993.

Nelli, Humbert S. *The Business of Crime: Italians and Syndicate Crime in the United States.* Chicago: University of Chicago Press, 1976.

Ness, Eliot, and Oscar Fraley. *The Untouchables.* New York: Simon & Schuster, 1957. Reprint, New York: Barnes & Noble, 1996.

Newark, Tim. "Hunting Down Vito Genovese in WWII Italy." *Crime Magazine,* June 1, 2007. http://crimemagazine.com/hunting-down-vito-genovese-wwii-italy.

———. *Lucky Luciano: Mafia Murderer and Secret Agent.* New York: St. Martin's Press, 2010.

Newton, Michael. *Mr. Mob: The Life and Crimes of Moe Dalitz.* Jefferson, N.C.: McFarland, 2009.

Ogden, Christopher. *Legacy: A Biography of Moses and Walter Annenberg.* New York: Little, Brown, 1990.

O'Grady, Joseph. *How the Irish Became Americans.* New York: Twayne Publishers, 1973.

Okrent, Daniel. *Last Call: The Rise and Fall of Prohibition.* New York: Scribner, 2010.

Olla, Roberto. *The Godfathers: Lives and Crimes of the Mafia Mobsters*. Richmond, U.K.: Alma Books, 2007.

Ouseley, William. *Open City: True Story of the KC Crime Family, 1900–1950*. Overland Park, Kan.: Leathers Publishing, 2008.

Pace, Denny F., and Jimmie C. Styles. *Organized Crime: Concepts and Control*. Englewood Cliffs, N.J.: Prentice-Hall, 1975.

Pasley, Fred D. *Al Capone: The Biography of a Self-Made Man*. Salem, N.H.: Ayer Company, 1930. Reprint, Whitefish, Mon.: Kessinger Publishing Rare Reprints, 1984.

Peterson, Virgil. *Barbarians in Our Midst: A History of Chicago Crime and Violence*. Boston: Little, Brown, 1952.

———. *The Mob: 200 Years of Organized Crime in New York*. Ottawa, Ill.: Green Hill Publishers, 1983.

"Philadelphia Justice for Chicago's Al Capone," *Literary Digest* 101 (June 15, 1929): 32–42.

Pietrusza, David. *Rothstein: The Life, Times, and Murder of the Criminal Genius Who Fixed the 1919 World Series*. New York: Carroll & Graf, 2003.

Porrello, Rick. *The Rise and Fall of the Cleveland Mafia: Corn Sugar and Blood*. New York: Barricade Books, 1995.

Poulson, Ellen. *The Case against Lucky Luciano: New York's Most Sensational Vice Trial*. Oakland Gardens, N.Y.: Clinton Cook, 2007.

Powell, Hickman. *Ninety Times Guilty*. New York: Harcourt Brace, 1939. Reprint, as *Lucky Luciano: The Man Who Organized Crime in America*. New York: Barnes & Noble, 2006.

Prassel, Frank Richard. *The Great American Outlaw*. Norman: University of Oklahoma Press, 1993.

Raab, Selwyn. *Five Families: The Rise, Decline, and Resurgence of America's Most Powerful Mafia Empires*. New York: St. Martin's Press, 2005.

Reddig, William M. *Tom's Town: Kansas City and the Pendergast Legend*. Columbia: University of Missouri Press, 1947.

Reppetto, Thomas. *American Mafia: A History of its Rise to Power*. New York: MJF Books, 2004.

———. *Bringing Down the American Mob: The War against the American Mafia*. New York: Henry Holt, 2006.

Reuter, Peter. "The Decline of the Mafia," *National Affairs* 120 (Summer 1955): 89–99. http://www.nationalaffairs.com/doclib/20080709_19951207thedeclineofthe americanmafiapeterreuter.pdf.

Roberts, Garyn. *Dick Tracy and American Culture: Morality and Mythology, Text and Context*. Jefferson, N.C.: McFarland, 1993.

Roemer, William F., Jr. *Accardo: The Genuine Godfather.* New York: Donald I. Fine, 1995.

Runyon, Damon. *Trials & Other Tribulations: The Best of His True Crime Writing.* New York: Dorset Press, 1946; reprint, 1991.

Russo, Gus. *The Outfit: The Role of Chicago's Underworld in the Shaping of Modern America.* New York: Bloomsbury, 2001.

Ruth, David. *Inventing the Public Enemy: The Gangster in American Culture, 1918–1934.* Chicago: University of Chicago Press, 1996.

Salerno, Ralph, and John S. Tompkins. *The Crime Confederation: Cosa Nostra and Allied Operations in Organized Crime.* Garden City, N.Y.: Doubleday & Company, 1969.

Sann, Paul. *Kill the Dutchman: The Story of Dutch Schultz.* New Rochelle, N.Y.: Arlington House, 1971.

Schoenberg, Robert J. *Mr. Capone:* New York: William Morrow, 1992.

Schwarz, Daniel R. *Broadway Boogie Woogie: Damon Runyon and the Making of New York City Culture.* New York: Palgrave Macmillan, 2003.

Smith, John L. "The Double Life of Moe Dalitz." *Las Vegas Review Journal.* http://www.1st100.com/part2/dalitz.html.

Smith, Mack. *Mussolini.* New York: Knopf, 1982.

Smith, Richard N. *Thomas E. Dewey and His Times.* New York: Simon & Schuster, 1982.

Spiering, Frank. *The Man Who Got Capone.* New York: Bobbs-Merrill, 1976.

Stolberg, Mary M. *Fighting Organized Crime: Politics, Justice, and the Legacy of Thomas E. Dewey.* Boston: Northeastern University Press, 1995.

Strauss, William. *Generations: The History of America's Future, 1584 to 2069.* New York: William Morrow, 1991.

Stuart, Mark. *Gangster #2: Longy Zwillman, the Man Who Invented Organized Crime.* Secaucus, N.J.: Lyle Stuart, 1985.

Taggert, Ed. *Bootlegger: Max Hassel, The Millionaire Newsboy.* New York: Writer's Showcase, 2003.

Talese, Gay. *Honor Thy Father.* New York: First Harper Perennial Edition, 2009.

Thrasher, Frederick Milton. *The Gang: A Study of 1,313 Gangs in Chicago.* Chicago: University of Chicago Press, 1929.

Thompson, Craig, and Allen Raymond. *Gang Rule in New York: The Story of a Lawless Era.* New York: Dial Press, 1940.

Tonelli, Bill. *Mob Fest '29: The True Story Behind the Birth of Organized Crime.* San Francisco: Byliner Originals, 2012.

Tucker, Kenneth. *Eliot Ness and the Untouchables: The Historical Reality and the Film and Television Depictions.* Jefferson, N.C.: McFarland, 2000.

Turkus, Burton B. *Murder, Inc.: The Story of "the Syndicate."* New York: Farrar, Strauss and Young, 1951.

Tully, Andrew. *Treasury Agent: The Inside Story.* New York: Simon & Schuster, 1958.

Unger, Robert. *The Union Station Massacre: The Original Sin of J. Edgar Hoover's FBI.* Kansas City: Andrews McMeel Publishing, 1997.

U.S. Circuit Court of Appeals for the Second Circuit. *U.S. v. Wexler.* Transcript of Record on Appeal from the District Court of the United States for the Southern Districrt of New York. n.d.

U.S. Congress. House. Committee on Immigration and Naturalization. *Biological Aspects of Immigration: Hearing before the Committee on Immigration and Naturalization.* 66th Congress, 2nd sess., April 16, 1920, 3–4.

Vizzini, Sal, Oscar Fraley, and Marshall Smith. *Vizzini: The Secret Lives of America's Most Successful Undercover Agent.* New York: Arbor House, 1972.

Waugh, Daniel. *Gangs of Saint Louis: Men of Respect.* Charleston, S.C.: History Press, 2010.

Wilkerson, W. R. III. *The Man Who Invented Las Vegas.* Beverly Hills, Calif.: Ciro's Books, 2000.

Wilson, Frank, and Beth Day. *Special Agent: A Quarter Century with the Treasury Department and the Secret Service.* New York: Holt, Rinehart, and Winston, 1965.

Winchell, Walter. *Winchell Exclusive.* Englewood Cliffs, N.J.: Prentice-Hall, 1975.

Wolf, George, with Joseph DiMona. *Frank Costello: Prime Minister of the Underworld.* New York: William Morrow, 1974.

Woodward, Frank B., and Arthur M. Woodford. *All Our Yesterdays: A Brief History of Detroit.* Detroit: Wayne State University Press, 1969.

Index

About the Author

Marc Mappen has a Ph.D. in American history. He has six books to his credit and has written articles for the *New York Times* and other publications. He was formerly the executive director of the New Jersey Historical Commission and is now a lecturer in the History Department at Rutgers University. You can contact Marc at mappen@rci.rutgers.edu.